Practical Google Analytics and Google Tag Manager for Developers

Jonathan Weber
and the Team at LunaMetrics

Apress®

Practical Google Analytics and Google Tag Manager for Developers

ISBN-13 (pbk): 978-1-4842-0266-1

ISBN-13 (electronic): 978-1-4842-0265-4

Managing Director: Welmoed Spahr
Acquisitions Editor: Susan McDermott
Developmental Editor: Douglas Pundick
Editorial Board: Steve Anglin, Mark Beckner, Gary Cornell, Louise Corrigan, James DeWolf, Jonathan Gennick, Robert Hutchinson, Celestin Suresh John, Michelle Lowman, James Markham, Susan McDermott, Matthew Moodie, Jeffrey Pepper, Douglas Pundick, Ben Renow-Clarke, Gwenan Spearing, Matt Wade, Steve Weiss
Coordinating Editor: Rita Fernando
Copy Editor: Kimberly Burton-Weisman
Compositor: SPi Global
Indexer: SPi Global

To Robbin, whose determination to figure out Google Analytics in its earliest days led to all of this, and whose relentless pursuit of the very best people makes LunaMetrics an extraordinary place to work.

Contents at a Glance

Contents

Foreword

A long, long time ago, some smart people understood that distributing water from a centralized place would provide more control and be faster. This was the beginning of irrigation, a more organized and effective way to bring water to plants.

Fast-forward a few thousand years, and some other smart people invented even more advanced ways to irrigate hundreds of millions of acres around the globe. Let's say you own a plantation with multiple crops: coffee (of course!), corn, and soya—each of those plants require a different amount of water and a different amount of fertilizers. Without irrigation, it would be impossible to create and maintain a constant and precise flow of those two essential resources (and others) to your crops in an effective and timely manner.

You are probably asking yourself by now: What is this guy talking about? Well, in the same way that irrigation is used to deliver resources to multiple crops, Google Tag Manager (GTM) is used to deliver different tags to different pages quickly and effectively. So, in our case, instead of crops, we have pages, instead of resources we have tags, and in both we have rules to define what to do in each case.

In the same way that irrigation powered farmers to manage their resources in a more scalable way, so does Google Tag Manager for developers. GTM is a powerful tool that enables multiple professionals from different departments and locations to work together to create and deploy solutions to digital challenges, such as agility and performance.

This is not to say that all problems will vanish and that in three steps you will be rocking the Web; no, GTM is not an Asterix magic potion. As you will learn in this book, creating a powerful GTM implementation requires discipline and hard work, but you will also learn that the hard work will pay for itself many times over.

As Jonathan and the LunaMetrics team accurately and comprehensively describe in the chapters to come, you can do wonders with Google Tag Manager, both when it comes to Google Analytics implementations and other types of data collection.

Now turn the page and put your hand to the plow!

—Daniel Waisberg
Analytics Advocate, Google

About the Author

Jonathan Weber is the data evangelist at LunaMetrics. He spreads the principles of analytics through training seminars on Google Analytics and Google Tag Manager, and works with clients on challenging strategic issues in measuring and interpreting analytics data. He holds a master's degree from the University of Pittsburgh School of Information Sciences. Away from the computer, you can find him out in the sunshine as a flower farmer and plant geek.

LunaMetrics is a cool Google Analytics Certified Partner and Authorized Premium Reseller, located in the heart of Pittsburgh, PA—one of the US's newly techie towns.

Jonathan and the rest of the team at LunaMetrics are constantly working to make themselves authorities in the area of GTM and GA. The team doesn't really act that nerdy, but they get excited by creating new GTM workarounds and celebrate by playing board games.

Acknowledgments

There's a reason the cover of this book reads "Jonathan Weber and the team at LunaMetrics", because it couldn't have happened without everyone here. It's a privilege to be able to just pop over to someone's desk and talk over an idea with some of the top folks working on Google Analytics and Google Tag Manager implementations anywhere. The breadth and depth of experience of the LunaMetrics team is the foundation of this book. Thanks especially to Robbin Steif and Jon Meck for their tireless reviews and feedback from front cover to back; again to Jon and to Jimmy Keener for assembling the first drafts of several chapters; to Sayf Sharif and Dan Wilkerson for reviewing technical issues; and to Alex Moore and his entire analytics team here for all of their support, encouragement, and feedback.

Beyond LunaMetrics, there's a larger community devoted to GA and GTM who come together to sharpen our practices and our collective wisdom on these tools, in the Google Analytics Certified Partner program, the Google+ GTM community, and elsewhere. Thanks especially to Simo Ahava for being as obsessed with GTM as we are, and for creating so much valuable writing about it on his blog.

None of this would be possible without the excellent teams at Google working on Analytics and Tag Manager, both past and present. Thanks especially to Paul Muret, who got all of this started way back when; Daniel Waisberg, who penned the foreword for us (and whose excellent book on GA integrations you should also check out); to Avinash Kaushik, for getting so many people excited about web analytics; and to Brian Kuhn and Lukas Bergstrom on the GTM team, who have tirelessly provided support for a new and rapidly developing tool.

And finally, eternal gratitude to Jimmy, who put up with a lot of days and nights of "clicky-clicky" in the quest to finish this book.

Introduction

Who Is This Book For?

"What is the use of a book," thought Alice, "without pictures or conversations?"

—Lewis Carroll, *Alice's Adventures in Wonderland*

Google Analytics is used on millions of websites to measure and understand user behavior. But for many of those sites, implementation of Google Analytics goes like this:

1. Sign up for an account.

2. Paste the tracking code into your site template according to the simple instructions.

3. View site data in reports.

That's certainly better than no data at all! But stopping your planning there misses many of the most powerful features of Google Analytics (GA): those that customize the data to your organization, your website, and your audience. This book will show you how to measure special interactions, conversions, and other types of data, so that you have reports and analysis with real impact.

One of the hurdles in further implementation can be IT resources necessary to deploy and test tracking code tags on the pages of your website to make additional measurement possible. Google Tag Manager (GTM) helps you overcome this hurdle by managing and deploying those tags from a web-based tool.

GA and GTM go together like peanut butter and jelly. While you can certainly implement all the things in this book without GTM, GTM makes the process so much more streamlined and testable that it's strongly recommended for all GA implementations. Throughout this book, GTM will be introduced alongside GA features, and you'll learn about using GTM to implement them.

Do I Need to Be a Developer?

The title says "for Developers", but what does that really mean?

Web analytics, by its nature, measures web pages. GA and GTM use JavaScript code to do that measurement. Because of that, you should be familiar with the basic technologies that make web pages work in your browser: HTML, CSS, and JavaScript.

But do you need to be able to sit down at a blank computer screen and code a fully functioning website from scratch? Certainly not. The majority of work you'll do involves adding a few lines of code here and there to existing, functioning pages in order to measure some element of that page. If your job title is "Developer", you'll have no problems, but if you work in marketing, content creation, or some other role, as long as you have some basic HTML skills you should be able to follow along and implement the examples in this book.

How Should I Read This Book?

Especially if you're just getting started with GA & GTM, *Part I: Implementing Google Analytics with Google Tag Manager* covers the basics you need to know about your implementation and getting the foundations of your website measurement in place, along with the processes for deploying and testing. Even if you have an existing implementation, Part I may provide a good refresher of basics, especially Chapters 3 and 4 if GTM is new to you.

Part II: Enhancing Website Data with Google Tag Manager covers a whole variety of additional kinds of data you'll want to send to GA from your website, while *Part III: Collecting Data from Other Sources* provides information about sending GA data from mobile apps, back-end systems, and more. The chapters of Parts II and III are collections of topics for growing and enhancing your implementation that you can approach in any order you like. Pick out the topics that are most valuable or highest priority for you and tackle those first. Chapter 5 is a good starting point, as it covers a number of the most common kinds of additional tracking in GA, as well as general approaches to implementation in GA and GTM. From there, feel free to skip around as your interest or needs dictate.

The *Bonus Chapter: Using GA with BigQuery for Big Data Analysis* provides an overview of the newest way of getting at your GA data, through Google's BigQuery service, enabling deep statistical analysis and data mining techniques on your website data. The *Appendix* provides an overview of GA and GTM APIs for setting up and reporting on your data.

Links to Resources and Code Examples

Throughout this book you'll find references to the GA and GTM documentation and other resources, as well as numerous code examples. You can also find these, organized by chapter, at this book's web page: `http://www.lunametrics.com/gtm-book/`. This page includes a number of helpful resources, organized by chapter:

- Clickable links to resources referenced in the text.

- Code for example tags and variables in GTM that appear in this book, provided in GTM's import/export format to easily bring them into your own setup.

- Resources to learn more about ancillary topics touched on in GA and GTM, such as regular expressions.

- Links to further relevant examples, beyond those included in the text.

Summary

- This book teaches you best practices for Google Analytics and Google Tag Manager implementation.

- You don't need to be a developer. You should have a basic understanding of HTML and JavaScript.

- Read Part I for a strong foundation for your implementation, and then pick and choose from Part II and Part III depending on your interest and needs.

PART I

■ ■ ■

Implementing Google Analytics with Google Tag Manager

CHAPTER 1

Google Analytics Fundamentals

"What a funny watch!" she remarked. "It tells the day of the month, and doesn't tell what o'clock it is!"

"Why should it?" muttered the Hatter.

—Lewis Carroll, *Alice's Adventures in Wonderland*

Google Analytics (GA) is an easy-to-use tool to measure activity on a website. A basic setup might take as little as a few minutes, and many of the standard reports are quite accessible and understandable without any special training or prior knowledge of web analytics. Because of this, many users jump into GA without knowing much about its underpinnings—how the data is structured and gathered—and that's fine for the basics. But eventually, users can outgrow this intuitive understanding of GA and its data, and need deeper insight into how it works and what it can do.

You may already be using GA, or just starting out. In either case, this chapter will help you get a handle on what's in GA:

- How Google Analytics accounts are structured

- How your data gets into Google Analytics

- How reports are generated from that data

GA Account Structure and Administration

If you're just creating your Google Analytics account from scratch, either because you are starting a new website or switching from another tool, congratulations! You have the opportunity to set everything up from the beginning.

On the other hand, if you're like most users of GA, you're inheriting some accounts that already exist, set up at some point in the dim past. There may or may not be any record, documentation, or organizational memory of what was set up and why.

To make sense of all this, let's take a look at the structure of GA accounts, starting with the email address you use to log in.

Getting a Google Login

Whether starting from scratch or accessing an existing implementation of Google Analytics, you will need a way to log in. For GA (and all other Google-y tools, such as Tag Manager, AdWords, Search Console, Google+, and so on), this requires that you have a Google Account.

If you sign up for an email address through Gmail, that's automatically a Google Account. But you can sign up any email address (alice@aliceswonderlandresorts.com, for example) as a Google Account. Look no further than the "Sign in" option at the top right of pretty much anything Google, which will allow you to sign in with an existing account or create a new one. It will ask you a few security questions and allow you to choose a username for a new Gmail address or to use an existing email address.

■ **Tip**   You're better off using company email addresses than Gmail addresses for official business using Google tools, since you have more control over your own email addresses (being able to reset the password with email verification if someone leaves your organization, for example).

You'll want anyone who needs a login to your organization's data and settings in Google Analytics (and later, Google Tag Manager) to create an account this way. You can have many different logins, with different levels of access to your GA data.

■ **Tip**   You might wonder: "Should we share a single login?" Whether you want a shared login (e.g., analytics@aliceswonderlandresorts.com) or separate logins for different personnel (e.g., alice@aliceswonderlandresorts.com, lewis@aliceswonderlandresorts.com, etc.) depends on the structure of your organization's departments, business units, or teams, as well as your internal security policies. Think about whether multiple people sharing a password works. (For small organizations, maybe. For larger organizations, you're going to want more granularity, control, and accountability for individuals.)

Google Analytics Structure

Google Analytics organizes data into a three-level hierarchy: *accounts*, *properties*, and *views*. Each login (email address) can have access at any of these levels.

> ***Account*** is the highest level, and generally corresponds to a single business or organization. In many cases, you may have access to just one GA account. But you might have multiple accounts for various reasons: you have a work account (for your employer's websites) and a personal account (for your blog on trends in the millinery industry); you might be an agency that works with multiple clients, each of whom has an account; or you might work for a large and complex organization that has multiple accounts (the North American division vs. the European division).

> The ***property*** is the next level of organization. Each account may have multiple properties. The property corresponds to a website (or group of websites), mobile app, or other source of data. Your organization might have multiple websites (aliceswonderlandresorts.com, madhatterheadwareinc.com, etc.), and so your account might contain multiple web properties.

> The ***view*** is the third and lowest level of organization. Each view is a specific set of data from the property from which the reports in GA are generated. By default, GA creates a view for each property that simply contains all the data for that property. You get to specify what data are included in each view, so you can create additional views for subsets of your site's content (just a particular section of the site, or just a particular marketing channel, for example).

On the Home tab for GA, you'll see a hierarchical listing of all the accounts, properties, and views to which your login has access, through which you can browse by collapsing and expanding the sections. Each view shows a short summary of metrics, and clicking on a view takes you to its reports.

Administration and Access Controls

The Admin tab of Google Analytics gives you access to all of GA's settings, and you'll find that it's organized in the same way, by account, property, and view (from left to right). Each of the three columns is a menu of settings for that level, and the drop-down menus at the top of each column control which account, property, or view you're seeing.

What you'll see in the Admin tab depends on which level of permissions your login has to GA. There are several levels of permissions that can be assigned to a login:

- *Read & Analyze* is the most basic level of permissions. This allows a user to view reporting data and create personal customizations, such as custom reports, alerts, dashboards, or segments.

- *Collaborate* is the next level. It includes everything that Read & Analyze can do, as well as the ability to share customizations with other users.

- *Edit* includes everything that Collaborate can do, with the addition of the ability to change settings in the Admin area.

- *Manage Users* is a separate permissions level from Read & Analyze, Collaborate, or Edit, and does *not* include those abilities (though it can be given in addition to them for a user). Manage Users gives the ability to add or remove permissions for other logins.

These permissions can be assigned at the account, property, or view level, which gives great flexibility. For example, Alice might be in charge of analytics across all company websites, so she could have Edit and Manage Users access at the account level. The Mad Hatter, who manages the ecommerce store portion of the website, may have Edit permissions to only that view.

If you have the Manage Users permission, you'll be able to see a Manage Users menu listed in the Admin tab. Clicking through shows a list of users and their permissions, as well as the ability to add a new user. Note that the login email needs to be a Google Account (see earlier) before you can add it to GA.

■ **Tip**   Most commonly, you will probably use Collaborate permissions for the majority of users, at whatever account, property, or view is appropriate for them to use. Typically Edit and Manage Users are reserved for a limited number of administrators (again, at the account, property, or view level that's appropriate).

Further chapters explore the other settings in the Admin area. The property-level settings largely pertain to what data is collected by GA: the tracking code itself (Chapter 2), custom data (Chapter 11), and data import (Chapter 14). The view-level settings control what data shows up in reports, and you'll learn ways to use those to track conversions (Chapter 6) and clean up and organize your data (Chapter 8).

Google Analytics Premium Properties

Google Analytics is a free tool. People often ask, "Why does Google give it away for free?" Organizations with better data about their websites and marketing are more likely to spend money on advertising, which is where Google brings in the money.

As a free tool, however, it does have some limitations on how much data you can collect and process. Google also offers Google Analytics Premium, which is a paid subscription service that includes higher limits on data collection and processing, service-level and uptime guarantees, and customer support and training. GA Premium also offers some more processing-intensive reports and ways of retrieving data beyond what's available in the free tool, as well as early access to beta features.

GA Premium is activated at the property level in GA, and you'll see a flag next to any properties in your account list that are enabled for GA Premium.

Most of the features discussed in this book are available for everyone—Premium or standard. Differences will be called out so you'll know.

How Google Analytics Collects Data

Google Analytics captures a wide variety of data. Data is sent to GA by means of a tracking *hit*. Each hit is a bundle of data about some specific type of interaction (viewing a page, for example).

GA specifies the format for this hit data with a data collection specification called the Measurement Protocol. The Measurement Protocol is agnostic about the source of the data—as long as the hit is in the right format, the data will be collected into Google Analytics. This means that you can send data to GA from anywhere: a website, a mobile app on iOS or Android, or from your own custom applications. (You can learn more about the Measurement Protocol in Chapter 14.)

In most cases, you'll be sending data to GA from your website, and that's the focus of the bulk of this book. For websites, GA provides a JavaScript library that generates the tracking hits for you and automates much of the nitty-gritty of the data collection so that you don't have to worry about the details of the Measurement Protocol.

This JavaScript code is loaded in each page of your website (Chapter 2 has all the details). By default, this code captures the view of each page (and a slew of associated data) each time a page loads. By adding more code, you can track other interactions or occurrences, such as clicking a button, scrolling the page, and more.

For standard (non-Premium) GA, you are limited to collecting ten million tracking hits per month by the terms of service. If you exceed that limit, Google may contact you about purchasing a GA Premium subscription or reducing the amount of data you collect. (Premium accounts have higher hit limits, starting at one billion hits per month.)

Hits, Sessions, and Users

Each hit sent to Google Analytics represents one interaction. A collection of hits that occur together is called a *session*. For example, a user might come to your website and view several pages in succession—each page generates a hit, and all of the hits together comprise the session. The typical rule for grouping hits into sessions is that not more than 30 minutes pass until the next hit (although you have the ability to change this time window in the GA settings).

■ **Example**   Alice visits a website and goes to pages A, B, and C. Then she follows a rabbit down a hole and returns an hour later, viewing pages D and E. Alice has two sessions: the first containing A, B, and C, and the second containing D and E. If only 29 minutes had passed between C and D, there would be a single session with all five pages.

Google Analytics also tracks the ***user***, who may have multiple sessions. When the same user comes back to the site repeatedly, GA keeps track of how many times they've been there and how recently. (Chapter 2 discusses how GA tracks website users with cookies; Chapters 10 and 11 give more detail on how to track individual users and record additional information about them.)

Privacy Considerations

Of course, you are interested in tracking user activity to make your website better. But you have to remember that the users visiting your website are real human beings, not just a collection of data, and you need to be clear about what you're collecting and careful about what you do with it.

Google Analytics' Terms of Service for the United States[1] require the following:

- That you disclose that you are using Google Analytics to track the behavior of your website users (typically by linking to Google's description of how it collects data in your site's privacy policy).

- That you must not circumvent any methods that GA allows users to opt out of tracking.

- That you must not collect any ***personally identifiable information*** within GA (names, email addresses, or billing information).

The terms for other regions may be different, and you should also become familiar with the privacy regulations in the countries in which you operate to understand your obligations.

Reports and Data Structures in GA

Once the data is sent to Google Analytics, it will appear in all of the standard reports you can access in the Reports tab (or in Custom Reports in the Customization tab, if you've created any of those). Let's take a look at how this data is organized into those reports and how the numbers are calculated.

Dimensions and Metrics

Dimensions and metrics are the building blocks of every report in Google Analytics, and understanding the dimensions and metrics available and how they fit together will give you a deep understanding of how GA really works, and what you can do with the data.

Dimensions are labels that describe data. They typically appear as the rows of reports. Examples include:

- *URLs*: Hostname, Page, Landing Page, Exit Page, Previous Page, Next Page

- *Traffic sources*: Source, Medium, Campaign, Keyword, Referral Path, Social Network

- *Geography*: Country, Region, City, Metro

---

[1]http://www.google.com/analytics/terms/us.html

Metrics are measurements. They are always numerical and typically appear as the columns of reports. Examples include:

- *User metrics*: Users, % New Sessions

- *Session behavior metrics*: Bounce Rate, Pages/Session, Avg. Session Duration, Conversion Rate

- *Campaign metrics*: Impressions, Clicks, CTR, CPC

Each report in GA—whether a standard report, a custom report, or even data extracted through the GA APIs—is a combination of dimensions and metrics that are extracted and calculated from the tracking hits received. Most standard reports have some sensible defaults, but allow you choices to show the data in different ways by changing the dimensions or metrics displayed. Custom reports allow you to select completely customized combinations of dimensions and metrics. Reports also allow filtering and segmentation of data based on dimensions and metrics. For example, you can say "Show me all the Pages with Bounce Rate greater than 50%" or "Show me the Campaigns only for users located in Florida".

You'll get a sense for the dimensions and metrics available simply by browsing through the standard reports in GA. A comprehensive reference to dimensions and metrics is available in the GA developer documentation,[2] which includes the labels used in the reporting interface as well as the programmatic identifiers used in the APIs. The dimensions and metrics reference also indicates which combinations are allowed—certain dimensions or metrics cannot be viewed in the same report, either because they are logically incompatible or because the underlying data on such a combination isn't available in GA.

Pre-Aggregation and Sampling

For the combinations of dimensions and metrics in most of the standard reports, all of the report data is pre-aggregated by Google Analytics. This means that the metrics in these reports are calculated and ready to go when you request the report for any date range.

Row Limits

For this pre-aggregated data, there is a limit of 50,000 unique rows daily that are shown in the aggregated reports. Once you exceed this limit, the report will group additional values into a single row labeled (other). This is uncommon for most dimensions, but for dimensions like Page (URL) or Keyword, there may be large numbers of unique values. (Additional limits apply in multiday or multidimension reports, but exceeding the daily limit is the most common scenario. The limits are higher for GA Premium users.) You may be able to overcome these limits by cleaning up unnecessarily specific query parameters or other information in your URLs, as discussed in Chapter 8.

Sampling

If you request a report that is not drawn from GA's pre-aggregated data—for example, by applying an additional dimension to a standard report, applying a segment, or creating a custom report—GA must calculate the metrics for the report on the fly by going back to the original tracking hit data.

---

[2]`https://developers.google.com/analytics/devguides/reporting/core/dimsmets`

For non-aggregated data, if the date range contains more than 500,000 visits, Google Analytics will employ *sampling* in calculating the metrics for the report. (Again, additional limits sometimes apply, but the session limit is the most common to trigger sampling. The limits are increased substantially for Google Analytics Premium users, who also have the ability to download completely unsampled reports.)

Sampling means that the totals are projected from a subset of the data. For example, if there were 1,000,000 sessions in your time period, Google Analytics might take 500,000 sessions to calculate the metrics, then multiply by 2 (1,000,000 / 500,000) for the totals.

GA will indicate when sampling occurred and what proportion of total traffic was used in calculating the report by a notification at the top right of the report. It also gives you the ability to select between "Slower response, greater precision" (which uses close to the limit of 500,000 sessions, but takes longer to calculate the report) or "Faster response, less precision" (which is quicker, but uses fewer sessions).

You can eliminate sampling if you can reduce the date range of your report to encompass fewer than 500,000 sessions. (In this scenario, you would have to add results back together for multiple date ranges to get totals for the entire time period of interest. You can also use the GA APIs to apply this technique programmatically.) However, this approach makes analysis in GA's reports cumbersome, and it does not make it possible to address user-level metrics (which cannot be simply totaled across time periods).

Tool Overlap and Reconciliation

If you're like most folks, you're using multiple tools for measuring web activity, and more than likely, some of those overlap with what Google Analytics is also measuring. Your content management system, social media plugins, ecommerce system, email marketing tools, and more may all have metrics about web activity.

To the extent possible, it's worth trying to consolidate as much as possible in a single system that is flexible enough to handle most of the data that's most important to you, for the simple ability to see and analyze all these data side-by-side without having to stitch them together in some other way. GA is a good candidate for bringing together as much of your online (and even offline) customer interaction as possible because of its flexibility. Much of this book will focus on bringing these different categories of data together. However, collecting data in GA may not be practical for you in all cases, so there are many facilities for exporting data as well (see the bonus Chapter 16 and Appendix).

Where you are using GA data alongside data from other sources, you should be aware that metrics will not always match exactly. This can happen for a whole variety of reasons. Metrics that *seem* like they should be the same are often defined in subtly different ways between tools, or are measured in different ways. Compare carefully, and don't assume that numbers between different tools are comparable unless you understand their definitions clearly and do some cross-checking of your own. Overall, though, you should expect metrics to agree directionally and proportionally between tools, and you shouldn't get bogged down in the minutiae of reconciling tools when you could better spend your time making decisions based on data that is *good enough*.

Google Analytics Documentation

Even with this excellent book in hand, you'll probably need to reference the documentation for Google Analytics at some point. There are actually two major documentation collections for GA:

- The Help Center,[3] accessible from the top menu, provides information about the reporting and administration functions in Google Analytics. If there's a report or setting you don't quite understand, it should give you some context on what it's for and how it works.

- The Developer Center[4] has all the documentation of the Google Analytics JavaScript tracking codes, APIs, and other technical information about GA. It makes a great supplement to this book, and some of its reference documentation and handy tools will be referred to for further background.

Summary

- Google Analytics has a three-level structure: accounts, properties, and views. Access to Google Analytics is through Google Accounts, which are logins based on a Gmail address or any other email address. Each login may have different levels of permission at any level in the GA account structure.

- Google Analytics collects data through tracking hits, packages of data about an interaction that are sent from your website using JavaScript, or from another source of data such as a mobile app. Hits are grouped together in sessions, and users are tracked over multiple sessions. There are privacy provisions for notifying your users about your data collection practices and restricting the data you can collect.

- Google Analytics data is based on dimensions (labels that describe data) and metrics (numeric measurements). All reports, including standard reports, custom reports, and APIs are based on GA's dimensions and metrics. Standard reports are pre-aggregated, meaning the numbers are precalculated. Non-pre-aggregated reports, such as a custom report or a standard report with an added segment, can be sampled, meaning that the numbers are calculated on the fly from a subset of the data if the dataset is large.

---

[3]https://support.google.com/analytics/
[4]https://developers.google.com/analytics/

CHAPTER 2

■ ■ ■

Basic Google Analytics Measurement

"Begin at the beginning," the King said, very gravely, "and go on till you come to the end: then stop."

—Lewis Carroll, *Alice's Adventures in Wonderland*

Google Analytics' measurement of your website is based on JavaScript tracking code installed on the site. Although for most of this book we'll be using Google Tag Manager (GTM) to manage and install this code (beginning in Chapter 3), it's instructive to understand the basics of the GA tracking code and how it is intended to work. Practically speaking, you probably won't use this tracking code directly. However, having a basic understanding of it will help you to interpret the options in GA tags within GTM, as well as to decipher GA documentation and examples to set up GTM for your site.

Basic Google Analytics Tracking Code

When you first create a Google Analytics account, you supply some basic information, such as your site's domain and time zone. Then, GA presents a snippet of JavaScript code with the instruction to "copy and paste this code into every web page you want to track" (see Figure 2-1).

This is your tracking code. Copy and paste it into the code of every page you want to track.

```
<script>
(function(i,s,o,g,r,a,m){i['GoogleAnalyticsObject']=r;i[r]=i[r]||function(){
(i[r].q=i[r].q||[]).push(arguments)},i[r].l=1*new Date();a=s.createElement(o),
m=s.getElementsByTagName(o)[0];a.async=1;a.src=g;m.parentNode.insertBefore(a,m)
})(window,document,'script','//www.google-analytics.com/analytics.js','ga');

ga('create', 'UA-XXXXX-YY', 'auto');
ga('send', 'pageview');

</script>
```

Figure 2-1. GA's tracking code instructions

11

If you need to find this suggested code after the initial setup process, you can find it in the Admin settings in the Property column in the section Tracking Info ➤ Tracking Code.

How the Tracking Code Works

Let's break this code down and take a look at what it does. The first part looks like this:

```
(function(i,s,o,g,r,a,m){i['GoogleAnalyticsObject']=r;i[r]=i[r]||function(){
(i[r].q=i[r].q||[]).push(arguments)},i[r].l=1*new Date();a=s.createElement(o),
m=s.getElementsByTagName(o)[0];a.async=1;a.src=g;m.parentNode.insertBefore(a,m)
})(window,document,'script','//www.google-analytics.com/analytics.js','ga');
```

Don't even bother reformatting this piece of code to make it more readable, because it's the same for every site and you would almost never make changes to it. It fetches the GA tracking library (analytics.js) from a Google server and inserts it into the page. (The only part of this script you would possibly want to change is the very last bit: 'ga' is the name that will be given to the GA tracking function. You can rename this function should you need to avoid a conflict with the name of an already existing object in your page.)

The second part is where you tell Google Analytics what to do. The default code includes two commands:

```
ga('create', 'UA-XXXXX-YY', 'auto');
ga('send', 'pageview');
```

The ga function accepts a sequence of parameters, the first of which is the name of a GA command. Here you see two different commands: create and send.

Create the GA Tracker

The create command sets up the GA tracker. Each tracker sends data to a specific GA property, which is identified in the second parameter in this command, called the ***property ID***. The property ID is of the form UA-XXXXX-YY, where XXXXX is a number that identifies your GA account, and YY is a number that identifies a property within the account. You can find the property ID listed next to each property in the Home screen of GA, or in the Admin settings in the Property column.

The last parameter, auto, is a configuration parameter for the tracker that relates to how it sets cookies for the site. (More about this later in the chapter.)

Send the Pageview

The second command, send, sends a tracking hit to GA.

The second parameter of this command is the ***hit type***, which in this case is pageview. There are a number of different hit types, which collect different kinds of data and are reported in different ways in GA, such as the event hit type for user interactions (described in Chapter 5) or the screenview hit type for mobile applications (see Chapter 13).

Whenever a send command occurs, data is sent to Google Analytics. An HTTP request is generated to www.google-analytics.com/collect that includes a payload of data about the hit (the data from which the dimensions and metrics in GA will be populated).

Because the GA tracking code is included on every page of your site, each time a page loads, the command to send a pageview executes, recording that the page was viewed. It's that simple. The two commands represented here (create to create the tracker, send to send the pageview) are the bare-bones minimum for GA tracking to function on your site.

Now, this default code doesn't capture everything you might want—it's just recording pageviews each time a page loads. So what about an AJAX form, where the user completes several steps but the page doesn't reload? What about other interactions within pages, like playing an embedded video? These are going to require additional code (to execute *only* when some action is completed, like loading new AJAX content or playing the video). Chapter 5 provides both general approaches for this additional tracking (using GTM), as well as specific recipes for common scenarios.

THE GENERATIONS OF GA TRACKING CODE

This book focuses on the latest generation GA tracking library, `analytics.js`, which is part of GA's suite of upgrades and expanded features called Universal Analytics. There are other, older GA tracking libraries, such as `urchin.js` and `ga.js`. These worked in similar ways, but the specifics of syntax are different, and not all features described in this book are available with older libraries.

The `analytics.js` library has been the default code for new properties in Google Analytics since 2014, and an upgrade process is available for properties that predate the change. You will see a notification about the upgrade process in the Admin section if you haven't updated (and you'll be able to see the older code on your site). Although the older code will continue to work and gather data for some period of time, if you want to take advantage of any of the newer features of GA, you will want to upgrade as soon as possible (and eventually it will become mandatory).

The GA Developer Center contains documentation for the legacy code and an upgrade center to guide you through the process.[1]

Multiple GA Trackers

One last important detail about creating a GA tracker: every tracker has a *name* that identifies it. (The default tracker's name is actually t0, although that's not indicated anywhere.) The name of the tracker is nothing to worry about if you're only using one, but in some cases, you might have multiple trackers running in parallel on a web page. If there are multiple trackers, each command must specify which tracker it is being called on. (It's not necessary to specify the name for the default tracker t0, however.)

Why might you want multiple trackers? In some cases, you might want to send data to more than one property in GA, which can happen for many reasons:

- Joint interest in a website by two distinct parties (your organization and its parent company, for example) with different GA accounts.

- Adding your tracking code to content provided by a third-party vendor or app that may have its own GA tracking already in place.

- In some situations, for testing upgrades to ensure your implementation is correct (see Chapter 4).

---

[1]https://developers.google.com/analytics/devguides/collection/upgrade/

Here's an example of naming a tracker and then calling a command on it. The name can be any string; here you use t1.

```
ga('create', 'UA-XXXXX-YY', 'auto');        // default tracker
ga('create', 'UA-WWWWW-ZZ', 'auto', 't1'); // additional tracker named t1

ga('send', 'pageview');                      // sends pageview for default tracker
ga('t1.send', 'pageview');                   // send pageview for t1
```

The commands for named trackers are prefixed with the tracker name before the command name, separated by a dot: t1.send, for example.

Arguments and Field Names

Depending on the command, Google Analytics accepts values for additional fields that affect how it works or the data gathered. As you saw earlier, for example, the create command indicates the property ID, for example.

In many cases, there are two ways you can specify these values. For some, you can specify them as arguments directly in the ga function call:

```
ga('create', 'UA-XXXXX-YY', 'auto');
```

This is the format you've already seen, and it is a convenient way to provide some of the most common field values. Since it uses function arguments, notice that the *order is important*, and the function expects the arguments to occur in a particular position.

There's an alternative syntax available as well, and it's the only way to specify some of the lesser-used fields, which do not have a parameter equivalent. This alternative syntax uses an object for the fields and values:

```
ga('create',
 {
   'trackingId': 'UA-XXXX-Y',
   'cookieDomain': 'auto'
 });
```

Since the object includes the name for each field, order doesn't matter. Both of these syntaxes are equivalent and work in the same way.

Getting the Code on the Page

So the instructions say "copy and paste this code into every web page you want to track," but fortunately that's probably easier than it sounds. In this era, chances are that you have a content management system with some manageable number of page templates (rather than individual, distinct HTML files for each page of the site).

If that's the case, you just need to get the code into one or more templates so that it's automatically included in each page of the site. You do want to make sure that you get all the templates, because any missing pages will not be measured in GA. As far as GA is concerned, if there's no tracking code on the page, it's as if it doesn't exist.

Code Placement

The GA tracking code is *asynchronous*, meaning that the browser doesn't need to wait for the code to finish loading to continue rendering elements that come after it in the page. This means that you can safely put the code at or near the top of your pages. The recommendation is to put the code in the `<head>` section of the page, although the beginning of the `<body>` is fine as well if that is easier in your templates.

▓ **Tip**   You do want to try to include the code as high in the page as possible. If the code is toward the end of the page and the page takes a significant amount of time to load, it's possible that the user could navigate away (click a link or close the browser window) before the tracking code has loaded, meaning you would miss capturing data about that pageview.

The GA code executes asynchronously from the rest of the page, but the *commands provided to GA execute in the order they are called.* Because of this, it's important for the `create` command to come *before* the `send` command, for example.

Cookies and Domains

Google Analytics employs a cookie to store a *client ID*, a randomly generated identifier for a particular browser and device. It uses the client ID in its calculation of the number of users and in user behavior across sessions (such as recency, loyalty, and the multichannel funnel reports).

Your browser stores cookies assigned to a particular domain (for security reasons, so that unauthorized sites can't read cookies from other domains). GA uses first-party cookies, meaning that its cookie, named _ga, is assigned to your domain. That is, if I have GA tracking code on `aliceswonderlandresorts.com`, I have a _ga cookie for that site (not for `google.com` or `google-analytics.com`, for example, which would be a *third-party* cookie).

In many cases, GA's use of cookies is pretty invisible to you, and if you have only a single domain, or several domains that are all separate sites, it isn't something you need to worry about. However, if you have multiple domains or subdomains that operate as a single website, you may need to specify where the cookie is set and how domains share the client ID value.

Choosing a Cookie Domain

Google Analytics uses some default rules to decide the cookie domain, or you can explicitly specify which domain you'd like to use. There are three possible cases for the cookie domain:

- *Default*: `ga('create', 'UA-XXXXX-YY')`
  GA uses the **full domain** shown in the hostname of the URL, except that it ignores a `www.` prefix, if any. If subdomains of your main domain should be treated **separately**, this is the desired option.

- *Automatic Configuration*: `ga('create', 'UA-XXXXX-YY', 'auto')`
  GA uses the **highest-level domain** possible from the hostname of the URL. This is the suggested code when first installing GA. If subdomains of your main domain should be treated **together**, this is the desired option.

- *Manual Configuration*: ga('create', 'UA-XXXXX-YY', 'store.aliceswonderlandresorts.com')
  GA uses the **domain you specify**. The domain must be an ancestor of the domain in the hostname of the URL.

■ **Note**   The create command can accept the cookie domain as the third argument, or you can use the field object. The following are equivalent:

ga('create', 'UA-XXXXX-YY', 'store.aliceswonderlandresorts.com');
ga('create', 'UA-XXXXX-YY', { 'cookieDomain': 'store.aliceswonderlandresorts.com' });

Table 2-1. *Cookie Domains in GA Using Different Settings in the Create Command*

If the URL hostname is...	And the cookie domain setting is...			
	default	'auto'	'example.com'	'store.example.com'
example.com	example.com	example.com	example.com	not allowed
www.example.com	example.com	example.com	example.com	not allowed
store.example.com	store.example.com	example.com	example.com	store.example.com

In most cases, you want to treat multiple subdomains (such as www and store) as a single site, with a single set of cookies, which the auto option does. If you wanted to treat subdomains as separate sites, you would want to specify the domains manually with separate cookies for each.

ALTERNATE COOKIES AND COOKIELESS SOLUTIONS

The default Google Analytics cookie is named _ga. Should you need to rename this cookie to prevent conflicts, you can do so with an additional field in your create command:

ga('create', 'UA-XXXXX-YY', { 'cookieName': 'my_ga_cookie' });

It's also possible to use GA without any cookies at all. To do so, you must supply the Client ID from your own source to identify the device. This option can be useful for syndicated content where you want to avoid first-party cookies, or use a third-party cookie, or supply data from an application on a shared kiosk—for example:

ga('create', 'UA-XXXXX-YY', {
    'storage': 'none',
    'clientId': '5aced0c9-1d2f-4da0-bbdf-5775d8ff7ad7' });

The clientId should be a universally unique identifier following the format of UUID Version 4.[2]

---

[2]www.ietf.org/rfc/rfc4122.txt

Multiple Domains As One Site

Sometimes, you need to treat multiple domains as a single site. This is most common with sites with third-party components, such as a shopping cart, donation site, or other application where some functionality is on a different domain. For example, your site might be aliceswonderlandresorts.com, but to book a hotel stay, users end up on aliceswonderland.example.biz instead, a third-party site.

If the regular GA tracking code were used on such a site, there would be a separate _ga cookie for aliceswonderlandresorts.com and aliceswonderland.example.biz. Since each site would have a different set of client IDs, GA won't connect behavior on one site with the other—for example, did someone who viewed a particular page on your site end up booking a hotel room on the third-party site? That's a question you would probably want to be able to answer, but to do so, you will have to coordinate the client IDs between the two sites (see Figure 2-2).

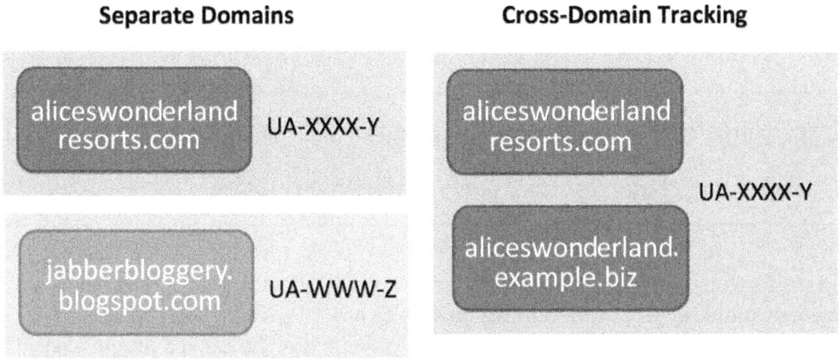

Figure 2-2. *Multiple domains and Google Analytics*

This is known as *cross-domain tracking* in GA. GA provides some functions to append a special parameter to the links or forms that take a user from one site to another that contains the client ID, so that the receiving site uses the same client ID. The links look like this:

```
http://aliceswonderland.example.biz/hotelbooking.php?_ga=1.1821195.1441315.1362115890410
```

The linker parameter _ga contains the client ID for the receiving site. Let's take a look at how to set this up.

Enabling Cross-Domain Tracking

First, in each site's create command, you have to turn on the cross-domain linker function:

```
ga('create', 'UA-XXXXX-YY', 'auto', {'allowLinker': true});
```

When allowLinker is set to true, GA will look in the URL of the page for the linker parameter containing the client ID. If it's present, it will use that value, rather than generating a new client ID for the cookie.

▪ **Note**   The cross-domain linker parameter also includes a timestamp, and the client ID will only be used by GA if the timestamp is within the last two minutes. This helps prevent a user from accidentally sharing a link with a linker parameter and causing multiple users to share the same client ID.

Decorating Links

Next, you have to append the linker parameter to links on either site that go to the other. This is known as "decorating" the links—like hanging a little ornament on the end.

GA provides several utility functions to do this in a plugin called `linker`. The simplest option is to use the `autoLink` command, which allows you to specify a list or pattern of domains to be included and automatically decorates links that appear on your web pages.

```
ga('require', 'linker');
ga('linker:autoLink', ['aliceswonderlandresorts.com', 'example.biz']);
```

The first line loads the `linker` plugin. The second calls the `autolink` command and supplies an array of domains for which you want links to be decorated. The domain list uses a substring match against the destination of the link—notice you can list example.biz or aliceswonderland.example.biz, depending on how specific you want to be.

░ **Tip**   Instead of a list of strings, you can also use a regular expression to match domains:

```
ga('linker:autoLink', [/^aliceswonderland(resorts\.com|\.example\.biz)$/]);
```

The `autoLink` command works well for automatically decorating links on most websites. Some pages may include scripts that prevent autolinking from functioning, so as with any JavaScript, you should test thoroughly before deploying on your site. If autolinking doesn't work for your site, the `linker` plugin also provides a function `linker:decorate` for manually decorating your links. This function is useful in a number of situations aside from standard links:

- Decorating an HTML `form` that posts from one site to another.

- Decorating the destination of an `iFrame` of one site's content within the other.

- Decorating links if the `autoLink` function doesn't play nicely with existing scripts on your site.

Specific examples of these cases are available in the GA Developer Center.

Summary

- Google Analytics uses JavaScript tracking code to track users' activity on a website. The `analytics.js` tracking library is included on each page of the site along with a `create` command (to set up the GA tracker) and a `send` command (to send pageview data to GA).

- Google Analytics uses a first-party cookie named _ga to store a client ID to identify a browser and device. With multiple subdomains or domains, there are options to specify the domain for the cookie.

- With multiple domains, Google Analytics provides cross-domain tracking to share client IDs between sites with different cookies via a parameter in links between the domains. The `linker` plugin provides the functionality to decorate links with this parameter.

CHAPTER 3

■ ■ ■

Introducing Google Tag Manager

At this moment the King, who had been for some time busily writing in his note-book, cackled out "Silence!" and read out from his book, "Rule Forty-two. All persons more than a mile high to leave the court."

—Lewis Carroll, *Alice's Adventures in Wonderland*

The basic Google Analytics code (see Chapter 2) isn't very complicated. Put it in your template and you're all set. Except... Well, there are still a bunch of chapters left in this book with additional types of data you might want to track with GA, many of which involve adding more code. A little piece here for PDF tracking, another little bit over there to track user logins, and so on. The more code you add, the harder it becomes to keep track of all the little pieces, and which of those pieces should be included and under what circumstances, and what happens when you make a change.

And that's just GA. Chances are, you also have other little bits of JavaScript on your site for other tracking tools that capture other kinds of data that are useful—maybe other Google tools like conversion and remarketing tags for AdWords or DoubleClick, or maybe for third-party ad platforms and analytics tools. Sometimes you might have to measure the same pageview or click for two, or three, or four different tools to serve different purposes, and each one takes a JavaScript tag.

If all of that sounds like it could get a little messy, it's because it can. That's where a tag management tool steps in to organize and standardize all those tags.

Why Use a Tag Manager?

Just like your content management system manages the *content* of your website—by allowing you to insert text, headings, and images in a web-based interface—a tag management system manages the *tags*—allowing you to insert those bits of JavaScript, such as the Google Analytics tracking code. It offers a web-based interface to choose, edit, and manage those tags when they are included in your web pages.

This approach offers a number of advantages:

- There's no need to make changes to the actual source code of the site or its templates when updating or adding tags.

- You can keep track of and organize tags to avoid duplication and mistakes.

- There are built-in debugging, testing, and preview tools.

- You can use version control to keep track of changes.

- There are multiple levels of permissions to view, edit, and publish tags.

Tag management tools separate the process of adding and updating tracking tags from the process of altering your site's templates and code. There are a number of good tag management tools available, but this book focuses on Google Tag Manager (GTM), since it's a free tool that works very well with GA. (And if you're a GA Premium subscriber, GTM is also covered by the service-level agreement for GA Premium.)

How Does Google Tag Manager Work?

Google Tag Manager has two components that work together to include tags on your website:

- A web-based interface to set up tracking tags to be included on your site.

- A container script that is placed in your site's template that loads the tags.

Let's take a look at each of these pieces to get your GTM account set up.

Creating a GTM Account

Since GTM is another Google tool, you can use the same Google Account login you use for GA. You can be granted access to a previously existing GTM account or you can create a brand-new one. Just like GA, your login can have access to multiple GTM accounts.

GTM Account Structure

GTM accounts are organized into *containers*. Each container corresponds to a *container script* (see the upcoming "GTM Container Script" section) that is included on a website using GTM. When you sign up for a GTM account, it creates your first container, and you are able to create additional containers as needed. GTM shows an overview of your accounts and containers when you log in (see Figure 3-1).

Alice Worldwide Industries AG		⋮
Container Name ▲	**Container Type**	**Container ID**
aliceswonderlandresorts.com	Web	GTM-593ZN3
iOS app	Mobile	GTM-WQTHQZ

Figure 3-1. *GTM's list of accounts and containers*

In some ways, it seems that there is an obvious parallel between *accounts* and *properties* in GA and *accounts* and *containers* in GTM. At the account level, this analogy holds up well: an account usually represents a single organization or business, in either tool.

The GTM container can be a somewhat broader concept than the GA property, however. For example, while you might have separate GA properties for your development, test, and production websites, you might have a single GTM container to manage the tags across those sites, since you want very similar tags deployed across all of them. A general rule of thumb for GTM containers is that if the tags are mostly the same across websites, use a single container. If they differ greatly between websites, separate containers might be more appropriate. (You'll see more of how these tags are set up over the next several chapters, so you may want to get a feel for how tags work in GTM before you make a final decision about how to structure your account.)

GTM Permissions

Just as in GA, logins in GTM can have different levels of permission at the account and container levels that give them different abilities. You can assign permissions in the User Management section of GTM's Admin area.

At the account level, there are two different levels of permissions:

- *View* allows the user to see the list of users and the account settings, but not to make any changes.

- *Manage* allows the user to add and remove other users and to edit the account settings.

At the container level, there are more detailed permissions:

- *View Only* allows the user to view the tags in the container, but not to make any changes.

- *View and Edit* allows the user to make changes to the tags in the container.

- *View, Edit, Delete, and Publish* allows the user to make changes to tags, delete them, and publish them to the live website.

Changes to your website don't take effect until they are published in GTM. By managing the container permissions, you can ensure that only the users who should be able to change tags or publish them to your website are able to. (The next chapter will take a look in greater detail at the publishing process in GTM.)

▪ **Note**   The GTM account settings additionally enable you to require two-step authentication for certain activities, such as modifying permissions or editing custom tags. Two-step authentication is an additional security measure for Google Account logins that sends a verification code to a phone or other device to verify the user's identity.

GTM Container Script

In order to include tags on your website, you have to add the GTM container script.

On the surface, the GTM container script is just another snippet of code you're adding to your website templates (just like GA or any other tracking code). But the GTM container script is meant to *replace all those other bits of code* as a single script that you won't need to update on your site; all updates will be made through GTM.

When you first create a container, GTM will provide you with the container script and instructions. Or, you can find the container script by selecting the Admin tab at the top and choosing Install GTM in the right-hand column.

The GTM container script looks something like this:

```
<!-- Google Tag Manager -->
<noscript><iframe src="//www.googletagmanager.com/ns.html?id=GTM-XXXXXX"
height="0" width="0" style="display:none;visibility:hidden"></iframe></noscript>
<script>(function(w,d,s,l,i){w[l]=w[l]||[];w[l].push({'gtm.start':
new Date().getTime(),event:'gtm.js'});var f=d.getElementsByTagName(s)[0],
j=d.createElement(s),dl=l!='dataLayer'?'&l='+l:'';j.async=true;j.src=
'//www.googletagmanager.com/gtm.js?id='+i+dl;f.parentNode.insertBefore(j,f);
})(window,document,'script','dataLayer','GTM-XXXXXX');</script>
<!-- End Google Tag Manager -->
```

This code contains your GTM container ID, which is an identifier of the form GTM-XXXXXX that uniquely identifies your container. This code loads a script called gtm.js, which includes all the tags you have set up in GTM.

Like the GA tracking script, the GTM script is asynchronous, so it should be placed as high in the page as possible. However, note that the GTM code contains two parts: a <noscript> tag and a <script> tag. The <noscript> portion allows GTM to include some types of tags even if JavaScript is not enabled in the client browser. These tags are included in an <iframe> element, which means that the GTM code must go in the body of the web page (iframe elements are not officially supported in the head section). Because of this, the recommendation for the location of the GTM code is at the beginning of the body, immediately after the opening <body> tag.

Once the GTM container code is included on your website, tags can be added and published through the GTM web interface.

The Building Blocks of GTM

Once you've created a container, you'll see it listed in GTM's list of accounts and containers. Selecting a container takes you to the container overview (see Figure 3-2). The container overview shows information about recent changes to the container, and prompts you to add your first tag (which we'll do in an upcoming section). In the top navigation, you'll notice tabs for Accounts (which takes us back to the list of accounts and containers), Container (this overview screen), Versions (past versions of the container, discussed in Chapter 4), and Admin (the account and container settings).

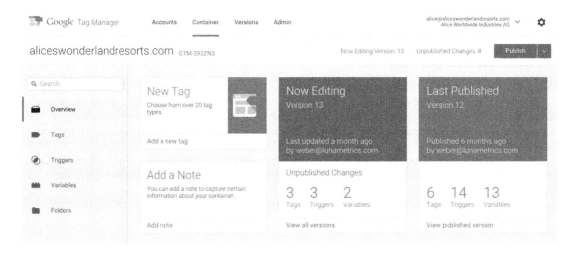

Figure 3-2. *GTM's container overview*

GTM has three building blocks that work together:

- ***Tags***, the tracking components for GA or other tools, which are typically composed of JavaScript or an image (tracking pixel).

- ***Triggers***, which are rules that specify when a tag should be executed by the GTM container.

- ***Variables***, which extract pieces of information from the page for use in tags and triggers.

■ **Note** If you've been using GTM since its beginning, you may remember that triggers were once called "rules" and variables were called "macros". Some older documentation may still contain these terms.

Note that these three building blocks correspond to the items in GTM's left-hand navigation (see Figure 3-2). Clicking on any of these navigation items displays a list of existing tags, trigger, or variables, and allows you to create new ones.

In addition, there's the ability to organize these tags, triggers, and variables into folders. This can be a handy organizational tool as the number of items in your container grows.

Tags

Tags, the first building block of GTM, are the tracking scripts or pixels that tools use to record data. GTM supports any kind of asynchronous tag. It has built-in templates for a number of Google products and third-party tools, as well as the ability to add completely custom HTML or image tags.

For tag templates, GTM handles all of the necessary JavaScript, providing a form with various options and entry fields for filling in settings or data within the tag's code. For example, the GA tag requires you to fill in the property ID. Instead of editing JavaScript, there's a simple form field to fill in this value. (You'll see the entire setup of a GA tag using GTM later in this chapter.) Each different tag template has its own settings based on the options available and the data it gathers.

The tag templates support GA, AdWords conversion and remarketing tags, DoubleClick Floodlight counter and conversion tags, as well as a variety of third-party (non-Google) tools. However, GTM also supports completely custom tags—either custom HTML (into which you can insert any custom HTML, including scripts), or custom image tags (which can be used for tools that use a simple tracking pixel, without scripting). Custom HTML tags, in particular, give great flexibility in using tags from tools for which templates aren't provided, or in using completely custom code to track page elements or user interactions (see Chapter 5).

Triggers

Triggers, the second of GTM's building blocks, describe under which circumstances a tag should be fired. Triggers can evaluate a variety of conditions on variables to determine whether a tag should be executed (see the following section for examples of variables).

When you create a GTM container, it includes one default trigger, All Pages, which executes on any pageview (which would be appropriate for your basic GA tag, for example). However, in many circumstances you want tags only to execute under more specific circumstances (for example, when a conversion occurs or when a certain user interaction takes place). You can create additional triggers, each of which includes one or more conditions. If more than one condition is included in a trigger, all of the conditions must be fulfilled for the trigger to apply (logical AND).

The conditions specified in triggers can specify an exact value, values containing a string, numerical value comparisons such as greater than and less than, or they can use regular expressions to match patterns.

Triggers, once created, can be used on any number of tags. For each tag that you create in GTM, you can assign both *firing triggers* and optional *blocking triggers*. Firing triggers say when the tag should execute. If any of the firing triggers apply, the tag would be executed (logical OR). Blocking triggers specify when a tag should NOT execute, and take precedence over firing triggers.

A tag needs at least one firing trigger to be executed. If you don't assign any triggers to a tag, it will never fire.

Variables

Variables are the third building block of GTM, and they allow you to pull information from a web page for use in tags and triggers. Variables let you customize the information you collect based on the actual content of the page.

GTM variables can be used to fill in the data and settings used in tags and the criteria specified in rules. In entry fields in GTM, you'll see a small building block icon, which allows you to access a drop-down of existing variables within your container. You can also type a variable directly into any text entry field or custom code within GTM using its name enclosed in double curly braces: {{Variable Name}}. GTM will automatically insert the value of the variable. (When referring to variables in this book, we'll use this format as well.)

Your container already includes a number of useful built-in variables, such as {{Page URL}} and {{Referrer}}. You'll see these listed in categories at the top of the Variables section (Figure 3-3).

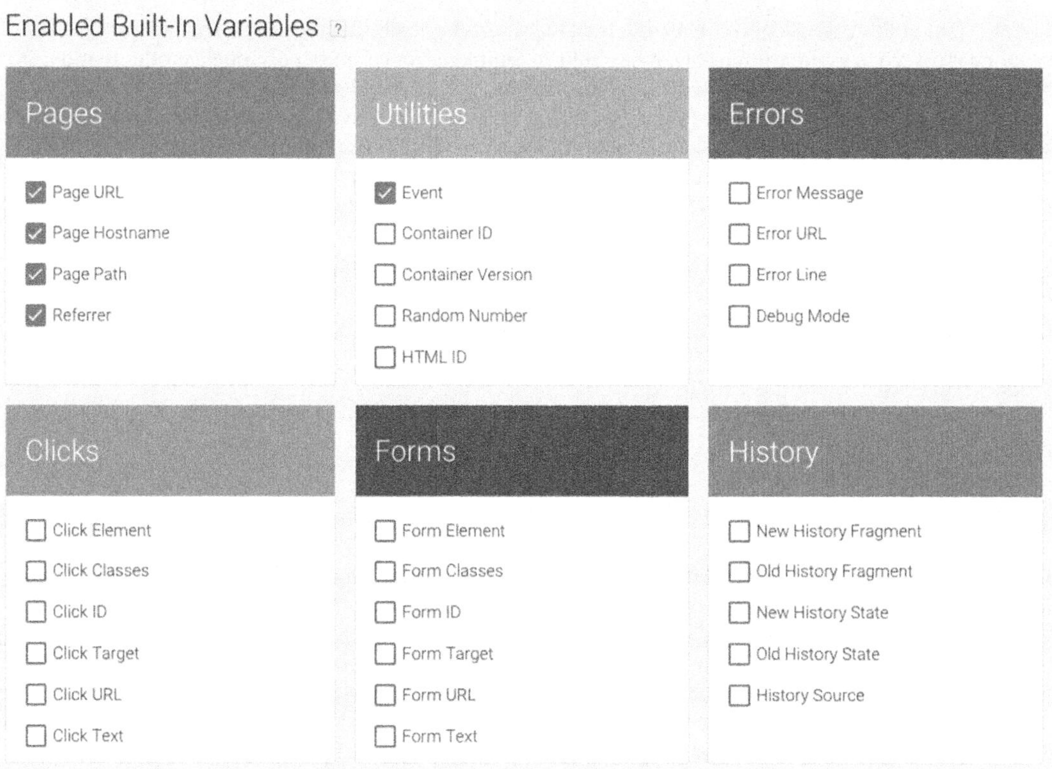

Figure 3-3. Built-in variables available in GTM

Notice that the built-in variables can be enabled or disabled. In a brand new container, a few of the built-in variables will be enabled by default. Those will be sufficient for now, but as other needs arise in later chapters, you'll enable more of these. We'll look at the types of variables and what values they contain below.

You can also create user-defined variables. When creating a new variable, you can select from among a number of different types. The variable types available include the following, which are grouped together into some categories based on their usage:

- *Basic page attributes*: URL, HTTP Referrer

- *Gleaning data from page content*: DOM Element, JavaScript Variable, First-Party Cookie, Data Layer Variable, Custom JavaScript

- *User interactions*: Custom Event, Auto-Event Variable

- *GTM attributes*: Container Version Number, Debug Mode

- *Others*: Constant String, Lookup Table, Random Number

Basic Page Attribute Variables

These variables are based on basic attributes of the page, URL and Referrer.

- *URL*: Your container already has three built-in variables available for the URL of the current page, {{Page URL}} (the full URL from beginning to end), {{Page Hostname}} (just the domain name), and {{Page Path}} (just the pathname portion of the URL, after the domain). The URL variable type additionally allows you to create variables to access individual pieces of the URL (see Table 3-1) for the current page or any other URL. It's a convenient way to avoid having to create regular expressions to match particular parts of a URL string.

Table 3-1. *URL portions available using the URL variable*

protocol	hostname	port	path	query	fragment
http://	aliceswonderlandresorts.com	:8080	/folder/ page.html	?category= hats&sort=mad	#returns

- *HTTP Referrer*: The previous page through which the current page was accessed (via a link or form submission). GTM again includes a built-in variable {{Referrer}} with the entire referring URL, but the variable type allows you to access individual parts of the URL string.

Page Content Variables

The next group of variable types makes use of information that's part of your web page. They use the HTML elements of the page through the browser's Document Object Model (DOM) or via JavaScript to extract page content. You'll make extensive use of the following types of variables in Chapter 5 and further explore their capabilities.

- *DOM Element*: You can specify an element of the page by its id attribute. The contents of the variable can be the text content of the element or the text of an attribute.

- *JavaScript Variable*: You can specify the name of a global JavaScript variable for the page. This includes any global variables available in custom code for your page, but note that you may also access standard DOM variables such as document.title.

- *First-Party Cookie*: You can specify the name of a cookie and access its values.

- *Data Layer Variable*: You can provide information to GTM in a standardized object known as a data layer. See "Providing Data to GTM with a Data Layer" later in this chapter for further information.

- *Custom JavaScript*: The most flexible type of variable, this allows you to include any JavaScript function. The value of the variable is the value returned by the function.

User Interaction Variables

The *Custom Event* and *Auto-Event Variable* types are used for capturing interactions with the page. The built-in variables in the Clicks, Forms, and History categories cover these types. These variables are covered in Chapter 5.

GTM Attribute Variables

These variables, both available as built-in variables, access information used internally by GTM.

- *Container Version Number*: This variable's value is the version number of the currently published GTM container.

- *Debug Mode:* This true/false variable indicates that the page is being viewed using GTM's debug mode (see Chapter 4).

Other Variable Types

- *Constant String*: This variable type can be used for a simple string. Even though it's not dynamic, this variable can be useful for a string that's used in multiple tags or triggers, because it allows a single place to update the value.

- *Lookup Table*: The lookup table variable type allows a series of comparisons to pick a value from a list.

- *Random Number*: This variable contains a random number between 0 and 2,147,483,647. This is available as a built-in variable.

Providing Data to GTM with a Data Layer

In some cases, you'll be able to capture information of interest directly from the page using variables for URLs, DOM Elements, and so on. But at times, there is information you might like to capture that is not part of the page—metadata about the page itself or the user viewing it that is not explicitly displayed in the page's content. Examples could include information such as a page's category (where that isn't made explicit in the URL) or a user's identity (for a site where users log in).

GTM uses an object for communication of this type of information, called a ***data layer***. The data layer provides a centralized list of information made easily accessible to GTM, but which remains invisible to the user viewing the page.

Structure of the Data Layer

The data layer is a JavaScript array named `dataLayer` that contains objects with properties. You can include a data layer in your page by declaring the data layer *before* the GTM container script, like this:

```
<script>
  dataLayer = [{
    'pageCategory': 'hats',
    'userId': '12345'
  }];
</script>
```

Each property provided in the data layer object has a name (which you can retrieve using a variable) and the value that applies to the particular page or user. The property names here, `pageCategory` and `userId`, are merely examples. The data layer properties can have any names you wish, although GTM uses several property names (such as `event`) with special meaning, which you'll see in more detailed uses of the data layer described in Chapter 5 and beyond.

Filling In the Data Layer

Filling in the values of the data layer typically involves server-side code in your website's templates. Your content management system or application server knows the category of the page or the user's login id, for example, and you'll need to pull that data from the appropriate places in those systems to fill in values in the data layer.

Implementing GA Basics with GTM

Now that you've looked at the basic building blocks of GTM, let's work through creating your first functioning tag: the standard GA pageview tracking tag (described in Chapter 2). Let's assume you've already created a GTM container and added the container code to your site.

PART 1: CREATE THE GA TAG

First, create a GTM tag for GA.

1. In the container's Tags section, select the New button.

2. Edit the tag name at the top ("Untitled Tag") to give the tag a name: "GA - Pageview" (see the screenshot below).

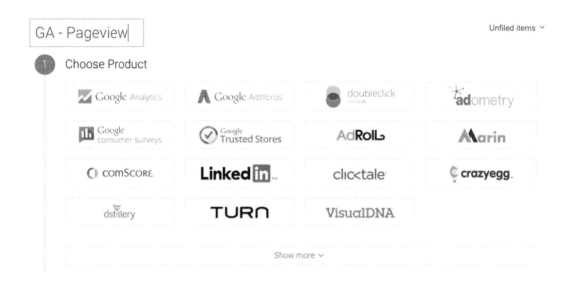

▓ Note   You'll want to devise a sensible naming convention for your tags, triggers, and variables, especially if more than one person adds and edits them in GTM. Typically, tags are named by starting with the type or tool (in this case, "GA"), what's being measured ("Pageview"), and then any additional information needed to describe the tag.

3. Select the tag from the list of supported tag templates: Google Analytics. Select the Continue button.

4. Choose Universal Analytics as the tag type. (Universal Analytics is the current version of the GA tracking code. You could select Classic Analytics to use the previous version if you needed to for some reason.) Select the Continue button to fill in the GA tag's options.

5. Enter your property ID in the Tracking ID field (see the screenshot below). This is the UA-XXXXX-YY identifier for your web property in GA. GTM uses this field to fill in the value in the GA code's `create` command.

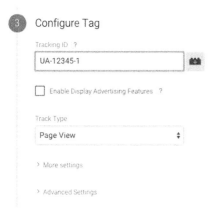

6. Select Track Type ➤ Page View as the type of GA tracking you'd like to use (see the screenshot above). This corresponds to the `send` command with the hit type `pageview`, as seen in the GA tracking code.

These are all of the settings you need to supply if you are using the standard, out-of-the-box GA tracking code, since they correspond to the two commands in GA (`create` and `send`). However, you'll notice that there are many more settings available under More Settings. These correspond to additional settings passed in the GA tracking code. You'll find items discussed in the customizations in Chapter 2, such as a tracker name (Advanced Configuration ➤ Set Tracker Name) and cross-domain tracking features (Cross Domain Tracking). There are fields that affect additional types of data, such as content groups, ecommerce data, and custom dimensions and metrics, which are features explored in further chapters.

Although many additional fields in GA are available as settings in these categories, you can also use the Fields to Set section, which is equivalent to using the field object in your GA code (see Chapter 2). If there are any settings that you need to change in GA that do not have a corresponding setting in GTM, you can use Fields to Set.

Two important notes about the default GA tag settings in GTM:

- **If no tracker name is specified, GTM assigns a random tracker name to each GA tag.** In this way, every tag in GTM creates a differently named tracker.

- **If no cookie domain is specified, GTM uses the default option (the full domain name, minus www.), not the** `auto` **option.** If we'd like to use the `auto` option, we need to use the Fields to Set to set `cookieDomain` to `auto` (like the screenshot below).

Both of these options in the GA code are discussed in Chapter 2.

PART 2: ASSIGN A TRIGGER

Before you save your new GA tag, you need to assign at least one trigger so that it executes.

1. Still in the tag creation screen, select the Continue button to assign triggers to your tag.

2. You have the opportunity to select from some basic trigger types. Since you want your default GA pageview tag to execute on every page, you can select the All Pages trigger provided (see the screenshot below).

3. At this point, you are ready to save your tag. Select the Create Tag button at the bottom of the page to save and return to the container overview.

PART 3: ADD FLEXIBILITY WITH VARIABLES

So far, you've set up your GA pageview tag to execute on every page, and that's all you really need it to do. However, it pays to do a little planning and use variables for any piece of information you might reuse. Is there anything you've configured so far that might benefit from using a variable?

You'll remember that you just typed the GA property ID into the corresponding setting in the GA tag. If you've got just one tag, that's not a big deal, but as you add additional types of tracking as you go forward, you're going to use that property ID again. If you create a variable, you can use it over and over without worrying about typos, and it will be easy to update everywhere if you need to change it.

Let's create a variable for the GA property ID.

1. In the container's Variables section, select the New button.

2. Give the variable a name: "GA Property ID".

3. Select the type of variable: Constant String.

4. Enter your property ID (UA-XXXXXX-YY) as the value of the variable.

5. Select Save to save and return to the container overview.

Now that you have a variable for the property ID, let's update the GA tag to use it.

1. In the container overview, select your GA tag to edit.

2. In the Tracking ID field, delete the existing value that you typed in directly earlier.

3. Select the building block icon on the right of the Tracking ID field to see a list of macros to fill in.

4. Choose the {{GA Property ID}} variable that you created (see the screenshot below).

5. Select Save to save and return to the container overview.

When you include a variable in a field in GTM, you can either select it from the block drop-down, or type it in directly. Either way, at the time the tag executes {{Variable Name}} will be filled in by GTM with the value of the variable.

What Comes Next

So far, you've set up a tag with a trigger and a variable. However, note that so far *nothing has changed on the website*. None of the changes in GTM are made live until you publish them to the site. Chapter 4 will talk about the publishing process and testing tools that you can use to ensure that everything is in order before you make the code live.

What you've set up so far covers the basic GA pageview tracking. In further chapters, you'll look at all the other types of data you might send to GA, and how to accomplish that with GTM.

SIDEBAR: MIGRATING TO GTM

If you're just starting out with GA, you have the opportunity to create all of your tags in GTM from the start. But what about sites that already have an existing implementation of GA (with code directly on the pages), where you'd like to migrate to using GTM to manage the tags?

You want to go through this migration without disrupting your data collection in GA. Here's the recommended process:

1. Create a GTM container and add the container script to your website. Do not change or remove any of the existing GA code at this point.

2. Create a new property in GA. This will be a temporary property for testing, which you can delete after the migration is complete.

3. Implement GA tags in GTM using the new property ID. The goal is to re-create any existing GA tracking on the site, using tags in GTM. This includes the standard pageview tracking, as well as any additional tracking, such as events, ecommerce, custom dimensions, and so forth. Since you have both your existing property and the new property tracking from GTM, you'll be able to compare to ensure that you're tracking all the same things and that the numbers match. Continue to refine until you are confident that you have replicated your existing implementation with GTM.

4. Last, the tricky part. At approximately the same time, you want to do two things:

    a. Remove *all* existing GA code from the website. This includes both the standard pageview tracking code as well as any additional custom code you've added.

    b. Switch the property ID in the GA tags in GTM from the new property to the old. (This is quick—especially if you use a variable for the property ID as recommended earlier).

Removing the old code can be the tricky part here. Ideally, you can do it all in a single push, but it depends on your site's deployment process and your content management system. Remember that any gap between removing the old code and switching the property ID in GTM means a gap of time in which you weren't capturing data to your property in GA. (Conversely, any overlap would result in double counting.) So you want to time this transition carefully and do it during a noncritical time.

Summary

- Google Tag Manager is a free tag management system that provides capabilities to manage, version, and publish tracking tags to your website. As with Google Analytics, you can log in to GTM using a Google login, and there are multiple levels of permissions that can be assigned to users.

- A GTM container is managed through a web interface and is a collection of tags (JavaScript or image code snippets to be included), triggers (rules to specify when to fire or block tags), and variables (pieces of information pulled from the page to fill in tag data or trigger criteria). The GTM container script goes on every page on the website(s) being managed with GTM, replacing the need for adding tags directly to those pages.

- GTM variables can access information in the page, such as the URL and HTML elements. GTM can also use a data layer, which is a way of providing information in a central place for GTM using a JavaScript object. The data layer can be used to provide additional information about a page or the user viewing it when that information is not readily apparent or available from the page itself. The data layer is typically filled in with server-side code.

CHAPTER 4

Testing Your Implementation

She generally gave herself very good advice, (though she very seldom followed it).

—Lewis Carroll, *Alice's Adventures in Wonderland*

That Publish button is really enticing in Google Tag Manager (GTM), but you should know what you're about to do before you click it. This chapter explores the testing and publishing process in GTM, as well as testing and evaluating data accuracy in Google Analytics to ensure that you've set up your tags correctly.

Publishing in Google Tag Manager

You can set up a collection of tags, triggers, and variables in your container. Until you deploy them using Tag Manager's publishing process, GTM won't include them in the container when it's loaded on a web page. You have to explicitly choose to publish your changes before they take effect.

The container overview always includes information about the current draft, the published version, and how many tags, triggers, and variables have changed between them. When you're ready to try out the changes you've made, you should first preview them on the site before publishing.

Preview and Debug Mode

You can enter GTM's Preview mode by selecting the drop-down on the Publish button in the top-right corner and then choosing Preview.

You'll see a banner indicating that you are in Preview mode in the container overview (see Figure 4-1). Behind the scenes, GTM has set a cookie so that only your web browser will receive the new tags, triggers, and variables you've set up, while all other visitors to the site continue to get the previous published version. This is the most important thing to understand about Preview mode: *it works on your live website, but only for you.*

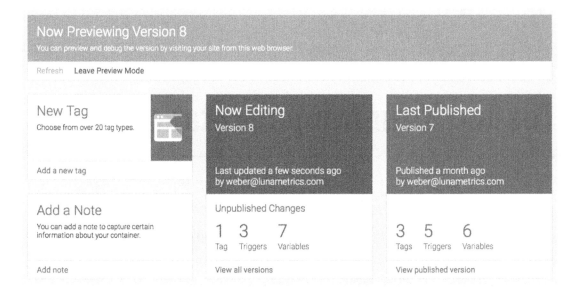

Figure 4-1. *Google Tag Manager container overview indicating Preview mode*

You can now visit your website to see what GTM is doing. GTM's Preview mode adds a debug panel at the bottom of the page when loading the site; it includes information about which tags fired (and didn't) for the page (see Figure 4-2).

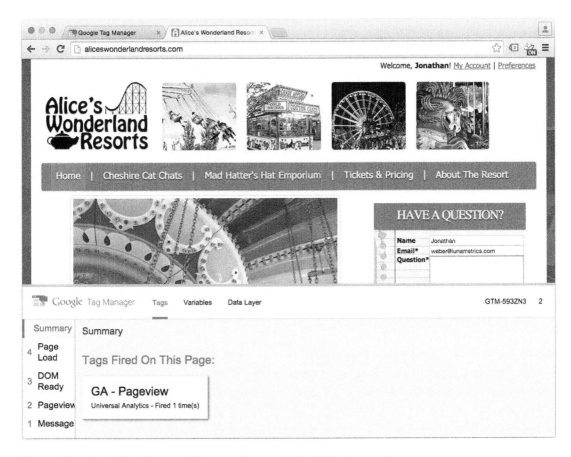

Figure 4-2. *Google Tag Manager debug panel on a website in Preview mode*

___

■ **Note**   Some types of ad-blocking software may prevent GTM's debug panel from loading. If you don't see the debug panel after entering Preview mode, disable these tools in your browser for your website and try again.

___

You can click a tag to see more information about its properties that were filled in by GTM and the triggers that caused it to fire (see Figure 4-3).

Figure 4-3. *Details available in the GTM debug panel*

■ **Note**   You can also see the value of variables and messages pushed to the data layer for the page with the additional tabs at the top of the debug panel. In Chapter 5 you'll explore using these for measuring additional interactions.

Every time you make changes in GTM, before publishing you should use Preview mode to inspect the changes and to make sure that your tags are firing when you expect them to (and not when you don't). Remember, Preview mode only affects what you see in your browser, not what others who visit your website see.

If you make changes to GTM while in Preview mode (such as altering a tag or trigger), select Refresh to update your site. You can exit Preview mode at any time by selecting Leave Preview Mode. Both of these options are found in the Preview mode banner at the top of GTM.

Beyond GTM's debug panel, there are a number of additional browser tools that can be useful for seeing the GTM and GA code that is included on the page, which you'll take a look at later in the chapter.

GTM AND DEVELOPMENT, TEST, AND STAGING SITES

Beyond the testing enabled by Preview mode in GTM, you may have additional processes already in place for testing updates to your site, through development, test, or staging versions of the site. In some cases, GTM allows you to skip this process and simply use GTM's preview tools, since you can deploy changes in GTM without requiring changes to the source code of your site. For changes and additions in GTM that accompany changes to the content of the site itself, however, you will want to ensure that everything is working on these test sites before they are put into production through your normal processes.

Whatever your current testing setup, GTM's preview tools provide you with an additional layer of assurance that code will work correctly when published to your live production site. All these tools only work if you use them, however. *Don't skip straight to the publish button and use GTM as a way to avoid testing.* Thorough testing ensures accurate measurements in GA and other analytics tools, and more importantly, a website that doesn't malfunction for users.

Chapter 8 will discuss some best practices for separating data in GA for production vs. test sites, along with some tips and tricks for doing that most effectively using GTM.

Publish Your Container

If you're satisfied with what you see in Preview mode, you are ready to publish your changes and make them live for all viewers of your website.

To publish, click the Publish button. GTM will indicate the changes that are being updated in the currently published version, and then ask for a confirmation. Once you confirm, GTM publishes the changes to the website.

Version Management

Each time you publish your container, GTM creates a new *version*. Versions are sequentially numbered, fixed snapshots of the container's tags, triggers, and variables. While the container overview always shows the current draft contents, it also provides the ability to view the currently published version (right) or to view a list of all previous versions (center). You can also view the list of all versions in the Versions tab in the top navigation.

The list of previous versions includes information about when the version was created and published, and who published it. By selecting a version, you can see a more detailed audit trail of edits and publication history for the version, as well as the tags, triggers, and variables it contains.

You can give the version a name and record notes about it in the Actions drop-down (at the right of the listing in the list, or at the top right in the version details). Naming the version adds a descriptive label in addition to the version number (such as "Added GA tag"). Adding notes allows more extensive descriptions of changes or details.

For any version, you have the opportunity to Preview, Publish, or Edit as a New Version. This allows you to revert to an earlier working version of your container if you have inadvertently published something that isn't working correctly. You can also Share Preview, which gives you the ability to send a link to someone else to view the Preview version in their browser. (Remember that Preview mode uses a cookie and only appears in your browser. The shareable link allows someone else to see the same thing.)

Finally, you may delete a version if desired. Deleted versions are permanently removed, so you should only do this if you need to remove versions that are broken or that you want to prevent from being republished to the website.

GTM's version management tools create a very good record of what's been done in GTM and when changes were published to your site, as well as provide the ability to revert changes quickly if anything goes wrong.

You also have the opportunity to create a version from the current draft *without* publishing it, using the drop-down on the Publish button on the container overview. This allows you to create a saved checkpoint of progress you have made without publishing it yet.

Troubleshooting Tools for GA

GTM's debug panel (described in the previous sections) is useful for understanding which tags fired when in GTM, including tags for GA. Sometimes, however, you want to know exactly what information was sent to GA, either for published or previewed versions of your GTM container.

The following sections provide suggestions for a variety of tools that can assist you in delving into how your tags work. The focus is primarily on the Chrome browser, since there are several tools available from Google specifically for Chrome, but comparable functionality is available in all browsers, and options for other browsers are also discussed.

Chrome Tag Assistant

The best at-a-glance tool for inspecting which GA tags are included on a page and what they are doing is the Tag Assistant, an extension provided by Google for the Chrome web browser. It installs an icon onto the Chrome toolbar that contains information about Google-related tracking tags that are included in the page currently being viewed in the browser, such as GTM, GA, AdWords, and DoubleClick tags.

Clicking the Tag Assistant icon (see Figure 4-4) reveals information about the tags, such as the container ID for GTM or the property ID for GA, as well as suggestions or warnings for the tags if they seem to be implemented in a nonstandard way or don't seem to be functioning correctly.

Figure 4-4. *Tag Assistant extension for Chrome*

The Tag Assistant is an easy way to check whether Google tags are included in a page, and which GTM container or GA properties are being used to track the page.

Google Analytics Debug Mode

To see more information about the data gathered and sent by Google Analytics, GA has a debug mode of its own. Enabling the GA debug mode prints information on what GA has done to the JavaScript console, which is a log in your browser that tracks JavaScript warnings, errors, and messages.

Enabling GA Debug Mode

There are two ways that you can enable GA's debug mode: by altering the GA tracking code (through the GTM tag), or by using a browser extension in Chrome. Altering the GA tag in GTM requires publishing a new version of your container to take effect, while using the extension you can turn the debug mode on and off at will (in your browser only).

- *Alter the GA tag in GTM.* In your GA tag in GTM, in the More Settings ➤ Advanced Configuration section, there is a setting labeled Use Debug Version. Setting this option to True enables GA's debug mode.

  Although you could always set this option to True, keep in mind that this will enable GA's debug mode for all visitors to the site (although visitors won't see anything different unless they look at their browser's JavaScript console). A better solution is to use the {{Debug Mode}} variable in GTM, which is True only when GTM is in the Preview mode discussed earlier in the chapter. (You'll have to enable this variable before using it in your GA tag.)

  Of course, you need to publish the container for the altered tag to take effect.

- *Use the GA Debugger Chrome Extension.* If you are using Chrome as your browser, you can install the GA Debugger Extension, which allows you to turn on GA debug mode on any website that you are viewing.

  Like the Tag Assistant extension described earlier, this extension installs an icon in the Chrome toolbar that allows you to turn GA debug mode on and off. Simply click the icon to turn it on (which will reload the current page in your browser window). Click again to turn it off.

  Using the extension allows troubleshooting at any time, without entering GTM's Preview mode or publishing changes to your container.

Viewing GA Debug Information

Once GA debug mode is enabled by either of these two methods, you can view information on what data GA collected and sent by using the JavaScript console.

In Chrome, you can access the console via the Chrome menu under More Tools ➤ JavaScript Console. (You can also find it in the View menu under Developer, or Ctrl+Shift+J on a PC or Cmd+Opt+J on a Mac.) In other browsers, check your documentation for menu items or keyboard shortcuts to access the JavaScript console.

The console contains JavaScript errors, warnings, and messages. GA's debug mode prints several messages about the commands executed by GA (see Figure 4-5).

```
Q  [?]   Elements  Network  Sources  Timeline  Profiles  Resources  Audits  | Console |

⊘  ▽   <top frame>                    ▼  ☐ Preserve log

▼  Initializing Google Analytics.
  | ▼  Running command: ga("create", "UA-11111-1", {name: "gtm1421680844556", al
  | ⓘ   Creating new tracker: gtm1421680844556
  | ▼  Running command: ga("gtm1421680844556.set", "&gtm", "GTM-593ZN3")
  | ▼  Running command: ga("gtm1421680844556.set", "anonymizeIp", undefined)
  | ▼  Running command: ga("gtm1421680844556.set", "hitCallback", [function])
  | ▼  Running command: ga("gtm1421680844556.send", "pageview")
  |   ⓘ
  |     Sent beacon:
  |     v=1&_v=j31d&a=1701399377&t=pageview&_s=1&dl=http%3A%2F%2Faliceswonderlan
  |     bit&sr=1280x800&vp=1280x701&je=1&fl=16.0%20r0&_u=cACAAAQBI~&jid=&cid=755
  |
  |   ⓘ  <unknown>      (&gtm)  GTM-593ZN3
  |   ⓘ  _j1            (&jid)
  |   ⓘ  adSenseId      (&a)    1701399377
  |   ⓘ  apiVersion     (&v)    1
  |   ⓘ  clientId       (&cid)  755588149.1412614064
  |   ⓘ  encoding       (&de)   UTF-8
  |   ⓘ  flashVersion   (&fl)   16.0 r0
  |   ⓘ  hitType        (&t)    pageview
  |   ⓘ  javaEnabled    (&je)   1
  |   ⓘ  language       (&ul)   en-us
  |   ⓘ  location       (&dl)   http://aliceswonderlandresorts.com/
  |   ⓘ  screenColors   (&sd)   24-bit
```

Figure 4-5. *Viewing the JavaScript console with GA debug mode enabled*

The "Sent beacon" message indicates that GA has sent a tracking hit upon the execution of a send command. Below that message is a breakdown of the data included in the hit. This serves as your confirmation of any data that was sent to GA from the GA tag(s) included in GTM.

Other Browser Tools

Apart from the tools specifically for GTM and GA described in previous sections, browsers include a number of general-purpose web development tools that can be useful to view the GA and GTM scripts included in a page, the GA cookies, and the GA tracking hits generated.

In Chrome, beside the Console tab, the Developer Tools also include a browsable tree of the HTML document (the Elements tab; see Figure 4-6), a list of scripts included and cookies set for the current page (the Resources tab), and a list of outgoing requests from the browser window and the responses received (including the GA tracking hit, in the Network tab).

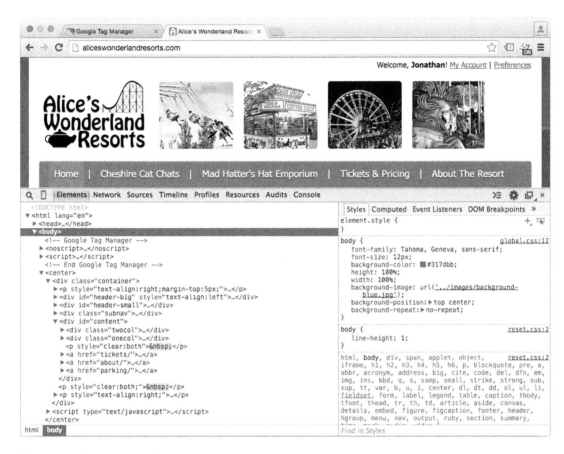

Figure 4-6. *Chrome's Developer Tools*

Internet Explorer, Firefox, and Safari all contain developer tools that are similar to Chrome's. Check your browser's documentation for menu items and keyboard shortcuts to access these tools.

Google Analytics Real-Time Reports

Browser-based tools check whether appropriate tracking code is included in a page and what data it sends. You can also take a look at the tracking data received by GA.

The majority of reports in GA take some time to calculate, and so aren't up-to-the-minute, but the Real-Time reports show a live stream of data just as it's received by GA. You can go to your site, view a page or trigger an event, and see the data appear in the Real-Time reports (see Figure 4-7).

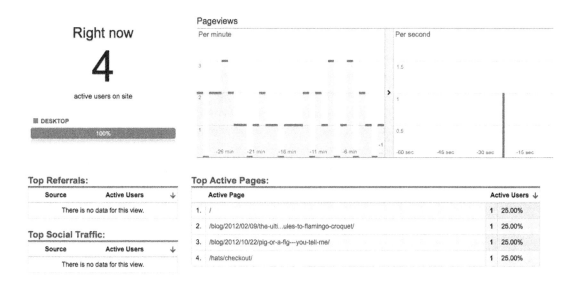

Figure 4-7. *The Real-Time reports in GA are useful for ensuring that data is received during testing*

These reports cover a variety of data, but the two reports most useful for troubleshooting are the Content report (which shows pageviews received by GA) and the Events report (which shows events received by GA). These will be especially useful in Chapter 5, which talks about measuring additional interactions within pages, such as link clicks.

Summary

- Google Tag Manager's Preview mode allows you to see the effects of new tags, triggers, and variables on your site in your web browser, before publishing them to the site for everyone. GTM loads a debug panel in your site's pages with information about which tags were triggered.

- Changes you make in GTM are not live on your site until you publish them. When publishing, GTM creates a numbered version of your container's contents. You can name and record notes about versions to document changes that were made, as well as publish a version if you need to revert to an earlier state of your container.

- Beyond GTM's preview tools, there are a number of browser tools that can help inspect code, cookies, and tracking hits. The Tag Assistant and GA Debug Chrome extensions are especially helpful, and you can also use your browser's developer tools and GA's Real-Time reports for verification that tags successfully sent data.

PART II

Enhancing Website Data with Google Tag Manager

███

CHAPTER 5

Tracking Interactions with Google Tag Manager

"Alice had begun to think that very few things indeed were really impossible."

—Lewis Carroll, *Alice's Adventures in Wonderland*

Beyond the basics of measuring pageviews, there are often other interactions, within pages, that you're interested in tracking with Google Analytics. These might include clicks on elements of the page, such as links to downloads or external websites, interactions with embedded video, or social media buttons on a page. This chapter discusses collecting data on those types of interactions using Google Tag Manager to send data to Google Analytics.

Tracking Interaction in Google Analytics

You'll recall that the basic Google Analytics tag captures pageviews. A pageview is only one of several *hit types* that represent different kinds of data that GA can collect. Besides the pageview hit type, two additional hit types, *event* and *social*, can be used to collect other kinds of interactions. (There are others as well, such as the *screenview* and *exception* types for mobile apps, and *transaction* and *item* for ecommerce, which you'll come to in later chapters.)

Event and social hits are similar to each other. Event hits are designed for any type of interaction within a page, while social hits are specifically for social media interactions. Each appears in its own set of reports (events in the Behavior reports in GA, social in the Acquisition reports). Let's start by focusing on events, and look at social interactions later in the chapter.

To send an event to GA, you can use the following JavaScript command:

```
ga('send', 'event', 'category', 'action', 'label', value, {'nonInteraction': false});
```

You'll see that there are several pieces of information used to describe the event:

- The *category* is required, and represents a way to group similar types of events for your site. For example, you might have categories such as Downloads, Outbound Links, and Videos.

- The *action* is also required, and describes the interaction within the category. For example, the Videos category might have actions like Play, Pause, or Finish.

- The *label* is an optional text field to further describe the event.

- The *value* is an optional integer that describes the event. There are no specific units associated with the value, so it might be dollars, seconds, points in a game, or any number that fits to describe the event.

- Finally, the *non-interaction* parameter controls whether the event affects bounce rate. By default, this is `false`, meaning that if a user lands on a page and then triggers an event, that session is no longer a bounce (which is usually what's desired if the event represents a user interaction). By setting it to `true`, the event no longer counts as an interaction and the session is still a bounce unless another interaction occurs (which may be what's desired for an event that automatically occurs when the page loads, such as a video that auto-plays, for example).

The category, action, and label appear as dimensions in GA, and the value as a metric. These dimensions and metrics appear in the Events reports in the Behavior section of GA, and whatever data you send with your event code are the values that appear in your GA reports. Because of this, it's important to design naming conventions for events that make sense and are consistent. The examples in this chapter have a number of suggestions for how you might name events, but you should do it in a way that is most useful and understandable for your GA users.

Of course, GTM has a built-in tag to include GA's event tracking code, just like for your pageview tracking. In the GTM tag, you still get to specify the same parameters (category, action, and so on).

CREATE A BASIC GA EVENT TAG IN GTM

You can add a GA event tag in GTM by following these steps:

1. Create a new tag. Select Google Analytics ➤ Universal Analytics as the tag type.

2. As you did in the pageview tag, you'll fill in the Tracking ID with the {{GA Property ID}} variable that you previously created (see Chapter 3).

3. Select Track Type ➤ Event. You'll notice that this reveals input fields for category, action, label, value, and non-interaction (see the following screenshot).

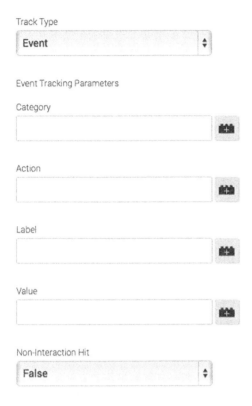

4. For now, you can fill values in by directly typing them into the event fields. In most cases you will use variables to fill them with relevant information from your page. This will be a key topic for this chapter. Select Continue to proceed to the next step.

5. Next, choose the tag's triggers. You can skip the triggers for now. Choosing the right triggers will be another key topic for this chapter.

6. Select the Create Tag button to save the tag, giving it a name: "GA – Event".

That's the basic process. In the rest of the chapter, you'll learn about the variables and triggers to use to fill in the blanks, and how those relate to measuring specific actions on your site.

Design Patterns for Events in GTM

The tag itself for event tracking is straightforward. The trick is to create the right triggers (to say when the tag should fire) and variables (to capture the right information about what interaction occurred, and to fill in the category, action, and other information). This chapter looks at several general design patterns for using GTM to track events, and then at a number of specific examples of the most common types of items to be tracked.

There are several approaches to tracking events in GTM because you can choose how much of the code is handled in GTM versus code that is included in the page itself. Whichever approach makes sense for you depends on your capabilities and your level of access to add or change code in your site's pages or templates.

All of these approaches make use of GTM's data layer. In addition to setting information in the data layer at the time the page loads (discussed in Chapter 3), you can send additional messages to the data layer at any time, which is how events within a page can be triggered in GTM. You can add information to the data layer about an interaction using the following code:

```
dataLayer.push({'event': 'event-name'});
```

This code adds a new message, or list of properties, to the data layer. The event property is used by GTM to trigger tags. You'll name different events that occur on your pages and use those names to trigger your tags. You can include additional properties with details about the event to pass additional information to GTM variables, which you'll see in examples throughout this chapter.

The data layer, then, comprises a sequential list of messages about different events that occur on the page. In fact, GTM creates several of its own events (the names of which are all prefixed with gtm). These GTM events are:

- gtm.js (labeled "Pageview" in the debug panel) is the first event in the data layer, and is sent as soon as the GTM container is loaded. This is the default event for tags with page-based triggers (such as your GA pageview tag).

- gtm.dom (labeled "DOM ready" in the debug panel) is sent when the DOM is ready. This means your browser has loaded the structure of the DOM, but not necessarily that all page content has been loaded or rendered.

- gtm.load (labeled "Page Load" in the debug panel) is sent when the page is completely rendered in the browser, including images, scripts, and other contents.

GTM's debug panel (see Chapter 4) will show any messages pushed to the data layer, as well as the current value of any variables after the message is pushed. You can click an event in the list on the left and select the Variables or Data Layer tabs at the top to see this information (see Figure 5-1).

Figure 5-1. *Viewing variables and data layer messages in the GTM debug panel*

SIDEBAR: JAVASCRIPT AND DOM EVENTS

The first challenge is to trigger the tag at the appropriate time: usually, when the user clicks something in the page in the browser.

Fortunately, JavaScript allows you to call a function when almost any user action occurs within the page. Browsers use a convention called the Document Object Model (DOM) to represent the content of the page and to allow JavaScript to interact with that content. The DOM allows you to access a certain element of the page (a link, button, form field, etc.) and to call a JavaScript function when a certain event happens (clicking the link, entering text in the form field). The DOM includes events for mouse interactions, keyboard interactions, and more. Most typically, you'll be interested in a click, but you'll see examples of other kinds of interactions as well.

The simplest possible example of calling JavaScript on a click might look like this:

```
<a id="link1" href="/some/link" onclick="someFunction();">Click me</a>
```

You can call a JavaScript function using attributes on the element in question. In this case, `someFunction()` is called when a user clicks on this link.

You can also add a click event to an element with an *event listener*, which is a function you add elsewhere in the page targeting that element by its id, position in the DOM, or other attributes.

```
<script>
    document.getElementById('link1').addEventListener('click', someFunction);
</script>
```

GTM uses the DOM and its events in its built-in auto-event tracking. Gaining an understanding of the DOM will be useful if you need to expand beyond the capabilities of GTM's auto-event tracking with custom JavaScript.

Several of the examples in this chapter use these techniques, and working with the DOM through JavaScript is a useful skill for you to develop to extend and adapt these examples. *Beginning JavaScript with DOM Scripting and Ajax* by Russ Ferguson and Christian Hellmann (Apress, 2013) is a step-by-step introduction to the topic and an excellent starting point.

Design Pattern 1: GTM's Auto-Event Tracking

The first design pattern uses features of GTM to move code from the page into GTM. In many cases, you may be able to use GTM's auto-event tracking capabilities to track page interactions without adding *any* additional code to the page.

GTM has built-in capabilities to listen for clicks, form submissions, errors, and more. These can be set up with a set of built-in variables and easy-to-configure triggers that don't require adding your own JavaScript code. This approach has the advantage of reducing or eliminating your reliance on adding code to the site itself.

When you create a tag in GTM, you are prompted to select a trigger from the types shown in Figure 5-2.

3   What triggers this tag to fire?

Choose one or more triggers from the following types:

All Pages	Some Pages	Click	Form	More

No triggers selected. This tag will not fire.

Continue

Figure 5-2. *Trigger type choices when creating a tag*

You previously used the All Pages trigger for your pageview tracking tag for GA, and Some Pages gives you the option to fire tags only on a subset of pages. The Click and Form trigger options allow you to track those types of interactions (the most common), while selecting the More button gives additional options. (The primary focus of this chapter is on the Click trigger, although Custom Event and Timer triggers are also discussed. The Form and History Change triggers are covered in Chapter 6 as part of tracking goal conversion funnels.)

These triggers use built-in capabilities for deploying event listeners on your site using GTM, without you needing to write any code to enable them.

In addition to the triggers, there are also variables that correspond to information collected about the element that was clicked, the form that was submitted, and so on. These built-in variables can be enabled or disabled, and you'll want to make sure that you enable the relevant variables before using the corresponding trigger type.

For clicks, GTM provides a number of variables:

- The {{Click Element}} variable returns the entire HTML object that was clicked from the DOM, including all its attributes.

- {{Click Classes}} and {{Click ID}} return the values of the class and id attributes (if any) on the element.

- {{Click URL}} includes the destination of a link element (the href attribute).

- {{Click Target}} includes the value of the target attribute (for example, target="_blank" to open the link in a new window/tab).

- {{Click Text}} includes the text content of the element.

Suppose the following link were clicked. GTM's auto-event variables would have the values listed in Table 5-1.

```
<a id="link1" class="button" href="http://example.com" target="_blank">Click me!</a>
```

Table 5-1. *Values for the built-in click variables for an example link*

Variable	Value
{{Click Element}}	HTML Object
{{Click Classes}}	button
{{Click ID}}	link1
{{Click URL}}	http://example.com
{{Click Target}}	_blank
{{Click Text}}	Click me!

CREATE A BASIC CLICK TRIGGER IN GTM

Let's look at the basic process for adding a click trigger in GTM.

1. In the Triggers section in the left-hand navigation, select the New button to create a new trigger.

2. For the event that causes the trigger, select Click.

3. Choose whether the trigger applies to clicks on all elements, or only clicks on links (see the screenshot below; more on this choice in the next section). Then select the Continue button.

4. (Optionally, if Just Links is selected) Choose to filter pages where this trigger is enabled. Then select the Continue button.

5. Choose to listen for All Clicks (it would be uncommon to want to trigger the same event on all clicks) or Some Clicks, which allows you to specify one or more filters. The filter can be based on the click variables described earlier, or any other variables you have in GTM (see the screenshot below). You'll see a variety of examples in this chapter.

6. Save the trigger, giving it a name describing the conditions it matches, such as "Clicks – Button Links".

All Elements and Just Links Target Types

When you create a Click trigger, there is a target type option with two choices: "All Elements" and "Just Links". Choosing All Elements allows you to listen for a click any element of the page, while Just Links applies only to links (<a> elements).

Why does GTM treat these differently? Opening a link typically replaces the current page in the browser window, which means that any JavaScript executing in the current page is interrupted. (This is not a problem for links that load in a separate window, or that merely trigger a tab, modal popup or other content within the same page, but it does affect any content that replaces the current page in the same browser window, including links to web pages or PDFs, for example.) The interruption of JavaScript could mean that as the destination page of the link begins to load, your tracking tags are prevented from executing. In order to work around this, Link Click triggers give an additional option (see Figure 5-3) to delay the link until the tags have finished or a short maximum time elapses (whichever occurs first; 2 seconds by default).

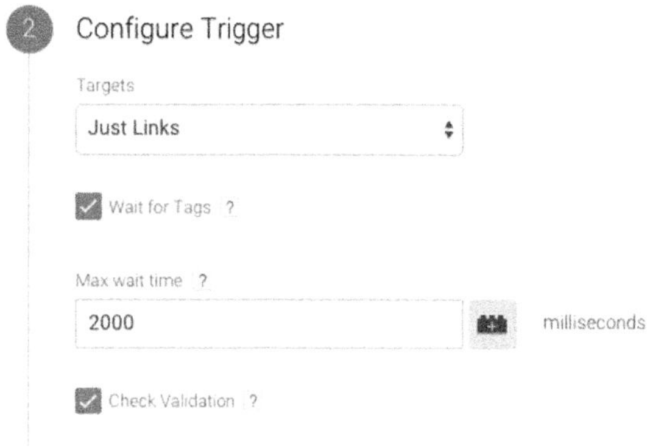

Figure 5-3. *Additional configuration options for link clicks*

For clicks on links, there's also the ability to limit the pages on which the listener is active (Figure 5-4). Since the "Just Links" option can temporarily interrupt other actions that result from clicking the link, you should be extra careful about testing before publishing to ensure that this behavior doesn't affect the functionality of your website. This option allows you to restrict the trigger to only pages where it is needed and thoroughly tested.

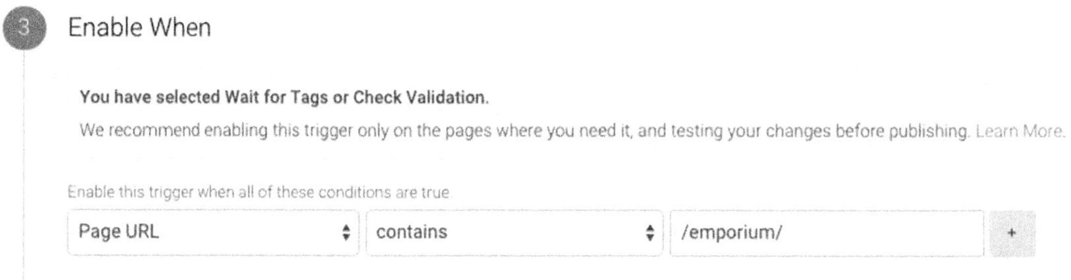

Figure 5-4. *Restrict the pages on which the link click trigger is enabled*

The Mechanics of Auto-Event Tracking

What GTM actually does for these auto-event tracking triggers is quite simple. It adds event listeners to the DOM and, when the event occurs, it does a `dataLayer.push` with a number of related pieces of information it uses to populate the variables described earlier. Here's an example of what a data layer message for a GTM auto-event looks like:

```
dataLayer.push({
        'event': 'gtm.click',
        'gtm.element': http://aliceswonderlandresorts.com,
        'gtm.elementClasses': 'button',
        'gtm.elementId': 'link1',
        'gtm.elementUrl': 'http://aliceswonderlandresorts.com',
        'gtm.elementTarget': '_blank' }
});
```

GTM's event names and properties are all prefixed with `gtm` to keep them separate from any events you may push to the data layer and prevent naming collisions. They are all string values, except for `gtm.element`, which contains the entire HTML object that was clicked.

Just like any other data layer message, you can see these in GTM's debug pane while in preview mode.

SIDEBAR: IDS, CLASSES, AND DESIGNING FOR TRACKABILITY

Being able to use GTM to find the elements you want to track within the content of your page is really important. This is most easily accomplished by providing some descriptors that will help identify the correct element(s). The `class` and `id` attributes are among the most useful.

The `class` and `id` attributes are an important part of the DOM. An element can have an `id`, which must be unique within the page (it applies to only that element). It can also have one or more `classes`, which represent a particular kind of element. Multiple elements can have the same `class`, and a single element can belong to multiple `classes` (separated by spaces).

GTM has variables for `{{Click ID}}` and `{{Click Class}}`, and they can be an easy way to select the correct elements. Without them, or some other attributes (like link URL) to help you select the correct element, as a last resort you would have to instruct GTM like so: Find the `<a>` element in the third `<li>` in the second `<ul>` in the `<div>` with `id=content`. You can see how this approach is fragile and easily breakable if the content of the page changes. Ensure that your site templates are adequately structured so that you can select the elements you want without resorting to these methods.

Design Pattern 2: Custom JavaScript in GTM

Auto-event tracking is great, but it works only under certain circumstances. If there are events that you'd like to track outside the situations GTM supports, you'll have to use some custom JavaScript to handle those. One option would be to include that JavaScript on your site (see the upcoming "Design Pattern 3" section). Better yet, though, you can include custom JavaScript in tags and variables inside GTM, so that you can manage them there, without needing to add or change code on the site.

GTM allows you to include custom JavaScript code in two different ways:

- A custom HTML tag can include a script tag, which can execute any JavaScript functions you desire. You can add event listeners, add or change elements, and push events to the data layer.

- A custom JavaScript variable can return a value, for example if you need to grab an element or property from the DOM, test if an element is visible, and so on.

You'll make use of both of these tools in the examples in this chapter. These tools will allow you to create custom event listeners for interactions outside what GTM can track using its auto-event tracking. These examples are where some knowledge of JavaScript and the DOM becomes useful (see the sidebar earlier in the chapter for more information).

SIDEBAR: PRO TIPS FOR JAVASCRIPT NINJAS

If you're already a developer familiar with JavaScript, this design pattern is right up your alley. It allows you all the flexibility of including custom JavaScript, with the advantages of versioning and testing in GTM. Here are a few recommendations.

For code you include in GTM, **follow JavaScript best practices** such as wrapping scripts in Custom HTML tags in anonymous functions and checking for the existence of variables (such as `dataLayer`) before using them. Such practices are an especially good idea to avoid conflicts if several independent developers may be adding JavaScript to the site.

Also, remember to **rely on GTM features rather than reinventing or obscuring them with JavaScript**. For example, use the built-in click listeners rather than attaching events with `addEventListener()`, and to give your triggers clarity use the `gtm.js` or `gtm.dom` events, rather than code in a tag that uses `window.onload` or other methods.

Design Pattern 3: Explicit Data Layer Events in Site Code

The last design pattern for event tracking in GTM uses code to specify the category, action, and other data for the event explicitly on the page.

```
<a onclick="dataLayer.push({'event': 'customEvent', 'eventInfo': {'category': 'Button',
'action': 'press'}})">...</a>
```

Here an event name (`'customEvent'`) is specified, as well as the category and action you'd like to send to Google Analytics. This is flexible for your site's developers, since you only need a single event tracking tag in GTM to handle many different possibilities. Its disadvantage is that you need to add information about the events to your pages by adding code directly.

■ **Note**   Although this example uses an inline `onclick` attribute to call the `dataLayer.push` function, the code could be used in an event listener or any other existing JavaScript code on the site.

This approach does work well if you already have GA event tracking code on your site and are migrating to GTM, and wish only to make a simple change to the existing code for these legacy events. For example, you might already have code like this:

```
ga('send', 'event', 'Button', 'press');
```

This would be easy to simply change to the following:

```
dataLayer.push({'event': 'customEvent',
               'eventInfo': {
                       'category':'Button',
                       'action': 'press' }
});
```

This approach doesn't really get you the full range of benefits of GTM (managing and testing code within GTM), since you're including code directly in the page. **There are, however, a number of advantages to this pattern.** It gives you a quick and easy path to update existing event code on the site to use GTM. It's also developer-friendly, in the sense that if you have developers creating site code, they can easily add events without needing to interact with GTM. Obviously, there is a trade-off between centralizing control in GTM and allowing flexibility for the site developers.

With this code on the site, you can create a GTM tag, trigger, and variables to send the data to GA.

CREATE A GENERIC EVENT TAG

Let's assume that you have script on your site of the following form:

```
dataLayer.push({
    'event': 'customEvent',
    'eventInfo': {
        'category':'someCategory',
        'action': 'someAction',
        'label': 'someLabel',
        'value': 0,
        'nonInteraction': false }
});
```

First, you'll have to create variables for each of your event data inputs: category, action, label, value, and non-interaction.

1. In the Variables section in the left-hand navigation, select the New button to create a new user-defined variable.

2. For the variable type, choose Data Layer Variable.

3. For the Data Layer variable name, enter eventInfo.category (which corresponds to the name in the preceding code).

4. Save the variable, giving it a name such as "Custom Event Category".

5. Repeat for eventInfo.action, eventInfo.label, eventInfo.value, and eventInfo.nonInteraction.

Now, you can create the tag and trigger to use these variables to send an event to GA.

1. Create a new tag. Select Google Analytics ➤ Universal Analytics as the tag type.

2. Fill in the Tracking ID with the {{GA Property ID}} variable that you previously created.

3. Select Track Type ➤ Event.

4. In each of the Category, Action, Label, Value and Non-Interaction fields, enter the corresponding variable you created earlier (see the following screenshot). Then select the Continue button.

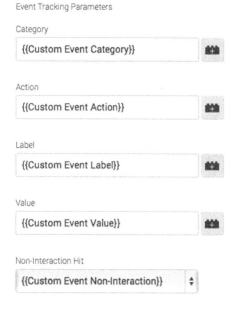

Event Tracking Parameters

Category

{{Custom Event Category}}

Action

{{Custom Event Action}}

Label

{{Custom Event Label}}

Value

{{Custom Event Value}}

Non-Interaction Hit

{{Custom Event Non-Interaction}}

5. For the trigger, choose More, which will bring up a list of existing triggers. To create a new trigger:

   a. Click the New button.

   b. Select Custom Event as the event to cause the trigger. Custom Event allows you to trigger on a dataLayer.push with any event name.

   c. For the Event name to match, enter customEvent (which corresponds to the name in the preceding code).

   d. Select the Create Trigger button, giving the trigger a name: "Custom Event – Click". GTM saves the trigger and returns to creating the tag.

6. Save the tag, giving it a name: "GA – Event – Custom".

Now, whenever a dataLayer.push occurs containing 'event': 'customEvent', this tag will be triggered to send an event to GA using the eventCategory, eventAction, and other values specified in the code.

Applications of Interaction Tracking

Given the three design patterns you've laid out, you can now take a look at some specific applications of tracking in GTM. As a guiding principle, you'll stick to GTM's auto-event tracking (design pattern 1) and use custom JavaScript within GTM for cases not covered by auto-event tracking (design pattern 2). The third design pattern always exists as a fallback should you need it, but the examples in this chapter will avoid it in favor of solutions that centralize tracking code in GTM and do not rely on adding code to your site.

Outbound Links

Let's start with one of the simplest and most common scenarios for tracking events in GA: recording clicks on links to other websites. Such links could range from merely informational links, to articles or content hosted on other websites, to important affiliate links, or to channel traffic to third parties with whom you have a relationship. In any of these situations, you might want to know who clicks on which links, and how often.

This scenario is a perfect application for your first design pattern: using GTM's auto-event tracking, since this is a straightforward use of tracking clicks on links.

▪ **Note** GA's pageview tracking already allows you to see the order of pages within your site that a user viewed during the session, so you don't need to use events to track *internal* links, unless you want to pay special attention to certain links (such as a particular promotional link, or a link in a particular position in dynamically rotating content, for example).

You can use the Click URL variable in the trigger to target only links that point to other sites. Although you can use the whole click URL (which includes the full URL, e.g., `http://aliceswonderlandresorts.com/directions?location=wonderland`), it would be handy to have a variable that has just the hostname (e.g., `aliceswonderlandresorts.com`). You can do this by setting up an additional variable. Let's walk through the whole process.

TRACK OUTBOUND LINKS

First, create the variable for Click URL Hostname. Then you can use that variable in creating your tag and trigger.

1. Select the Variables section in the left-hand navigation. Then select the New button to create a new user-defined variable.

2. For the variable type, choose Auto-Event Variable.

3. For the variable type, select Element URL (see the following screenshot). For the component type, instead of Full URL (which is what the built-in variable already has), select Host Name. Notice there's also an option to strip off a leading `www.` if you prefer.

4. Save the variable, giving it a name: "Click URL Hostname".

Now that you've created the variable, you can create the tag and trigger.

1. Create a new tag. Choose Google Analytics ➤ Universal Analytics as the type.

2. Use your previously created {{GA Property ID}} variable for the Tracking ID.

3. Select Track Type ➤ Event.

4. Fill in the Category, Action, and Label to be sent to GA. You'll want to choose your own conventions for how you'd like to see these in your reports, but one sensible choice might be:

    •   Category: Outbound Link

    •   Action: {{Click URL Hostname}} (e.g., example.com)

    •   Label: {{Click URL}} (the full URL, e.g., http://example.com/some-page.html)

5. Select the Continue button to specify a trigger for the tag.

    a. Choose Click, and then select the New button to create a new click trigger.

    b. Choose Just Links as the target type (which accounts for tracking of links that open in the same browser window; see earlier in the chapter for a discussion of the difference between All Elements and Just Links triggers). Choose the Wait for Tags option with the default two-second maximum.

c. Select the Continue button to filter pages on which the trigger is enabled, if needed. If you want to restrict this trigger to only listening for outbound links on certain pages, you can use a condition or regular expression to match certain pages. To listen on all pages, use a regular expression to match any URL:

```
{{Page URL}} - matches RegEx - .*
```

d. Select the Continue button to choose the firing conditions. Choose Some Clicks.

e. Select the `{{Click URL Hostname}}` variable you created from the drop-down, and then criteria to match (see the screenshot below).

```
{{Click URL Hostname}} - does not end with - aliceswonderlandresorts.com
```

■ **Note** If necessary, you could use a regular expression to match several hostnames (if you have the same GTM container across multiple sites).

---

f. Select the Create Trigger button to save the trigger, giving it a name: "Click – Outbound Links". GTM saves the trigger and returns to creating the tag.

6. Save the tag, giving it a name: "GA – Event – Outbound Links".

PDFs and Other Downloads

Another common type of link to track is any link to a downloadable file (PDFs, most commonly, but a link to any file that isn't a web page can also be tracked).

The process for tracking downloads will be similar to the outbound link tracking in the previous section. The Click URL variable you used would contain the file name of the linked file, and you could use some conditions based on this variable to trigger your tag (probably using a regular expression). However, it might be handy for you to pull out just the file extension (so you can check if it's a web page or a download). You can create a variable to do exactly that. Here's the process.

TRACK DOWNLOAD LINKS

First, create the variable for Click URL File Type. Then use that variable in creating a tag and a trigger.

1. Create a new variable.

2. For the variable type, choose Custom JavaScript. Here's the code to use[1]:

```
function() {
  var clickUrlParts = {{Click URL}}.pathname.split('.');
  return clickUrlParts.length > 1 ? clickUrlParts.pop() : 'html';
}
```

This uses the existing `{{Click URL}}` variable, gets just the pathname part (stripping off the domain, query parameters, and anchor), finds a dot (if there is one), and returns the characters after the dot. If there's no dot (thus, there's no file name), assume the URL is for a web page and return `html` as the file type.

3. Save the variable, giving it a name: "Click URL File Type".

Examples values for the `{{Click URL File Type}}` *variable*

URL of link	Value of variable
/alice/map.pdf	pdf
/alice/map.pdf?location=wonderland	pdf
/alice/index.html	html
/alice/	html

Now that you've created the variable, you can create the tag and trigger.

1. Create a new tag. Choose Google Analytics ➤ Universal Analytics as the type.

2. Use your previously created `{{GA Property ID}}` variable for the Tracking ID.

3. Select Track Type ➤ Event.

4. Fill in the Category, Action, and Label to be sent to GA. You'll want to choose your own conventions for how you'd like to see these in your reports, but one sensible choice might be:

   • Category: Download

   • Action: `{{Click URL File Type}}` (e.g., pdf)

   • Label: `{{Click URL}}` (the full file URL, e.g., http://aliceswonderlandresorts.com/park-map.pdf)

---

[1]This very elegant function was first proposed by Stephane Hamel on the GTM Google+ community.

5. Select the Continue button to specify a trigger for the tag.

   a. Choose Click, and then select the New button to create a new click trigger.

   b. Choose Just Links as the target type (which accounts for tracking of links that open in the same browser window; see earlier in the chapter for a discussion of the difference between All Elements and Just Links triggers). Choose the Wait for Tags option with the default two-second maximum.

   c. Select the Continue button to filter pages on which the trigger is enabled, if needed. If you want to restrict this trigger to only listening for download links on certain pages, you can use a condition or regular expression to match certain pages. To listen on all pages, use a regular expression to match any URL:

      `{{Page URL}} - matches RegEx - .*`

   d. Select the Continue button to choose the firing conditions. Choose Some Clicks.

   e. Select the `{{Click URL File Type}}` variable you created from the drop-down, and then criteria to match. You could just use "contains `pdf`" (for example), but then you'd need to create a separate trigger for each different type of file you're interested in. Instead, let's use a regular expression (see the screenshot below):

      `{{Click URL File Type}} - matches RegEx (ignore case) - pdf|doc|xls|zip`

Fire On

Fire this trigger when all of these conditions are true.

| Click URL File Type ⬍ | does not match RegEx (ignore case) ⬍ | pdf|doc|xls|zip | - | + |

   Feel free to extend this regular expression to take into account other types of files on your site. Alternatively, if you want to track anything that isn't a web page, a trigger like this one would work:

   `{{Click URL File Type}} - does not contain - htm`

   Note that this will track any non-HTML link, including images.

   f. Select the Create Trigger button, giving the trigger a name: "Click – Download Links". GTM saves the trigger and returns to creating the tag.

6. Save the tag, giving it a name: "GA – Event – Downloads".

```
┌─────────────────────────────────────────────────────────────────┐
│              PRO TIP: SESSIONS LANDING ON DOWNLOADS               │
└─────────────────────────────────────────────────────────────────┘
```

If you're paying close attention, you'll notice that this code doesn't really track *downloads*, it tracks *clicks on downloads*, which is a subtle but important distinction. What happens if someone lands directly on a PDF from a link from another website (like a search engine, for example), without going through one of your web pages?

Since you can't include JavaScript in PDFs or other files, they're not directly measurable with GA, GTM, and JavaScript. However, you could use server-side code to intercept a direct request for a PDF, send data to Google Analytics, and then seamlessly redirect the user to the PDF file. This is a perfect application for GA's Measurement Protocol (see Chapter 14).

Mail and Phone Links

It's possible to include links that launch a new email or dial a phone number by using link URLs like the following:

```
<a href="mailto:madhatter@aliceswonderlandresorts.com">Send me email!</a>
<a href="tel:14125550000">(412) 555-0000</a>
```

In these cases, you can see that it would be straightforward to adapt the approach you've used for outbound links and downloads in the previous sections in this chapter. You could trigger only when the {{Click URL}} variable begins with mailto: or tel:, for example.

Tabs, Hover, Scroll, and Other Content Interactions

There are many additional ways that users can interact with the content of the pages on your website. In this section, you'll look at a variety of examples of measuring engagement with page content.

Tabs and Other In-Page Content

Tabs, accordions, and other ways of showing and hiding content on the page are typically interacted with by clicking an element that you can use a click trigger to listen for. Ideally, the tabs or accordion links have a class or ids that you can leverage in your trigger criteria to select the correct elements.

```
<div class="tab">
        <span class="tab-title">Tweedle Dee</span>
        <div class="tab-content">...</div>
</div>
<div class="tab">
        <span class="tab-title">Tweedle Dum</span>
        <div class="tab-content">...</div>
</div>
```

You can see how to use the auto-event listeners that were already discussed with filters such as the following: {{Click Classes}} – contains – tab-title. What if you don't have nice neat class or id attributes on the items you'd like to track, however?

Recall that in addition to the variables like {{Click Classes}} and {{Click ID}}, there is also the {{Click Element}}, which contains a reference to the DOM for the element that was clicked. GTM provides the option to match by a CSS selector, which allows us to specify a hierarchy of elements, classes, or or id attributes to target (see Figure 5-5). Keep in mind that this approach can be fragile and broken by the arrangement of elements on the page changing, so it should be used carefully and only when other methods are insufficient.

Figure 5-5. *Using a CSS selector to target a link element (<a>) in a list item (<li>) contained in an element with id=content*

■ **Note**   Similar to tabs or other in-page content, a related issue is pages using AJAX, where a complex sequence of interactions may occur within a single page—an entire checkout or registration process, for example—without the page reloading. In cases like this, you may actually wish to record additional pageviews to GA in order to separate and track the process. This scenario is discussed further in Chapter 6.

Time Spent

GA calculates metrics like Time on Page and Session Duration in a very simple way: it simply subtracts the timestamp of one page from the next page the user views.

This isn't a perfect measure by any means. For example, what about the last page the user views? They might have spent 10 seconds or 10 minutes, but you don't really know. Since there isn't a subsequent timestamp to subtract it from, it doesn't have a time on page and isn't included in the session duration.

GTM includes Timer triggers that allow you to trigger an event every so often, which is a simple way for you to get a more accurate picture of how much time users spend on pages.

```
EVENTS FOR TIME SPENT ON PAGE
```

1. Create a new tag. Choose Google Analytics ➤ Universal Analytics as the type.

2. Use your previously created {{GA Property ID}} variable for the Tracking ID.

3. Select Track Type ➤ Event.

4. Fill in the Category, Action, and Label to be sent to GA. You'll want to choose your own conventions for how you'd like to see these in your reports, but one sensible choice might be:

   • Category: Time Spent

   • Action: 30 second interval

5. Select the Continue button to specify a trigger for the tag.

   a. Choose More, and then select the New button to create a new trigger.

   b. Choose Timer as the event to cause the trigger.

   c. Keep `gtm.timer` as the event name. (Notice that you could have multiple "stopwatches" running with different names, on different cycles or to time different things, but let's assume for now this is the only one.)

   d. As the interval, let's use 30000 (that's milliseconds, so 30 seconds). And for the limit, let's say 60 times (so it will stop counting after 30 minutes if the user is still on that same page).

▨ **Note**   Have some care about how rapid your timers are, and set a limit on them. GA has a limit of 500 hits per session, so let's not fire an event every second!

---

   e. Select the Continue button to filter pages on which the trigger has the timer count on (if needed). If you want to restrict this trigger to only timing certain pages, you can use a condition or regular expression to match certain pages. To user the timer on all pages, use a regular expression to match any URL:

      `{{Page URL}} - matches RegEx - .*`

   f. Select the Continue button to choose the firing conditions. Choose All Timers. (Note that, if you desired, you could have the trigger only fire on the first timer event, or every second one, or other conditions you impose. Here you just want all of them.)

   g. Select the Create Trigger button, giving the trigger a name: "Timer – 30s". GTM saves the trigger and returns to creating the tag.

6. Save the tag, giving it a name: "GA – Event – Time Spent".

▨ **Caution**   Please note that implementing these timer events will have a significant impact on time-based metrics in Google Analytics (Time on Page, Session Duration) as well as the Bounce Rate metric. You should be prepared for this, and make a conscious decision about how much time on a page you want to be considered "not a bounce" for a user.

You could go even further in measuring the time the user is truly engaged with the content, by checking things such as whether the tab is active, how far down the page they've scrolled, and so on. See the next section for an example using scrolling.

Scrolling

If you're trying to measure how people engage with the content on your site, you often want to know more than just that they viewed a page: did they really read it? One way of getting at that would be to measure the scroll depth (that is, how far down the page the user scrolled). This is the first example where GTM's auto-event tracking can't do what you need. Since the action you're interested in isn't a click or other action supported by auto-event tracking, you'll need to use custom JavaScript to create your own listener.

EVENTS FOR SCROLL DEPTH

This setup will involve two tags. The first is the custom tag with an event listener for scrolling events, which will push messages to the data layer to indicate the events of interest. The second will be the GA event tag to send data about these to GA.

First, let's create the event listener tag.

1. Create a new tag. Select Custom HTML as the type.

2. For the HTML, enter the following code:

```
<script id="gtm-scroll-tracking" type="text/javascript">
;(function(document, window, config) {

  // Browser dependencies, script fails silently
  if (!document.querySelector || !document.body.getBoundingClientRect) {
    return false;
  }

  // Get our dataLayer ready, in case we're not in GTM or we've got a special name
  var dataLayerName = config.dataLayerName || 'dataLayer';
  var dataLayer = window[dataLayerName] || (window[dataLayerName] = []);
  var cache = {};

  // Initialize our distances, for later
  config.distances = config.distances || {};

  checkDepth();
  addEvent(window, 'scroll', throttle(checkDepth, 500));

  function getMarks(_docHeight, _offset) {
    var marks = {};
    var percents = [];
    var pixels = []
```

```
      if(config.distances.percentages) {
        if(config.distances.percentages.each) {
          percents = percents.concat(config.distances.percentages.each); }
        if(config.distances.percentages.every) {
          var _every = every_(config.distances.percentages.every, 100);
          percents = percents.concat(_every); }
      }

      if(config.distances.pixels) {
        if(config.distances.pixels.each) {
          pixels = pixels.concat(config.distances.pixels.each); }

        if(config.distances.pixels.every) {
          var _every = every_(config.distances.pixels.every, _docHeight);
          pixels = pixels.concat(_every); }
      }

    marks = addMarks_(marks, percents, '%', _docHeight, _offset);
    marks = addMarks_(marks, pixels, 'px', _docHeight, _offset);
    return marks;
  }

  function addMarks_(marks, points, symbol, _docHeight, _offset) {
    var i;
    for(i = 0; i < points.length; i++) {
      var _point = parseInt(points[i], 10);
      var height = symbol !== '%' ? _point + _offset : _docHeight *
      (_point / 100) + _offset;
      var mark = _point + symbol;
      if(height <= _docHeight + _offset) { marks[mark] = height; }
    }
    return marks;
  }

  function every_(n, total) {
    var n = parseInt(n, 10);
    var _num = total / n;
    var arr = [];
    for(i = 1; i < _num + 1; i++) { arr.push(i * n); }
    return arr;
  }

  function checkDepth() {
    var _bottom = parseBorder_(config.bottom);
    var _top = parseBorder_(config.top);
    var height = docHeight(_bottom, _top);
    var marks = getMarks(height, (_top || 0));
    var _curr = currentPosition();
```

```
    for(key in marks) {
      if(_curr > marks[key] && !cache[key]) {
        cache[key] = true;
        fireAnalyticsEvent(key); }
    }
}

function fireAnalyticsEvent(distance) {
    dataLayer.push({
      'event': 'scrollTracking',
      'attributes': { 'distance': distance }
    });
  }
}

function parseBorder_(border) {
  if(typeof border === 'Number' || parseInt(border, 10)) {
    return parseInt(border, 10); }

  try {
    // If we have an element or a query selector, poll getBoundingClientRect
    var el = border.nodeType && border.nodeType === 1 ? border :
    document.querySelector(border);
    var docTop = document.body.getBoundingClientRect().top;
    var _elTop = Math.floor(el.getBoundingClientRect().top - docTop);
    return _elTop;
  } catch (e) { return void(0); }
}

// Adapted from https://developer.mozilla.org/en-US/docs/Web/API/Window/scrollY
function currentPosition() {
  var supportPageOffset = window.pageXOffset !== undefined;
  var isCSS1Compat = ((document.compatMode || "") === "CSS1Compat");
  var currScrollTop = supportPageOffset ?
                      window.pageYOffset :
                      isCSS1Compat ?
                        document.documentElement.scrollTop :
                        document.body.scrollTop;
  return parseInt(currScrollTop, 10) + parseInt(viewportHeight(), 10);
}

function viewportHeight() {
  var elem = (document.compatMode === "CSS1Compat") ?
             document.documentElement :
             document.body;
  return elem.clientHeight;
}
```

```
function docHeight(_bottom, _top) {
  var body = document.body;
  var html = document.documentElement;
  var height = Math.max(body.scrollHeight, body.offsetHeight,
                        html.clientHeight, html.scrollHeight, html.offsetHeight);
  if(_top)    { height = height - _top; }
  if(_bottom) { height = _bottom - _top; }
  return height - 5;
}


/*
 * Throttle function borrowed from:
 * Underscore.js 1.5.2 http://underscorejs.org
 * (c) 2009-2013 Jeremy Ashkenas, DocumentCloud and Investigative
   Reporters & Editors
 * Underscore may be freely distributed under the MIT license.
 */
function throttle(func, wait) {
  var context, args, result;
  var timeout = null;
  var previous = 0;
  var later = function() {
    previous = new Date;
    timeout = null;
    result = func.apply(context, args);
  };
  return function() {
    var now = new Date;
    if (!previous) previous = now;
    var remaining = wait - (now - previous);
    context = this;
    args = arguments;
    if (remaining <= 0) {
      clearTimeout(timeout);
      timeout = null;
      previous = now;
      result = func.apply(context, args);
    } else if (!timeout) {
      timeout = setTimeout(later, remaining); }
    return result;
  };
}

// Cross-browser compliant event listener
function addEvent(el, evt, fn) {
  if (el.addEventListener) { return el.addEventListener(evt, fn); }
```

```
    if (el.attachEvent) {
      return el.attachEvent('on' + evt, function(evt) {
        // Call the event to ensure uniform 'this' handling, pass it event
        fn.call(el, evt);
      });
    }

    if (typeof el['on' + evt] === 'undefined' || el['on' + evt] === null) {
      return el['on' + evt] = function(evt) {
        // Call the event to ensure uniform 'this' handling, pass it event
        fn.call(el, evt);\
      }
    }
  }

})(document, window, {
  // False if you just use the default dataLayer variable, otherwise
    enter it here
  'dataLayerName': false,
  'distances': {
    // Configure percentages of page you'd like to see if users scroll past
    'percentages': {
      'each': [10,90],
      'every': 25
    },
    // Configure for pixel measurements of page you'd like to see if
      users scroll past
    'pixels': {
      'each': [],
      'every': null
    }
  },
  // Accepts a number, DOM element, or query selector to determine the top
    of the scrolling area
  'top': null,
  // Accepts a number, DOM element, or query selector to determine the
    bottom of the scrolling area
  'bottom': null,
});
</script>
```

3. For the trigger for the tag, select All Pages. (Alternatively, if you only wish to track scrolling on some pages of your site, you could specify a more restrictive trigger here.)

4. Save the tag, giving it a name: "Listener – Scroll Events".

You don't necessarily need to understand all the details of this script to use it, but in a nutshell what it does is this: it allows us to set some breakpoints (by percentages or pixels) in a configuration object (the bolded section at the end of the code), and then monitors for scrolling activity and sends a message to the data layer when those breakpoints are reached (which you can see in the earlier bolded section). A few smart things this script includes are the following:

- Careful cross-browser support so that it functions across the widest variety of browsers and versions.

- A cache that capture whether each of the events has previously been sent (so that there's only one 25% scroll event for the page, for example).

- A timer that throttles how often the scroll position is checked (in this case at most every 500 milliseconds), so that you're not running your function every time the screen moves one pixel.

These are good concepts to incorporate in any custom event listeners you create.

Next, let's create a variable for the `distance` data layer property.

1. Create a new variable.

2. For the variable type, choose Data Layer Variable.

3. For the Data Layer variable name, enter `attribute.distance` (which corresponds to the name in the preceding code).

4. Save the variable, giving it a name: "Scroll Progress".

Finally, create a tag to send this data as events to GA.

1. Use your previously created {{GA Property ID}} variable for the Tracking ID.

2. Select Track Type ➤ Event.

3. Fill in the Category, Action, and Label to be sent to GA. You'll want to choose your own conventions for how you'd like to see these in your reports, but one sensible choice might be:

    - Category: Scrolling

    - Action: {{Scroll Progress}}

4. Select the Continue button to specify a trigger for the tag.

    a. Choose More, and then select the New button to create a new trigger.

    b. Select Custom Event as the event to cause the trigger. Custom Event allows you to trigger on a `dataLayer.push` with any `event` name.

    c. For the Event name to match, enter `scrollTracking` (which corresponds to the name in the preceding code).

    d. Select the Create Trigger button, giving the trigger a name: "Scroll Tracking Event".

5. Save the tag, giving it a name: "GA – Event – Scroll Tracking".

Hover and Other Interactions

When a user *clicks* on an element, GTM's auto-event tracking can be used. JavaScript additionally supports other types of interactions, such as *mouseover* (that is, moving one's mouse over an element, so that you could track hovering that doesn't necessarily result in a click), *change* (for entering text or changing a selection in a form element), and many others as well. These aren't built in to GTM's auto-event tracking, but you can build on the model with custom JavaScript to track these interactions using GTM.

Extending GTM's Auto-Event Tracking Model

A sensible way to model the data for an interaction like hovering would be to parallel the same pieces of data GTM captures for a click.[2] You might use the following data layer message to indicate a mouseover:

```
dataLayer.push({
        'event': 'mouseover',
        'gtm.element': http://aliceswonderlandresorts.com,
        'gtm.elementClasses': 'button',
        'gtm.elementId': 'link1',
        'gtm.elementUrl': 'http://aliceswonderlandresorts.com',
        'gtm.elementTarget': '_blank' }
});
```

Look familiar? It's just like the data layer message that GTM's auto-event tracking creates for a click, except the name of the event is mouseover instead of gtm.click. This lets you use the same set of familiar variables to set up your event tags. The only thing you'll need to add is a tag that generates this message to the data layer when the desired interaction occurs.

To do that, you'll need to write some of your own JavaScript; consult the sidebar earlier in the chapter for resources. The addEvent and sendAnalyticsEvent functions in the scroll tracking code in the previous section are also a good foundational example for extending to your own event listeners.

Social Interactions

Another common type of interaction within a page is a social action: the now nearly ubiquitous "Like This" and "Tweet This" buttons (and every other social network you can think of). Although you could measure these with event tracking in Google Analytics, GA actually has a separate, specific hit type specifically designed to capture information particular to social interactions, with its own report (in the Acquisition ➤ Social ➤ Plug-ins report in GA, where it is brought together with other data about social traffic to your website).

The GA code for tracking a social interaction is very similar to event tracking:

```
ga('send', 'social', 'network', 'action', 'target');
```

Instead of an event's category, action, and label, a social interaction has a network, action, and target:

- The ***network*** is the social network (Facebook, Twitter, etc.)
- The ***action*** is what the user did (like, unlike, follow, tweet, retweet, etc.)
- The ***target*** is the thing that is being liked or tweeted, usually a URL (and often simply the URL of the current page)

---

[2]Credit to Doug Hall at Conversion Works for first suggesting this pattern.

Of course, GTM has a tag that generates the GA code for you, just like for events, where you can fill in the network, action, and target with variables (see Figure 5-6).

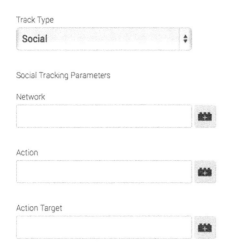

Figure 5-6. *GA's social tag in GTM*

Social Actions: Initiation vs. Completion

Based on the examples that you've already seen in this chapter, it would be easy enough to set up a GA social tag with a click trigger for a Tweet button (for example). The challenge, though, is that clicking the Tweet button may only be the first step of several: first, if the user isn't already logged in, Twitter will prompt her to do so, and then the user may edit the tweet before finally publishing it. The click that initiates the process, then, may not really be what you would like to capture, but rather the successful completion of the tweet. (And an additional wrinkle may be that the button exists in an iFrame element, which presents additional challenges to directly track the click.)

Your page and its code don't have direct access to the user's Twitter activity (for obvious security and privacy reasons). As a result, to measure completion of the social action, you typically have to interface with an API for the social network in question. Twitter's API (which allows you to include a Tweet button on your page in the first place) also provides for a callback function when certain events occur (such as a tweet, retweet, etc.). Facebook has similar functionality for likes (and unlikes). Let's take a look at a specific example for Facebook here; you can extend this model for other social interactions using this basic structure, although the particulars will depend on the social network and what APIs it provides.

Facebook Likes

The basic methodology for tracking Facebook likes will be similar to other examples in this chapter where you've created custom listeners:

1. Create a Custom HTML tag with an event listener for your social action completion, to be triggered on every page (or at least, all pages where social interaction could occur). This tag will create a data layer message with the appropriate information about the social action.

2. Set up any variables you need to extract information from the data layer message.

3. Set up a GA tag with track type social, and fill in the network, action, and target using variables.

Since the pattern remains the same, let's dispense with step-by-step instructions here and just take a look at the part that is different: the Custom HTML tag listener. (See the scroll tracking section for a detailed, step-by-step example of the whole process.)

A Custom HTML tag to listen for Facebook likes might look something like this:

```
<script type="text/javascript">
    (function(window) {
    var n = 0;
    function checkIfSocialExists(n) {
        if(typeof window.FB !== 'undefined') { bindSocial()
            } else if(n < 30) {
                    n++;
                setTimeout(function() { checkIfSocialExists(n); }, 500); }
     }
    checkIfSocialExists(0);

    function socialTrack(network, action, socialTarget, el) {
        var target = typeof socialTarget === 'undefined' ? '' : socialTarget;
        dataLayer.push({
            'event': 'socialShare',
            'attributes': {
                'network': network,
                'action': action,
                'link': target }
        });
    }

    function bindSocial() {
        FB.Event.subscribe('edge.create', function(targetUrl, el) {
          var lowerTarget = targetUrl.toLowerCase();
          var type = 'share';
          var trackTarget = targetUrl;
          socialTrack('facebook', type, trackTarget, el)
        });
      }
    })(window);
</script>
```

■ **Note**   This code assumes you've already loaded the Facebook API in your page and checks for existence of the FB object before adding its listener.

This listener uses the Facebook API method `FB.Event.subscribe` to call a function when a share occurs. A data layer message is pushed with the details. You can now trigger a tag in GTM using a Custom Event of `socialShare` and create variables for the data layer properties `attributes.network`, `attributes.action`, and `attributes.link` to fill in the GA social tag.

This listener only captures events for likes, but can easily be adapted to capture unlikes as well.

Video

Another common type of interaction within a page is with embedded media, often a video that's included in a page. Like social network buttons, each video platform has its own player with unique implementation details. Let's take a look at YouTube, the most common video player.

By now you'll be familiar with the basic pattern of this code: first, a custom JavaScript listener tag (using the YouTube API), and then a Google Analytics event tracking tag to send the data to GA. Again, let's dispense with the step-by-step instructions and cut right to the chase.

The listener tag looks like this:

```
<script type="text/javascript">
    ;(function( document, window, config ) {
      'use strict';
      window.onYouTubeIframeAPIReady = (function() {
        var cached = window.onYouTubeIframeAPIReady;
        return function() {
          if( cached ) { cached.apply(this, arguments); }
          // This script won't work on IE 6 or 7, so we bail at this point if we detect that UA
          if( !navigator.userAgent.match( /MSIE [67]\./gi ) ) { init(); }
        };
      })();

      var _config = config || {};
      var forceSyntax = _config.forceSyntax || 0;
      var dataLayerName = _config.dataLayerName || 'dataLayer';
      // Default configuration for events
      var eventsFired = { 'Play': true, 'Pause' : true, 'Watch to End': true };

      // Overwrites defaults with customizations, if any
      var key;
      for( key in _config.events ) {
        if( _config.events.hasOwnProperty( key ) ) {
          eventsFired[ key ] = _config.events[ key ]; }
      }

      // Invoked by the YouTube API when it's ready
      function init() {
        var iframes = document.getElementsByTagName( 'iframe' );
        var embeds  = document.getElementsByTagName( 'embed' );
        digestPotentialVideos( iframes );
        digestPotentialVideos( embeds );
      }
```

```
var tag            = document.createElement( 'script' );
tag.src            = '//www.youtube.com/iframe_api';
var firstScriptTag = document.getElementsByTagName( 'script' )[0];
firstScriptTag.parentNode.insertBefore( tag, firstScriptTag );

// Take our videos and turn them into trackable videos with events
function digestPotentialVideos( potentialVideos ) {
  var i;
  for( i = 0; i < potentialVideos.length; i++ ) {
    var isYouTubeVideo = checkIfYouTubeVideo( potentialVideos[ i ] );
    if( isYouTubeVideo ) {
      var normalizedYouTubeIframe = normalizeYouTubeIframe( potentialVideos[ i ] );
      addYouTubeEvents( normalizedYouTubeIframe ); }
  }
}

// Determine if the element is a YouTube video or not
function checkIfYouTubeVideo( potentialYouTubeVideo ) {
  var potentialYouTubeVideoSrc = potentialYouTubeVideo.src || '';
  if( potentialYouTubeVideoSrc.indexOf( 'youtube.com/embed/' ) > -1 ||
      potentialYouTubeVideoSrc.indexOf( 'youtube.com/v/' ) > -1 ) {
    return true; }
  return false;
}

// Turn embed objects into iframe objects and ensure they have the right parameters
function normalizeYouTubeIframe( youTubeVideo ) {
  var a             = document.createElement( 'a' );
      a.href        = youTubeVideo.src;
      a.hostname    = 'www.youtube.com';
      a.protocol    = document.location.protocol;
  var tmpPathname = a.pathname.charAt( 0 ) === '/' ? a.pathname : '/' + a.pathname;
  // IE10 shim

  // For security reasons, YouTube wants an origin parameter set that matches our
      hostname
  var origin = window.location.protocol + '%2F%2F' + window.location.hostname +
  ( window.location.port ? ':' + window.location.port : '' );
  if( a.search.indexOf( 'enablejsapi' ) === -1 ) {
    a.search = ( a.search.length > 0 ? a.search + '&' : '' ) + 'enablejsapi=1'; }

  // Don't set if testing locally
  if( a.search.indexOf( 'origin' ) === -1  && window.location.hostname.indexOf(
  'localhost' ) === -1 ) {
    a.search = a.search + '&origin=' + origin; }

  if( youTubeVideo.type === 'application/x-shockwave-flash' ) {
    var newIframe     = document.createElement( 'iframe' );
    newIframe.height  = youTubeVideo.height;
    newIframe.width   = youTubeVideo.width;
```

```
      tmpPathname = tmpPathname.replace('/v/', '/embed/');
      youTubeVideo.parentNode.parentNode.replaceChild( newIframe, youTubeVideo.
      parentNode );
      youTubeVideo = newIframe; }
    a.pathname        = tmpPathname;
    if(youTubeVideo.src !== a.href + a.hash) {
      youTubeVideo.src = a.href + a.hash;
    }
    return youTubeVideo;
}

// Add event handlers for events emitted by the YouTube API
function addYouTubeEvents( youTubeIframe ) {
  youTubeIframe.pauseFlag  = false;
  new YT.Player( youTubeIframe, {
    events: {
      onStateChange: function( evt ) {
        onStateChangeHandler( evt, youTubeIframe ); }
    }
  } );
}

// Returns key/value pairs of percentages: number of seconds to achieve
function getMarks(duration) {
  var marks = {};
  // For full support, we're handling Watch to End with percentage viewed
  if (_config.events[ 'Watch to End' ] ) {
    marks[ 'Watch to End' ] = duration * 99 / 100;
  }

  if( _config.percentageTracking ) {
    var points = [];
    var i;
    if( _config.percentageTracking.each ) {
      points = points.concat( _config.percentageTracking.each );
    }

    if( _config.percentageTracking.every ) {
      var every = parseInt( _config.percentageTracking.every, 10 );
      var num = 100 / every;
      for( i = 1; i < num; i++ ) { points.push(i * every); }
    }

    for(i = 0; i < points.length; i++) {
      var _point = points[i];
      var _mark = _point + '%';
      var _time = duration * _point / 100;
      marks[_mark] = Math.floor( _time ); }
  }
  return marks;
}
```

```
function checkCompletion(player, marks, videoId) {
  var duration     = player.getDuration();
  var currentTime  = player.getCurrentTime();
  var playbackRate = player.getPlaybackRate();
  player[videoId] = player[videoId] || {};
  var key;

  for( key in marks ) {
    if( marks[key] <= currentTime && !player[videoId][key] ) {
      player[videoId][key] = true;
      fireAnalyticsEvent( videoId, key ); }
  }
}


// Event handler for events emitted from the YouTube API
function onStateChangeHandler( evt, youTubeIframe ) {
  var stateIndex    = evt.data;
  var player        = evt.target;
  var targetVideoUrl = player.getVideoUrl();
  var targetVideoId = targetVideoUrl.match( /[?&]v=([^&#]*)/ )[ 1 ];
  // Extract the ID
  var playerState   = player.getPlayerState();
  var duration      = player.getDuration();
  var marks         = getMarks(duration);
  var playerStatesIndex = {
    '1' : 'Play',
    '2' : 'Pause'
  };
  var state = playerStatesIndex[ stateIndex ];
  youTubeIframe.playTracker = youTubeIframe.playTracker || {};
  if( playerState === 1 && !youTubeIframe.timer ) {
    clearInterval(youTubeIframe.timer);
    youTubeIframe.timer = setInterval(function() {
      // Check every second to see if we've hit any of our percentage viewed marks
      checkCompletion(player, marks, youTubeIframe.videoId);
    }, 1000);
  } else {
    clearInterval(youTubeIframe.timer);
    youTubeIframe.timer = false; }

  // Playlist edge-case handler
  if( stateIndex === 1 ) {
    youTubeIframe.playTracker[ targetVideoId ] = true;
    youTubeIframe.videoId = targetVideoId;
    youTubeIframe.pauseFlag = false; }

  if( !youTubeIframe.playTracker[ youTubeIframe.videoId ] ) {
    // This video hasn't started yet, so this is spam
    return false; }
```

```
      if( stateIndex === 2 ) {
        if( !youTubeIframe.pauseFlag ) {
          youTubeIframe.pauseFlag = true;
        } else {
          // We don't want to fire consecutive pause events
          return false; }
      }

      // If we're meant to track this event, fire it
      if( eventsFired[ state ] ) {
        fireAnalyticsEvent( youTubeIframe.videoId, state );
      }
    }

    // Fire an event to Google Analytics or Google Tag Manager
    function fireAnalyticsEvent( videoId, state ) {
      var videoUrl = 'https://www.youtube.com/watch?v=' + videoId;
      window[dataLayerName].push({
          'event'    : 'youTubeTrack',
          'attributes': {
            'videoUrl': videoUrl,
            'videoAction': state }
        });
    }

  } )( document, window, {
    'events': {
      'Play': true,
      'Pause': true,
      'Watch to End': true
    },
    'percentageTracking': {
      'every': 25,
      'each': [ 10, 90 ]
    }
  } );
</script>
```

This follows the same model as the scroll listener earlier in the chapter. It uses YouTube's player API to detect changes to the state of the video player as Play, Pause, or Watch to End and pushes an event to the data layer (indicated in bold). It also measures percent completion, which is configurable at breakpoints in a configuration object (the bold section at the end of the code).

Each data layer push looks like the following example:

```
dataLayer.push({
    'event'      : 'youTubeTrack',
    'attributes' : {
    'videoURL'   : 'https://www.youtube.com/watch?v=msvOUUgv6m8',
    'videoAction' : 'Play' }
});
```

The property `attributes.videoAction` is the state of the video player, while `attributes.videoURL` is a link directly to the video on YouTube (which also include the video identifier). You can now trigger a tag in GTM using a Custom Event of `youTubeTrack` and create variables for the data layer properties `attributes.videoURL` and `attributes.videoAction` to fill in the GA event tracking tag's action and label.

Summary

- Google Analytics has two hit types, *event* and *social*, for tracking interactions within pages. GTM has built-in tags for each of them. Events are used for general interactions with page content, including such examples as download links, outbound links, tabs and accordions, video plays, and more. Social interactions are used for social network actions, such as liking a page on Facebook or tweeting it on Twitter.

- The challenge for tracking interactions in GTM is selecting the appropriate triggers for the interaction and the appropriate variables to capture data about them. There are three basic approaches:

  - Using GTM's auto-event tracking, which has built-in capabilities to track clicks on items within the page (as well as a few other scenarios, such as forms and timers).

  - Using custom extensions to GTM's capabilities with Custom HTML tags and Custom JavaScript variables. Knowledge of JavaScript and the DOM are especially useful in being able to create scripts to listen for custom events and extract information from the page.

  - Using JavaScript on the page to send data to GTM, which is a flexible, developer-friendly method, but it keeps management of this code outside GTM's control.

- Interaction events are represented as messages in GTM's data layer. You can use these messages to create triggers and populate variables for your interaction tracking tags.

CHAPTER 6

Goals: Measuring Conversions

"Would you tell me, please, which way I ought to go from here?"

"That depends a good deal on where you want to get to," said the Cat.

"I don't much care where—" said Alice.

"Then it doesn't matter which way you go," said the Cat.

—Lewis Carroll, *Alice's Adventures in Wonderland*

One of the most important concepts in web analytics is the *conversion*, the transformation of a mere website visitor into a customer. The actions that define conversion may be any type of user interaction that is valuable to you, from major (purchases, contact requests) to minor (content engagement, newsletter signup). Google Analytics allows you to specify the interactions that you want to consider as conversion through **goals**.

GA has four kinds of goals:

- **Destination** goals, the most common type, are based on the URLs of pageviews. Typically they are used for a confirmation or thank-you page of some kind that indicates the user has completed a process. Destination goals can also have a *funnel*, a series of steps leading up to the final destination page (a series of forms that must be filled out, etc.).

- **Session Duration** and **Pages Per Session** goals are based on those metrics exceeding a given threshold (the user spent more than 5 minutes on the site, or viewed more than 3 pages).

- **Event** goals are based on events, the non-pageview interactions for measuring activities such as downloads, outbound links, or video plays (described in Chapter 5).

In many cases, these goals are straightforward to create, based on the tags and triggers you're already using in GTM. However, in some cases where URLs don't change, such as dynamic, AJAX-driven processes, you might require additional tags and triggers in GTM to accommodate. This chapter explores the setup of goals in GA and any tags and triggers in GTM that are necessary to deal with such situations.

SIDEBAR: WHY SET UP GOALS?

Notice that none of these goals represents actions by the user that aren't already available in GA data. What good, then, are these goals?

First of all, creating goals forces you to actually *think* about why your site exists and what you'd like your users to accomplish.

Within GA, creating goals elevates these particular actions in importance in the way GA presents them in its reports. Goal metrics such as conversion rate are easily accessible across all of the types of reports in GA, as well as enabling further analysis through tools such as the multi-channel funnel reports. The accessibility of goal metrics in reports makes it easy and straightforward to make comparisons and find your most valuable audiences and marketing channels. Without goals, you'd have to dig harder, using segments and other tools in reports, to come to these answers.

You can also assign monetary values to the goals you create in GA, and there are metrics that let you compare these values in your reports as well. If there are actual purchases being made on a website, you can capture those with ecommerce tracking (see Chapter 7); but for other types of sites, you may still be able to assign a real-world value to the goals. For a lead generation process, for example, you may be able to gather data from outside GA (out of 1000 leads from the website over the last year, 10% resulted in a sale, and the average value of a sale was $500), resulting in an average value per lead (in this case, $50, if you do the math).

Alternatively, if there aren't any conversions on your site that you can tie to real-world monetary values, you can still use the goal values as a way of weighting their importance. Maybe your primary goal is $100, a couple of secondary goals are $50 each, and some minor goals are $10 each.

Creating and Organizing Goals

Goals are created within each view in GA. You'll find any goals you've created and the ability to create new ones in the view column of GA's Admin settings (see Figure 6-1).

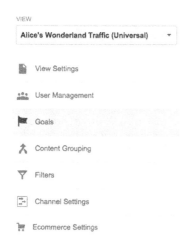

Figure 6-1. *Goal settings in the GA Admin section*

Each view has slots for up to 20 goals (see Figure 6-2). You'll need edit permissions for the view to edit or create goals. (See Chapter 8 for more information on creating views.)

	Goal ↓	Id	Past 7 day conversions	Recording
☐	5+ pages viewed	Goal ID 3 / Goal Set 1	242	ON
☐	5+ Time On Site	Goal ID 2 / Goal Set 1	298	ON
☐	Booked Reservation	Goal ID 1 / Goal Set 1	14	ON
☐	Button Click	Goal ID 4 / Goal Set 1	0	OFF

+ NEW GOAL   Import from Gallery   Search

16 goals left

Figure 6-2. *List of goals in GA*

Setting up goals, like any other changes to the Admin settings in GA, does not retroactively reprocess existing data in reporting views. Creating a goal will measure conversions for that goal going forward.

CREATE A GOAL IN GOOGLE ANALYTICS

Let's walk through how to create a goal in GA.

1. In the Goals section of the View column in GA's Admin tab, select the + New Goal button.

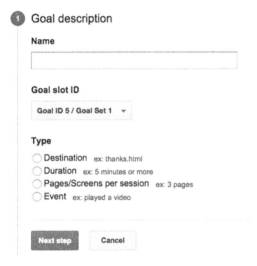

2. Enter a name for the goal. The name will be the label that displays for the goal in your GA reports, so be sufficiently descriptive that it's obvious to anyone using your data what the goal represents.

3. Optionally, choose a goal slot. As noted, each view has 20 goal slots. These are divided into four sets of five goals each, which correspond to groups of goals viewable in reports. By default, GA simply uses the next open slot, but you can change this (for example, if you want to put the most important goals first and less important ones last).

4. Choose a goal type: Destination, Duration, Pages/Screens per session, or Event. Then select the Next button to provide the goal details.

5. Depending on the type of goal you've selected, in the next step GA asks you for the details of the goal:

- For Destination goals, you enter the URL(s) of the goal page, and optionally of funnel pages for steps that lead up to the goal. This type of goal is explored in detail in the next section.

- For Duration goals, specify a time by entering numbers for hours, minutes, and seconds. If a session's duration is longer than the time you enter here, GA will count the goal conversion.

- For Pages/Screens per session goals, specify a number of pages. If a session contains more than that number of pages (or screens for mobile apps; see Chapter 13), GA will count the goal conversion.

- For Event goals, you can specify one or more criteria for the category, action, label, and value of the event(s) to count as a goal conversion. If you set more than one criterion, all of them must be true to count as a goal conversion. (See Chapter 5 for more about events and their properties.)

Event conditions

Set one or more conditions. A conversion will be counted if all of the conditions you set are true when an Event is triggered. You must have at least one Event set up to create this type of Goal. Learn more

6. Optionally, for any type of goal, set a currency value. (For Event goals, you have the additional option to use the event value for the goal value.)

7. Use the Verify this Goal option to double-check your goal setup. This compares your goal setup to data from the last seven days and shows the number of conversions that would have been recorded. If you get 0 but you know you have had conversions, check your setup for typographical errors in URLs, event properties, and so forth.

8. Select the Create Goal button to save the goal.

GA will start calculating conversions for this goal in your reports from this point forward.

Deleting Goals

If one of your goals is no longer relevant, you can disable it with a toggle in the list of goals, which hides it from view in your reports.

Notice, however, that there is no option to delete a goal. Like all GA data, once data is in reports, there's no going back in time to change it (including deleting the existing goal data). You can, however, reuse the slot for a goal by simply changing its name and all of its settings. From that point forward, data in that goal's slot will be for the new goal, and backward for the old.

▪ **Tip**   There's no indication in GA's reporting interface when a goal's setup has changed, so you should provide an annotation, and consider including a date in the goal's title to be clear about changes.

Destination Goals and Funnels

The most common type of goal in GA is the Destination goal, which indicates that the user has reached some particular page (defined by URL). Usually this is a page reached at the end of some process, a confirmation page reached upon completion. However, it could be any important page on your site you want users to reach.

For goals that have a set of steps leading up to the final destination, you can create a funnel. GA will show progression through this funnel so that you can understand where the process may have leaks or bottlenecks that prevent some users from completing the goal.

There are two reports in GA where the funnel data is shown, the Funnel Visualization and Goal Flow reports (both found in Conversions ➤ Goals). These reports offer different visualizations, with different levels of detail into behavior (see Figure 6-3).

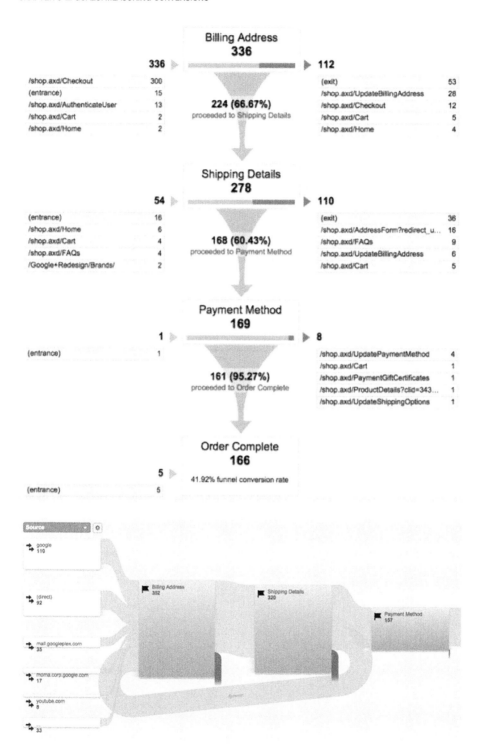

Figure 6-3. *The Funnel Visualization (top) and Goal Flow (bottom) reports show progression through the funnel steps*

▓ **Note**   A goal's funnel setup affects *only* these funnel reports. All other metrics in GA based on the goal (conversions, conversion rate, value) only look at whether the final goal destination is reached.

Funnels are designed for a sequence of steps that a user goes through in order to complete some process. This sequence might include an optional step, or have the possibility to go backward to a previous step, but there is an implied order to the funnel, from first step to last. You should only include steps in the funnel that a user progresses through to get to the goal in a particular order. If the pages can be viewed in any order, the funnel reports will not show especially useful data.

Setting Up a Funnel

Before setting up the goal funnel, you'll need to know the URL of each step in the process. Depending on what the process is, it might be easy to walk through on the site (fill out the contact form and say "Sorry, just testing") to see what the URLs are. In other cases (purchases, account registrations, etc.), the processes may be more complex or difficult to test. You may need to use a test version of the site or consult your documentation or developer to understand the process and the sequence of URLs involved.

In some cases, you may encounter a sequence of steps that doesn't have any distinction between URLs. You'll explore how to tackle these later in the chapter.

CREATE A DESTINATION GOAL WITH A FUNNEL

Assuming you've already gathered a list of URLs of the steps in your process, let's set up a destination goal with a funnel.

1. Complete steps 1–4 from "Create a Goal in Google Analytics" and choose Destination as the goal type.

2. For a Destination goal, the first goal detail setting to enter is the final URL destination for the goal (see the following screenshot). This represents the conversion: if the user reaches this page, the conversion occurred; if not, it didn't.

2 Goal details

Destination

| Equals to ▼ | App screen name or web page URL | ☐ **Case sensitive** |

For example, use *My Screen* for an app and */thankyou.html* instead of *www.example.com/thankyou.html* for a web page

Value OPTIONAL

| Off | | Assign a monetary value to the conversion. |

Funnel OPTIONAL

| Off | |

Specify a path you expect traffic to take towards the destination. Use it to analyze the entrance and exit points that impact your Goal.

Verify this Goal   See how often this Goal would have converted based on your data from the past 7 days.

Enter URLs here just as they appear in reports in GA, typically beginning with the path (excluding the hostname). There are three matching options:

- *Equals to*: The URL must match exactly what is entered, no more and no less. This is the default, and works fine in many cases, but where you need more flexibility, the next two options are available.

- *Begins with*: The URL must begin with the string entered, but could continue with additional text at the end of the URL. This is quite useful for URLs that have many possible variations according to the user making a choice or entering information in a form. For example:

  /locations/retail?zipcode=12345
  /request-a-quote/thank-you?Industry=Education&Country=US

- *Regular expression*: The URL must match the regular expression pattern. This allows a large degree of flexibility for matching patterns from general to specific.

You also have the option whether the URL you entered should be case-sensitive (which is almost never needed).

Enter the full URL, partial URL, or regular expression pattern for the final goal page.

3. Optionally, assign a monetary value to the goal.

4. To create a funnel, turn the funnel option to On. A list will appear for you to list labels and URLs for each step (see the following screenshot).

For each step, the Name is simply the label for the step in the funnel reports. The Screen/Page is a URL or regular expression pattern for the step. The funnel URLs follow the same rules—Equals to, Begins with, or Regular expression—chosen earlier for the final goal URL.

You can add as many steps as necessary that precede the final goal page (up to 20, although if a process is 20 steps long, you should probably rethink the user experience). You don't need to repeat the goal URL in the funnel steps; the final goal URL is always considered the last step.

Finally, notice that the first step has an additional option, whether it should be required. This is further discussed later in the chapter and situations where it's appropriate.

5. Use the Verify button to check the goal. Note that the Verify button only tests the final conversion, not each individual funnel step. (More advice on testing and verifying funnel URLs to come.)

6. Select the Create Goal button to save the goal.

GA will start calculating conversions and funnel data for this goal in your reports from this point forward.

Testing Goal and Funnel URLs

The Verify feature during goal setup is a quick check to see if your goal URL makes sense. However, it doesn't provide much detail, and it doesn't give you the ability to test the funnel steps. The best way to test the URL patterns used in your goal setup is by using the Behavior ➤ Site Content ➤ All Pages report in Google Analytics. The URLs shown in this report for your pages are the same ones GA is using to compare the goal settings and record conversions.

You can use the advanced option on the in-report filter (see Figure 6-4) to show URLs that match some criterion. Notice that the options available include *Exactly matching*, *Begins with*, and *Matching RegExp*, which correspond to the options in your goal setup. You want to make sure that the URL patterns in your goal setup match the pages you think they should (and don't match any pages they shouldn't).

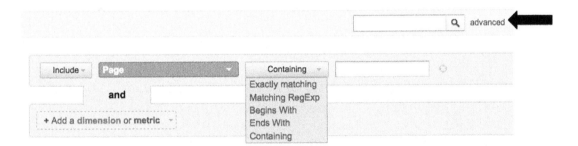

Figure 6-4. *Select the advanced option next to the filter in the All Pages report to test goal URLs*

Try URLs or regular expressions in this filter to see whether they work as expected, and refine as necessary. If some of the goal URL patterns are too broad, they can result in funnels that look like the Figure 6-5.

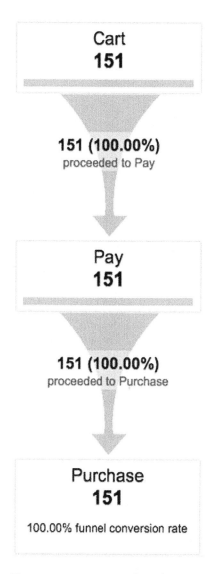

Figure 6-5. *A suspicious funnel*

It's a little too good to be true, isn't it? Although it would be great if 100% of sessions progressed all the way through the conversion funnel, this data seems fishy.

The cause of this type of problem is with URL patterns that match more than one step. Consider the following sequence of URLs and the goal setup for them:

	Funnel setup	URL of page
Step 1	/contact/	/contact/
Step 2	/contact/thank-you/	/contact/thank-you/

If you're using the "Equals to" option, everything is fine. Using the "Begins with" or "Regular Expressions" options, however, notice that your funnel URL for Step 1 *also* matches Step 2! You need to be more careful. In this case, you can use a regular expression:

	Funnel setup	URL of page
Step 1	`/contact/`	`/contact/$`
Step 2	`/contact/thank-you/`	`/contact/thank-you/`

By using a regular expression with the $ (dollar sign), meaning "ends with," you can ensure that Step 1 doesn't match the URL of Step 2. Problem solved!

Required First Step

Finally, there's one additional option that useful in some scenarios: the required step option on the first funnel step. Notice that the funnel reports show users entering the funnel at any step in the process (see Figure 6-6). Often, that's the first step, but it could be a subsequent step.

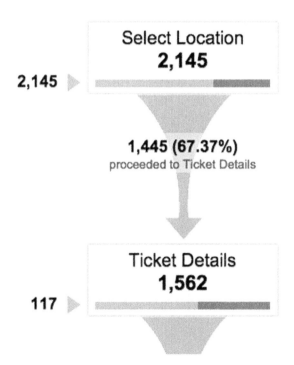

Figure 6-6. *In this partial funnel, 117 sessions entered in the second step*

91

How does this happen? You may think it's not possible; there's no way to get to Step 2 of the registration process without going through Step 1! Nevertheless, it can happen in a variety of edge-case scenarios, like this:

1. *Hey, we should get tickets to go to Alice's Wonderland Resorts!* I'll go to Step 1.

2. *Wait, I should ask the Mad Hatter if he wants to come along with me.* I'll just leave this open in my browser until I find out. More than 30 minutes go by, and my session expires in GA.

3. *OK, now I'm ready to reserve those tickets!* I go on to Step 2, but since my session expired, GA shows me entering the funnel at Step 2.

In most cases like these, the bulk of users enter at the first step, and a handful at subsequent steps. However, in some scenarios, you might only wish to see users who completed the full process. Consider the funnel in Figure 6-7.

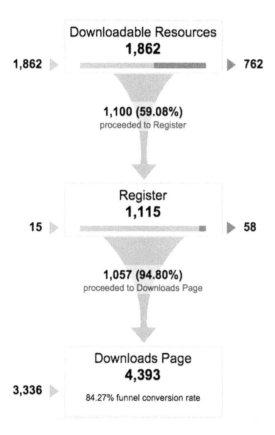

Figure 6-7. *A funnel where many users enter at the last page!*

The first two steps are a sign-up process, giving the users access to a page with some downloadable resources. The final page can be bookmarked and returned to by those users, who do that often (which is why you see so many of them enter at the final step). But the users you're really interested in are just those who actually signed up in Steps 1 and 2.

By setting the Required setting on the first step of the funnel, the funnel reports show you only users who began at Step 1. Note that this affects *only the funnel reports*; the number of conversions overall for the goal is always determined only by the final destination URL.

Funnels Without Distinct URLs

For funnels where the steps are easily differentiated by URL, the goal setup is pretty straightforward. What happens in a situation where the funnel steps aren't easily differentiated by URL, such as the following:

- A modal popup appears within a page

- A form and its confirmation page have the same URL

- A checkout or signup process has several steps that occur within a single page without reloading (known as AJAX)

- A process where one or more steps occur at an external, untracked website

The approach for setting up funnels in these situations is to use *virtual pageviews*—that is, to trigger a GA pageview on some interaction like a form submission or a click a button that advances to the next step, and use a concocted URL to represent the interaction. GTM's GA tag allows you to override the current page's URL with a URL of your choice using the page field in the Fields to Set section (Figure 6-8).

Figure 6-8. *The* page *field in GTM's GA tag allows you to override the URL recorded in GA*

For the virtual pageview, /drink-imaginary-tea is the URL chosen to be recorded—a URL that doesn't actually exist on your site, but that you'll see in your GA data to represent the action that was performed. Because these actions are recorded as pageviews in Google Analytics, you can then use the URLs you chose to set up the funnel (and you'll also be able to see the pageviews in the Site Content reports).

■ **Note**   For external websites, such as a third-party payment site, if you can put your GTM container code on the site, you can use cross-domain tracking to capture data (see Chapters 2 and 3). If the third party doesn't allow your code, activity by the user on their site is invisible to you, but you can at least track users leaving your site to go there.

Modals and iFrames

A ***modal*** is a popup that occurs within a page (rather than as a separate tab or window within your browser). This modal popup could contain two different types of information:

- Often they use the `iframe` HTML element to simply include another page within.

- In other cases, such as a lightbox for images, they might simply show/hide or restyle elements of the page content.

To check the content of a particular modal popup on your site, you can simply inspect the source code.

If the `iframe` element is used, there is actually a distinct page for the content of the modal. As long as your GTM container is on that page, you're measuring it just like any other, and a pageview for that URL will appear in GA, just like all your other pages show up.

■ **Note**   If the page within the `iframe` is on a different domain, you need to use cross-domain tracking. There are some additional browser and security issues regarding cross-domain iframes; see the GA developer documentation for details on handling this scenario.[1]

For modals that do not use an `iframe` element, you can use the Click trigger (described in Chapter 5) to trigger tags. It's up to you whether you want to trigger a GA event tag or pageview tag, depending on the nature of the interaction and how you want to be able to see the data in GA. For an image in a lightbox, an event tag might be most appropriate. If there's a form or other multi-step process within the modal popup, however, you might want to use a pageview so that you can set up a destination goal with a funnel.

TRIGGER A VIRTUAL PAGEVIEW FOR CLICKS

To create a virtual pageview for a click, think back to the process outlined in Chapter 5, when you triggered a GA event tag based on a click. Here, you'll swap out the GA pageview tag instead.

1. Create a new tag. Choose Google Analytics ➤ Universal Analytics as the type.

2. Fill in the Tracking ID with the {{GA Property ID}} variable that you previously created.

3. Select Track Type ➤ Pageview.

4. Under More Settings ➤ Basic Configuration, you'll find a field labeled Document Path (see Figure 6-8). This is the URL recorded by GA. By default the current page path is used, but you can override that label here. (This is the essence of your "virtual pageview": you're creating a URL that doesn't actually exist to represent the form submission.) You can use any combination of text and variables here to construct a URL. Often it makes sense to use the current page (the {{Page Path}} variable) and append some label to the end:

   {{Page Path}}/modal-newsletter-signup

---

[1] https://developers.google.com/analytics/devguides/collection/analyticsjs/cross-domain#iframe

5. Now specify a trigger for the tag.

    a. Choose Click, then select the New button to create a new click trigger.

    b. Specify some criteria to restrict the click trigger to the appropriate link, button, or other element. See Chapter 5 for more discussion and examples of using the Click trigger.

■ **Note**   Here it is not necessary to use the "Wait for tags" option of the Link Click listener, since the current page remains open after the click.

---

    c. Select the Create Trigger button, giving the trigger a name: "Modal Popup". GTM saves the trigger and returns to creating the tag.

6. Save the tag, giving it a name: "GA – Pageview – Modal Popup".

Forms and the Form Listener

HTML form elements allow the user to fill out a number of input fields and then submit the form. The contents of the input fields are submitted to a URL for processing by your site (represented in HTML by the action attribute of the form element).

```
<form id="red-queen" action="/off-with-her-head/">
        <input id="first-name" name="first-name" type="text" placeholder="Alice">
        <input type="submit" value="Submit!">
</form>
```

If the URLs are different for the page that includes the form and the action of the form, you can easily differentiate these steps in a funnel. In some cases, however, the action of the form may be the same as the current page. After the form is submitted, the page may show different content (a confirmation message, for example), but the URL is the same. In cases where you can't differentiate a form by URL, you can track submissions of the form using GTM's Form trigger. The Form trigger is similar to the Click trigger (described in Chapter 5), but instead listens to see if the HTML form element is submitted.

■ **Note**   Just as GTM includes built-in variables for the Click listener like {{Click ID}} and {{Click URL}}, it has the same set of variables available for the Form listener. You'll want to make sure these are enabled in the Variables section in GTM before setting up a Form listener.

TRIGGER A PAGEVIEW FOR A FORM SUBMISSION

Let's look at how to create the tag and trigger for a form submission.

1. Create a new tag. Choose Google Analytics ➤ Universal Analytics as the type.

2. Fill in the Tracking ID with the `{{GA Property ID}}` variable that you previously created.

3. Select Track Type ➤ Pageview.

4. Under More Settings ➤ Basic Configuration, you'll find a field labeled Document Path (see Figure 6-8). This is the URL recorded by GA. By default, it's just filled in with the current page path, but you can override that label here. (This is the essence of your "virtual pageview": you're creating a URL that doesn't actually exist to represent the form submission.) You can use any combination of text and variables here to construct a URL. Often it makes sense to use the current page (the `{{Page Path}}` variable) and append some label to the end:

   `{{Page Path}}/red-queen-submitted`

5. Now specify a trigger for the tag.

   a. Choose Form, and then select the New button to create a new form trigger.

   b. Like a link, the form typically submits to the same browser window, replacing the current page. Choose the Wait for Tags option with the default two-second maximum to give the tracking tags time to execute before the form is submitted.

   c. Use the Check Validation option to only trigger when the form will successfully submit. Typically a form includes validation checks such as checking that the user has completed required fields and entered values in the correct formats. With this option enabled, the trigger will only operate when the validation is successful and the form submits. If this option is disabled, the trigger would operate each time the user clicks the submit button, whether or not validation is successful.

   d. Under "Enable when", filter pages on which the trigger listens for the form submission. It's only necessary for this listener to operate on a page where the form could appear. If it's a form that appears in many places throughout the site, you can use a regular expression to match any URL:

   `{{Page URL}} - matches RegEx - .*`

   Otherwise, you can be more restrictive to include only the page or pages where this form appears.

e.   Under "Fire when", choose Some Forms and specify one or more criteria to restrict this trigger to the form you want to track. Most commonly, you might use the Form ID or Form URL variables to restrict to a specific form.

```
{{Form ID}} - equals - red-queen
```

f.   Select the Create Trigger button, giving the trigger a name: "Red Queen Form". GTM saves the trigger and returns to creating the tag.

6.   Save the tag, giving it a name: "GA – Pageview – Red Queen Form Submission".

Now that you have a distinct URL for the form submission, you can use that URL as a goal or funnel step.

AJAX and Dynamic Processes

Sometimes a multistep process may occur all within the same page, without the page reloading or the URL changing. The user interacts with the content to step through the process, and the content of the page dynamically changes, but the user is on the same page. It's even possible for a whole website or web application to be built as a single page, which changes content as the user "navigates" through, though the page never fully reloads or changes URLs.

This is commonly referred to as *AJAX* (short for *Asynchronous JavaScript and XML*, although the term has come to encompass a variety of related techniques that aren't necessarily asynchronous and don't necessarily use XML). AJAX can be an elegant and attractive option for dynamic content, but it also introduces several challenges because of the ways it differs from a "normal" website with distinct pages and URLs.

Since the page doesn't fully refresh, GTM only triggers the single, initial pageview. To capture further interactions, you'll have to use other event listeners to trigger tags. There are a couple of possible options, depending on how the site is set up.

- *The History Listener*. Most modern AJAX designs are browser- and search engine-friendly: they allow directly linking to dynamic content, and they allow the browser's back and forward buttons to operate correctly. They do this by several different methods of inserting entries into the browser's history to keep track of the state and path of the user. GTM's History Listener can be triggered on these changes.

- *The Click Listener*. For simple situations, or where dynamic interactions are not reflected in the browser history, you can use the Click Listener to trigger a click on a particular button, link, or other element.

Both of these are described in the following sections.

■ **Caution**   If you aren't the author of the AJAX processes on your website, make sure you speak to the developer and understand how they operate. GTM's listeners are pretty harmless and unlikely to interfere with the page's functionality, but you do want to ensure that the data accurately reflects the interactions you want to capture.

The History Listener

There are two major ways that dynamic pages can use to keep track of the state of the page in the browser: the URL fragment, or HTML5's window.history API.

The URL fragment is the portion of the URL after the hash (#). You may be familiar with this from links within a page, to jump to a particular location within the page. URL fragments don't change the base URL and don't trigger a reload of the page. Since the browser keeps track of these in its history, however, dynamic pages can use artificial labels for the URL fragment as one way to support the Back and Forward buttons. Dynamic pages using URL fragments might have URLs that look like these:

```
/ticketing/registration.php#signup
/ticketing/registration.php#billing
/ticketing/registration.php#confirmation
```

Additionally, HTML5 introduced the `window.history` API, which allows dynamic pages to directly insert entries into the browser history. The `window.history.pushState()` and `window.history.replaceState()` methods allow scripts to insert entries into the browser history, including both a JSON object that maintains the state as well as a new URL. Additionally, the `popstate` event allows for monitoring any changes to the history state, including use of the Back and Forward buttons.

To cover these, GTM has a History Listener trigger, which allows you to trigger tags on any of the following occurrences:

- The URL fragment changes

- The `window.history.pushState()` or `window.history.replaceState()` methods are called

- A `popstate` event occurs

Whenever one of these occurs, a message is pushed to the data layer that looks like the following:

```
dataLayer.push({
        'event': 'gtm.historyChange',
        'gtm.historyChangeSource': 'pushState',
        'gtm.newHistoryState': historyStateObject,
        'gtm.newUrlFragment': '',
        'gtm.oldHistoryState': null,
        'gtm.oldUrlFragment: ''
});
```

The new and old history state objects and URL fragments are included (if any), as well as the source of the history change (`pushState`, `replaceState`, or `popstate`). There are several built-in variables to access these; enable those in the list of variables before using the History listener. The `{{Page URL}}` variable is also updated if changed by `pushState` or `replaceState`, and you can create one or more variables to access properties of the state object (if used).

TRIGGER A PAGEVIEW FOR HISTORY CHANGES

Let's look at how to create the tag and trigger in GTM for a history change.

1. Create a new tag. Choose Google Analytics ➤ Universal Analytics as the type.

2. Fill in the Tracking ID with the `{{GA Property ID}}` variable that you previously created.

3. Select Track Type ➤ Pageview.

4. Under More Settings ➤ Fields to Set, set the `page` field (the URL recorded by GA). If calls to `pushState()` or `replaceState()` change the URL, you might simply use the `{{Page Path}}` variable, or you could use information from the state object as a virtual URL. For changes in the anchor portion of the URL, you could use the `{{New History Fragment}}` in conjunction with the `{{Page Path}}` variable to construct a virtual URL:

   `{{Page Path}}#{{New History Fragment}}`

5. Select the Continue button to specify a trigger for the tag.

   a. Choose More to see the list of all listeners. Then choose New to create a new trigger.

   b. Choose History Change as the trigger type.

   c. You can choose to trigger on All History Changes, which might be the right option for a completely AJAX-based website. If you're just measuring a certain page or process, you can specify some criteria to restrict this trigger. Depending on the scenario, you might restrict the trigger to certain pages (via the `{{Page URL}}` variable) or to certain types of history change interactions (using the built in history variables described above). Specify a condition that reflects the situation on your site.

   d. Select the Create Trigger button, giving the trigger a name: "AJAX Reservation Page". GTM saves the trigger and returns to creating the tag.

6. Save the tag, giving it a name: "GA – Pageview – Ticket Reservations".

Now that you have distinct URLs for the steps in the dynamic process, you can use those URLs as a goal or funnel step.

Using the Click Listener

An alternative for dynamic content without URL changes is to use the Click listener, discussed in Chapter 5. If the user causes a dynamic change in the page by clicking an element of the page, the Click listener can capture that interaction. This is especially useful as a workaround for AJAX processes that don't use URL fragments or the `window.history` API to properly support the Back and Forward buttons (described in the previous section).

In such a scenario, you can set up triggers on a link using criteria like the URL, `id`, or other properties, just as laid out in Chapter 5, but instead of using a GA event tag, you'll use the pageview tag like the examples in this chapter. Remember to specify a virtual URL for the page field to identify the interaction.

Flash and Other Browser Plugins

Interactive, dynamic content in a page may also be in an embedded object handled through a browser plugin, such as content developed using Adobe Flash.

In the browser's DOM, such objects are a black box: their content is not accessible via JavaScript, so neither GTM's built-in listeners nor custom JavaScript can give you detailed information about user interactions with the content of Flash. Instead, tracking can be built into the Flash object itself, using Flash's scripting language (ActionScript) to interface with the browser's JavaScript.

In the past, Adobe has provided a semiofficial ActionScript library for Flash tracking in Google Analytics,[2] although updates have not occurred in some time, and at the time of this book's publication it has not been updated to support GA's newest Universal Analytics tracking. (Microsoft Silverlight, an alternative to Flash, is in a similar situation, but Microsoft has announced the end of support for Silverlight, so it is unlikely that its GA tracking library[3] will be updated.) However, ActionScript in a Flash object can call JavaScript within the page containing the object, so you can push events to the data layer for GTM from your Flash widget or application. GTM can then trigger tags based on the data layer messages (see Chapter 5).

Conversions That Span Sessions

GA's model of conversions includes a funnel that occurs within a single session. For some more complicated processes, it's possible that the user might actually complete several steps in one session, and come back at a later time to finish.

Here's one common example of how that might happen in an account signup or registration process:

1. The user fills out details to create their account, going through one or several pages of forms on the website (Pages A, B, C).

2. An email is sent to the email address the user registered to confirm that it's correct.

3. The user clicks a link in the email, opening another page on the website, to confirm and finish the account registration (Page D).

You could create a single goal with a funnel all the way from Page A to Page D. However, it's certainly possible that a user completes the steps from Page A through C, and then returns at a later time, in a new session, to Page D (after receiving the email). A better approach might be to have two separate goals, one from Page A to Page C, and another for Page D. (Additionally, you might even measure email opens using the Measurement Protocol; see Chapter 14.)

In other scenarios, you might have a long or complicated process in which a user can save their progress and return later. Or, you might be interested in whether the same user comes back twice within a week. In such cases, you might keep track of specific behaviors or achievements with a cookie, and only trigger a pageview for your goal when some cumulative set of achievements is completed. You can set new cookies with custom JavaScript (using the `document.cookie` property), and GTM's variable types include the ability to read a value from a cookie.

Once you've created GTM variables based on cookie values you've set, you can use them in a trigger or in the URLs of virtual pageviews. (Also see Chapter 10 for tracking users across devices, which is very useful in situations where users log in and you want to tie together their behavior, regardless of the device or browser they're using to access the site.)

---

[2] https://code.google.com/p/gaforflash/.
[3] http://msaf.codeplex.com/wikipage?title=Google%20Analytics.

Summary

- You can set up goals in GA to easily allow you to make comparisons on conversion metrics. Goals can be based on URLs, events, or the number of pages or duration of a session.

- Goals based on destination URLs can include a funnel, which is a series of steps, also specified by URL, that lead up to the final conversion page.

- For interactions where URLs don't change, you can still set up URL-based goals using pageviews with virtual URLs. GTM includes a Form trigger for form submissions and a History Change trigger for dynamic AJAX-based interactions, as well as the Click trigger discussed previously. You can override the URL recorded by GA in the tag in GTM using variables or text to generate a virtual URL label.

CHAPTER 7

■ ■ ■

Ecommerce: Tracking Products and Purchases

"And if you take one from three hundred and sixty-five what remains?"

"Three hundred and sixty-four, of course."

Humpty Dumpty looked doubtful, "I'd rather see that done on paper," he said.

—Lewis Carroll, *Through the Looking Glass*

For sites that sell products, you can gather additional data about the purchases users make on the site. Google Analytics offers two levels of detail in tracking ecommerce:

- *Basic ecommerce* tracking tracks purchases only. Since it is only concerned with the completed purchase, you only need to make changes in GTM for the final purchase confirmation page.

- *Enhanced ecommerce* offers expanded tracking of users' interactions with products all through the site, from viewing a product in a list, adding it to the cart, and ultimately purchasing. It offers richer ways to categorize and track all types of product interactions. Because of this, you will generally have to make tracking changes throughout much of the website to take full advantage of enhanced ecommerce.

Which should you choose? If you need only very simple ecommerce tracking, the basic option may suffice. For many sites, the enhanced ecommerce offers much deeper and more actionable data, however, so if you have the resources to implement it, it's recommended.

With either ecommerce tracking option, implementation generally involves two sets of tasks:

- Changes to your website to provide the ecommerce data to GTM via the data layer.

- Changes to tags in GTM to accommodate sending ecommerce data to GA.

This chapter lays out the process for both basic and enhanced ecommerce, including walking through any GTM changes (the second item). For the first item, the information that needs to be present in the data layer and in what format will be detailed. This is normally accomplished by server-side changes to the website to provide this data in the data layer, and so the specific implementation will depend on your site and ecommerce platform.

ECOMMERCE TRACKING FOR NON-ECOMMERCE SITES

Although it's generally intended for measuring purchases, GA's ecommerce tracking features are well-suited to any type of transactional interactions, whether there's a monetary component or not. This might include scenarios such as the following:

- Selecting from a catalog or library of items, such as e-books, videos, or other content, and downloading, checking out, or viewing such items.

- Registering for classes or online courses.

- Applying for volunteer or job opportunities.

- Selecting or configuring products that are ultimately purchased offline (such as a car).

In many cases, you might find goals (see Chapter 6) sufficient for measuring these scenarios. If you want more detailed data about the particulars of each transaction, however, ecommerce tracking can be a good option. All of the ecommerce tracking functionality described in this chapter will still work even with $0.00 amounts.

The remainder of this chapter is divided into two sections, for basic ecommerce and enhanced ecommerce tracking. For implementation, you should choose one option or the other, and it's only necessary to read the relevant section.

Basic Ecommerce Tracking

Basic ecommerce tracks only completed purchases. Setting up basic ecommerce involves three steps:

1. Enable ecommerce tracking in Google Analytics.
2. Add ecommerce data to the data layer on the site.
3. Add a Google Analytics transaction tag in Google Tag Manager.

Let's walk through the process.

ENABLE BASIC ECOMMERCE TRACKING IN GA

First, you'll enable ecommerce tracking in GA. This enables the ecommerce reports in the Conversions section as well as ecommerce data available in other reports throughout GA. Ecommerce reports can be enabled or disabled in each view's settings.

1. In the Admin tab of GA, choose the desired account, property, and view from the drop-down lists.

2. In the view's settings (the rightmost column), select Ecommerce Settings (as seen in the following screenshot).

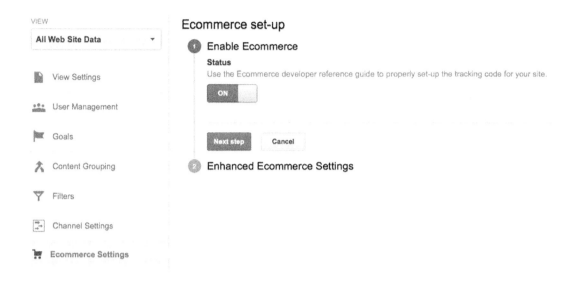

3. To enable ecommerce tracking, set the toggle to On. Select the Next Step button.

4. Leave the setting for enhanced ecommerce Off and select the Submit button.

You can also set the currency that you'd like to see in reports in this view. (GA will convert ecommerce data between currencies if you have a multicurrency store; see the following sidebar for more details.)

1. Still in the Admin tab of GA, choose View Settings in the rightmost column.

2. About halfway down this page of settings is a drop-down list of currencies. Choose the currency you wish to see in reports for this view.

3. Select the Save button.

Enabling ecommerce simply makes the appropriate reports available in GA, but you still have to send the ecommerce data to fill them up. Next, you'll add some information to your data layer about the purchase. Then, you'll create a tag in GTM to send this data to GA.

Ecommerce Data in the Data Layer

Data about the purchase will be provided on the final confirmation page of the purchase process using GTM's dataLayer object. GTM specifies a format and labeling for the pieces of information GA requires. Here's an example of purchase data in the data layer; let's break down the pieces afterward.

```
<script>
dataLayer = [{
    'transactionId': 'AW699168',
    'transactionAffiliation': 'Mad Hatter\'s Hat Emporium',
    'transactionTotal': 42.98,
    'transactionTax': 3.00,
    'transactionShipping': 3.99,
    'transactionProducts': [
```

```
      { 'sku': 'MH342',
        'name': 'Felt Fedora',
        'category': 'Hats',
        'price': 17.99,
        'quantity': 1 },
      { 'sku': 'MH007',
        'name': 'Purple Top Hat',
        'category': 'Hats',
        'price': 24.99,
        'quantity': 1 } ]
}];
</script>
```

■ **Caution**   You should only *declare* the data layer (with a statement like dataLayer = []) *once* within the page, and it should be *before* the GTM code (which automatically creates a data layer if there isn't one already). Declaring the data layer again at a later time will overwrite its previous values and can cause GTM to behave unexpectedly. To provide additional values to the data layer after it's been created, use dataLayer.push() (as seen in Chapter 5 for interaction tracking), which *appends* to the data layer, rather than overwriting it. In this case, you need the values to be included when the page loads, so you'll include the ecommerce data in the declaration.

This code should be included only when the transaction is completed—that is, on the final receipt page in the checkout process.

The first set of attributes summarizes the transaction:

- transactionId is required, and serves as a unique identifier for this particular purchase.

- transactionAffiliation is optional, and could denote a particular store (if you have multiple stores) or an affiliate code.

- transactionTotal is required and represents the total revenue for the transaction. (This total can be inclusive or exclusive of shipping and tax, depending on how you want to see revenue in your reports.)

- transactionTax and transactionShipping are optional and represent tax and shipping charges for the transaction.

The next part of the ecommerce data is an array called transactionProducts. The array has entries for each of the distinct products purchased. Each product entry contains the following attributes:

- sku and name are required, and represent an identifier and a label for the product.

- category is optional, and represents a categorization or grouping of products.

- price is required, and represents the unit price for the product.

- quantity is required, and represents the number of units purchased. It should be an integer.

You need to repeat this information in the data layer for each of the products that's part of the transaction. In our example, there are two products.

As mentioned previously, the values of the information in the data layer are included from your site's data, typically using server-side code to pull the values from your database or ecommerce platform. The specifics of how to do this are particular to your site and the tools you are using to process these transactions, but as long as you format the data in this way, GTM and GA can use it.

■ **Caution**   Since you're inserting values from your database into this JavaScript code, you need to be careful about formatting and syntax. Specifically, beware of apostrophes or quotation marks in text fields (note the apostrophe escaped using the backslash in `'Mad Hatter\'s Hat Emporium'` in the example code). Also note that currency values are numeric, and so should contain only digits and a decimal (no currency symbols or commas) — so `1342.57`, not `$1,342.57`.

SIDEBAR: CURRENCY CONVERSION

As you saw, you can choose a currency setting for your view in GA, which controls the currency shown in reports. If you have a single-currency store, you simply set your reports to show US Dollars, send your prices and transaction amounts in US Dollars, and the numbers appear in the reports.

However, you may have a situation where you have a store that accepts multiple currencies, or several country-specific stores where you want to aggregate reporting across the locales. In such a situation, currency conversions need to occur for reporting.

In the transaction data in the data layer, you can specify a currency using the `transactionCurrency` attribute (for the transaction total) and the `currency` attribute (for each product). The currency values are three-letter codes such as USD or EUR that represent the currency. The GA documentation includes a complete list of the currencies supported by GA.[1]

```
<script>
dataLayer = [{
    'transactionId': 'AW699168',
    'transactionAffiliation': 'Mad Hatter\'s Hat Emporium',
    'transactionTotal': 42.98,
    'transactionTax': 3.00,
    'transactionShipping': 3.99,
    'transactionCurrency': 'EUR',
    'transactionProducts': [
      { 'sku': 'MH342',
        'name': 'Felt Fedora',
        'category': 'Hats',
        'price': 17.99,
        'quantity': 1,
        'currency': 'EUR' },
      { 'sku': 'MH007',
        'name': 'Purple Top Hat',
        'category': 'Hats',
```

---

[1]https://developers.google.com/analytics/devguides/platform/currencies

```
        'price': 24.99,
        'quantity': 1,
        'currency': 'EUR' } ]
}];
</script>
```

This is the same transaction as before, with the added `transactionCurrency` and `currency` attributes to indicate the currency in euros. (Although it would be unusual to have different currencies for different products, you still need to include the currency for the transaction total as well as each product.)

If the currency code included in the transaction data differs from the currency setting in GA, the currency will be converted using a daily exchange rate, and the resulting amounts shown in the reports. (The exchange rate is taken from Google Billing, and is an average for the previous day. As a result, the exact amounts may have small variances from the exchange rates you actually obtain through your financial institutions.)

For basic ecommerce tracking, the data layer object described is the only additional code you'll need on the site. In the next section, you'll create the GTM tag to send this data to GA.

Basic Ecommerce Tag in GTMFor basic ecommerce tracking in Google Analytics, there's an additional hit type to send *transaction* data (just as you've previously seen hits to send data about *pageviews* or *events*). To send this data, you'll have to create an additional tag in GTM.

CREATE A BASIC ECOMMERCE TRANSACTION TAG IN GTM

You can add a GA transaction tag in GTM by following these steps:

1. Create a new tag. Select Google Analytics ➤ Universal Analytics as the tag type.

2. As you did in the basic pageview tag, you'll fill in the Tracking ID with the `{{GA Property ID}}` variable you previously created (see Chapter 3).

3. Select Track Type ➤ Transaction. You'll notice that a message is displayed indicating that you should set up the data layer appropriately (see the following screenshot), which you've already done. Select Continue.

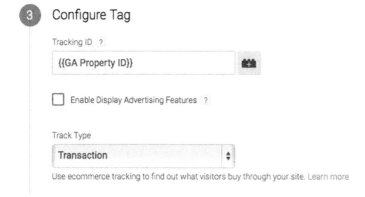

4. For the trigger, choose Some Pages. The list of any page triggers you've previously created is shown.

    a. Select New to create a new trigger.

    b. Name the trigger appropriately; for example, **Receipt page only**.

    c. Enter some criteria to trigger this tag only on the final checkout page (the page to which you added the ecommerce code in the data layer). Typically, you could do this with a criterion using the {{Page URL}} variable (see the following screenshot).

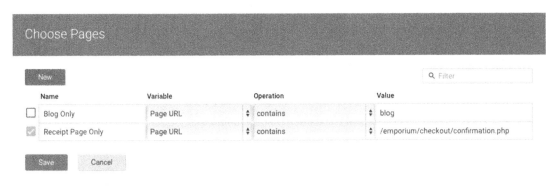

    d. Save the trigger.

5. Save the tag, giving it a name: "GA – Ecommerce".

That's it! This tag will now fire (after testing and publishing, of course) on the receipt page, where it reads the data you previously added to the data layer and sends it to GA.

Create a Goal in GA for the Checkout Process

The tasks in the previous sections are the only things you need to do to enable ecommerce reporting in Google Analytics and collect data on transactions. However, you probably also want to set up a goal with a funnel for the checkout process so that you can see how users progress through the steps leading up to their completed purchase (or fail to complete that process). Chapter 6 describes setting up such goal funnels.

Enhanced Ecommerce Tracking

The enhanced ecommerce features in Google Analytics go beyond just measuring completed purchases, to track ecommerce interaction activity throughout the entire website.

The data you can collect includes interactions of two types: with products (from viewing the product all the way through purchase) and with internal promotions (such as a banner or other offer). Information about all of these interactions will be handled by adding information to the data layer. GTM and GA expect a certain format and labeling for this data, which you'll look at with detailed examples. There are a variety of reports in the Conversions ➤ Ecommerce section of reports in GA that reflect the data you send.

For products, the interactions are as follows:

- *Product impression* (`impressions`): The user saw a listing of products, as in a category page, for example.

- *Product click* (`click`): The user clicked a product listing.

- *Product detail view* (`detail`): The user viewed a product detail page.

- *Add and remove products from cart* (`add` and `remove`): The user added or removed a product from the shopping cart.

- *Checkout* (`checkout`): The user proceeded through the steps of the checkout process (you'll be able to configure the number and sequence of steps).

- *Purchase* (`purchase`): The user successfully purchased a product or products.

- *Refund* (`refund`): A full or partial refund was issued.

For promotions, the interactions are as follows:

- *Promotion impression* (`promoView`): The user saw a promotion, such as a sale banner.

- *Promotion click* (`promoClick`): The user clicked a promotion.

Note that the types of interactions you're talking about fall into two categories: those that occur *when the page loads*, and those that occur only *when the user clicks* on some element of the page.

In the first category are `impressions`, `detail`, and `promoView`, which all indicate something being viewed on a page. For these measurements, you can include ecommerce data in the data layer declaration when the page is loaded.

In the latter category are `click` and `promoClick`, which both indicate a click. For these interactions, you'll need to push information to the data layer when the click occurs (using the same principles as in Chapter 5 for tracking clicks).

Other interactions, such as `add`, `remove`, `checkout`, and `purchase` could fit either category, depending on the site. Some sites might take the user to the cart page when adding a product, while others might merely add the product without refreshing the page, for example. For checkouts, each step (billing, shipping, etc.) may be a separate page, or they may all be within a single page (using AJAX). You can deal with either scenario.

Finally, `refund` is a type of interaction that may often take place outside a regular user interaction on the site (they may occur in conjunction with a customer service request, for example). You'll examine how to handle refunds separately.

SIDEBAR: A PHASED APPROACH TO ENHANCED ECOMMERCE

The types of interactions that can be tracked in enhanced ecommerce and the amount of data needed to support them can be overwhelming when you are considering implementation. However, recognize that it's not necessary to implement everything at once. There are no dependencies among the interaction types, so you can choose to implement some of them but not others (although of course the Google Analytics reporting will show only those you have implemented).

Because of this, it's common to start with only the most vital interactions, like the shopping cart, checkout, and completed purchases. More information about impressions and clicks can then be layered in, and finally you can address promotions and refunds, if desired.

Enabling Enhanced Ecommerce

Before sending data, you first need to enable enhanced ecommerce in Google Analytics and in Google Tag Manager. Here's the process.

ENABLE ENHANCED ECOMMERCE IN GOOGLE ANALYTICS

First, let's enable ecommerce tracking in GA. This enables the ecommerce reports in the Conversions section, as well as ecommerce data available in other reports throughout GA. Ecommerce reports can be enabled or disabled in each view's settings.

1. In the Admin tab of GA, choose the desired account, property, and view from the drop-down lists.

2. In the view's settings (the rightmost column), select Ecommerce Settings (see the following screenshot).

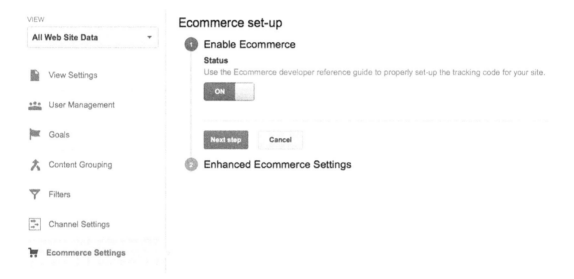

3. To enable ecommerce tracking, set the toggle to On. Select the Next Step button.

4. Change the setting for enhanced ecommerce to On.

5. In the Checkout Labeling settings, choose Add Funnel Step and add a label for each step in the checkout process (see the following screenshot). For example, if the checkout contains the following steps, you'd add each one as a labeled step in the funnel:

   - Shipping

   - Billing

   - Payment

   - Review

This is similar to a goal funnel setup (described in Chapter 6) but is specific to the enhanced ecommerce reports. You'll add code later that indicates where the user is in each of the steps in this process. Note that it's not necessary to add the purchase confirmation as a step; that's always assumed to be the final step in the process.

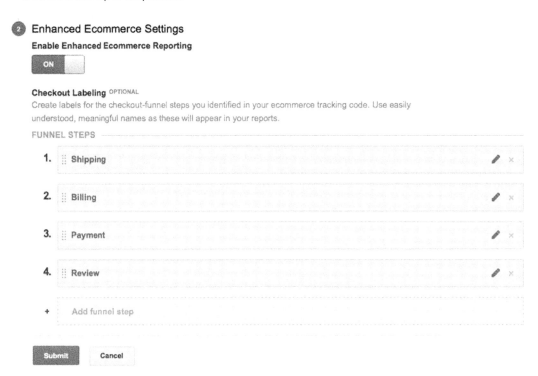

6.   Select the Submit button to save the settings.

You can also set the currency you'd like to see in reports in this view. (GA will convert ecommerce data between currencies if you have a multicurrency store; see the following sidebar for more details.)

1.   Still in the Admin tab of GA, choose View Settings in the rightmost column.

2.   About halfway down this page of settings is a drop-down list of currencies. Choose the currency you wish to see in reports for this view.

3.   Select the Save button.

ENABLE ENHANCED ECOMMERCE IN GOOGLE TAG MANAGER

Enhanced ecommerce sends additional ecommerce data along with existing GA tag(s), such as the basic pageview tag or an event tracking tag. You'll enable enhanced ecommerce for the basic pageview tag. Later in the chapter, you'll look at uses that require event or virtual pageview tags.

▓ **Note** *Do not use the GA "Transaction" tag type for enhanced ecommerce.* The transaction tag is used in basic ecommerce tracking. With enhanced ecommerce, product data is sent along with another hit, such as a pageview or an event; it does not require an additional tag type.

---

1. In the list of tags in GTM, select the basic GA pageview tag to edit.

2. Click the Configure Tag section to edit the tag.

3. Under More Settings ➤ Ecommerce Features, select the check box to Enable Enhanced Ecommerce Features (see the following screenshot).

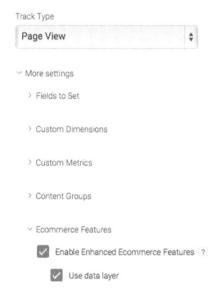

4. Check the box to use the data layer. (The other option allows you to read ecommerce data from a variable instead of the data layer. You'll see an example of when you might use that later in the chapter, but for all the basic tags, you'll be using the data layer.)

5. Save the changes to the tag.

The GA pageview tag is now ready for you to add ecommerce data to the data layer. When ecommerce data is present in the expected format, it will be sent along with the pageview automatically.

Ecommerce Data in the Data Layer Declaration

Now that you've enabled enhanced ecommerce, you can begin to include ecommerce data in the data layer, which will be sent along with the GA pageview tag. This is the approach you'll use for any data that's available at the time the page loads. Since the data is available on page load, you'll include it in the data layer declaration (dataLayer = []). (For data from a click or an AJAX interaction after the page loads, you'll use dataLayer.push() to send data; see the next section for details.)

You can declare a data layer before by including it in the page *before* the GTM container code. Your ecommerce data will be included in an object called ecommerce. The basic format for the object looks similar to the following:

```
<script>
dataLayer = [{
    'ecommerce': {
        'currencyCode': 'USD',    // optional, used for currency conversions
        'action': {               // one of the ecommerce actions: impressions,
                                     detail, add, etc.
            'actionField': {}, // optional, used for options for some actions
            'products': []     // an array containing product detail objects or other data
        }
    }
}];
</script>
```

Each action has slightly different details, and required and optional attributes. Detailed examples are provided in the following sections for all actions.

As mentioned previously, the values of the information in the data layer are included from your site's data, typically using server-side code to pull the values from your content management system or ecommerce platform. The specifics of how to do this are particular to your site and the tools you are using to process these transactions, but as long as you format the data in this way, GTM and GA can use it.

■ **Note**   The naming and hierarchy of data layer attributes is different for enhanced ecommerce from basic ecommerce. If you are updating from basic ecommerce, you'll need to make revisions to the fields in your data layer.

SIDEBAR: CURRENCY CONVERSION

As you saw earlier, you can choose a currency setting for your view in GA, which controls the currency shown in reports. If you have a single-currency store, you simply set your reports to show US Dollars, you send your prices and transaction amounts in US Dollars, and the numbers appear in the reports.

However, you may have a situation where you have a store that accepts multiple currencies, or several country-specific stores where you want to aggregate reporting across the locales. In such a situation, currency conversions need to occur for reporting.

In your transaction data in the data layer, you can specify a currency using the `currencyCode`. The currency values are three-letter codes, such as USD or EUR, that represent the currency. The GA documentation includes a complete list of the currencies supported by GA.[2]

If the currency code included in the transaction data differs from the currency setting in GA, the currency will be converted using a daily exchange rate, and the resulting amounts shown in your reports. (The exchange rate is taken from Google Billing, and is an average for the previous day. As a result, the exact amounts may have small variances from the exchange rates you actually obtain through your financial institutions.)

Product Data

There are many ecommerce actions that include product data, from product impressions, through viewing a product, adding it to the cart, and checking out. Throughout this process, there are a number of core attributes about products that can be captured:

```
{
    'name': 'Top Hat',
    'id': 'MH007',
    'price': '24.99',
    'brand': 'Mad Hatter\'s Hat Emporium',
    'category': 'Hats/Mens',
    'variant': 'Purple'
}
```

These attributes describe various characteristics of the product:

- name and id are required, and represent a label and an identifier (SKU) for the product.

- price represents the unit price for the product.

- brand, category, and variant are optional and are used to further describe and categorize products:

  - brand represents the brand name or designer of the product.

  - category represents a categorization or grouping of products. With enhanced ecommerce (unlike basic ecommerce), you can specify hierarchical categories up to five levels deep, separated by a slash (/). In this example, the top-level category is Hats with a subcategory of Mens. Typically, you would use this to represent the taxonomy the site uses to organize and present products.

  - variant represents some further differentiation of the product, such as color, size, and so forth.

In addition, there are other attributes, such as quantity, that only apply under certain circumstances; you'll see these in the detailed examples to follow. Additionally, you can use custom dimensions to capture even more information about products, if appropriate (see Chapter 11 for more on custom dimensions). As noted, many of these attributes are optional, but the more information you fill in, the richer your ecommerce reports in GA will be.

---

[2]https://developers.google.com/analytics/devguides/platform/currencies

■ **Caution**   Since you're inserting values from the database into this JavaScript code, you need to be careful about formatting and syntax. Specifically, beware of apostrophes or quotation marks in text fields (note the escaped apostrophe in `'Mad Hatter\'s Hat Emporium'` in the example code). Also note that currency values are strings that should contain only digits and a decimal (no currency symbols or commas) — so `'1342.57'`, not `'$1,342.57'`.

Product Impressions

The `impressions` action is used to record impressions of products as users see them throughout the site. Typically, ecommerce sites show lists of products in many places: on the home page, on category pages, on search results pages, and in related product recommendations. By sending data about which products are viewed in these lists (and then later, which products are clicked and purchased), you can better understand click-through and purchase behavior on a per-product and per-list basis.

Here's an example of impressions data in a data layer:

```
<script>
dataLayer = [{
    'ecommerce': {
        'impressions': [
            {
              'name': 'Top Hat',
              'id': 'MH007',
              'price': '24.99',
              'brand': 'Mad Hatter\'s Hat Emporium',
              'category': 'Hats/Mens',
              'variant': 'Purple',
              'list': 'Featured Products',
              'position': 1
            },
            {
              'name': 'Felt Fedora',
              'id': 'MH342',
              'price': '17.99',
              'brand': 'Mad Hatter\'s Hat Emporium',
              'category': 'Hats/Mens',
              'variant': 'Grey',
              'list': 'Featured Products',
              'position': 2
            }
        ]
    }
}];
</script>
```

Note that `impressions` is the name of an array containing the impressions data. The array is a list of products for which you wish to record an impression on this page (only two in this example, but as many as necessary on your site). These can include all the core attributes described previously, and also two additional attributes:

- `list` is a name for the list of products. You can use whatever names you want; choose names that are easily understood by users of your reports to represent the product lists on your site, such as "Category Page", "Recommended Products", "People Who Purchased This Also Liked", and so forth.

- `position` is numeric and represents the position of the product within the list (starting with 1).

You can include as many products in as many lists as are on the page.

■ **Note** There is an 8-kilobyte limit to the amount of data sent in any Google Analytics request (approximately 8,000 characters). In typical usage, this is not a barrier, but if you have many impressions on a page, you may run afoul of this limit. Keep track of how long your list of product data grows, and if necessary, you may need to split it into multiple requests (using `dataLayer.push()` to send additional events to GA with more product impressions).

SIDEBAR: IMPRESSIONS WITH LAZY LOAD OR INFINITE SCROLL

In some cases, a site might not load all the products at once, but only when the user begins to scroll down the list, an effect that is sometimes called *lazy load* or *infinite scroll*. In this case, product impression data for some sets of products might not be available until after the page loads, so you won't be able to include them in the data layer definition.

In this case, you could use `dataLayer.push()` to send additional product impression data to the page after page load. You'll also need an event to send this data to GA. The click and the AJAX interaction examples later in this chapter provide examples of sending ecommerce information after the initial page load.

Product Detail View

The `detail` action represents viewing a product detail page. Here's an example of a product detail view in a data layer:

```
<script>
dataLayer = [{
    'ecommerce': {
        'detail': {
            'products': [{
                'name': 'Top Hat',
                'id': 'MH007',
                'price': '24.99',
                'brand': 'Mad Hatter\'s Hat Emporium',
```

```
                    'category': 'Hats/Mens',
                    'variant': 'Purple'
               }]
          }
     }
}];
</script>
```

For this data, `detail` is the name of the object, which contains a `products` array with the core product attributes. (Typically for a product detail view, there is only a single product.)

The `detail` action has an optional property, `list`, that can be provided in the `actionField` object, like so:

```
<script>
dataLayer = [{
     'ecommerce': {
          'detail': {
               'actionField': { 'list': 'Featured Products' },
               'products': [{
                    // as above
               }]
          }
     }
}];
</script>
```

This allows you to capture which list a user came from to arrive at the product detail page. (If you're already tracking product impressions and product clicks, this is unnecessary, but may be useful if you're not capturing those details.)

Note that there may be more than one type of ecommerce data included in the data layer. For example, on a product detail page, there may also be a list of products with impressions (such as "Related Products" or "People Who Bought This Also Bought…"). You can combine these in the data layer:

```
<script>
dataLayer = [{
     'ecommerce': {
          'detail': {
               // as above
          },
          'impressions': [
               // as above
          ]
     }
}];
</script>
```

Cart Additions and Removals

The add and remove actions can be used to track products added to or removed from the shopping cart.

```
<script>
dataLayer = [{
    'ecommerce': {
        'add': {
            'products': [{
                'name': 'Top Hat',
                'id': 'MH007',
                'price': '24.99',
                'brand': 'Mad Hatter\'s Hat Emporium',
                'category': 'Hats/Mens',
                'variant': 'Purple',
                'quantity': 1
            }]
        }
    }
}];
</script>
```

The action object can be named add or remove as appropriate, and contains one or more products. The product objects include the core attributes as well as the quantity attribute, which is numeric and indicates the number of items added or removed.

Checkout Process

You can measure the checkout process using the checkout action. Recall that when you enabled enhanced ecommerce in GA, you labeled the steps of the checkout process. In the example, you included four steps:

1. Shipping

2. Billing

3. Payment

4. Review

The final step is always the completed purchase (which is a separate action addressed in the next section). For your site, you should include as many steps as you need. You'll include code in the data layer corresponding to each of the steps, as illustrated next.

■ **Note** This example assumes that each step of the checkout process is a separate page. For a site with an AJAX checkout process, see the "AJAX Cart and Checkout Interactions" section later in the chapter.

```
<script>
dataLayer = [{
    'ecommerce': {
        'checkout': {
```

```
                    'actionField': {
                        'step': 1,
                        'option': 'White Rabbit Delivery Service'
                    },
                    'products': [
                        {
                          'name': 'Top Hat',
                          'id': 'MH007',
                          'price': '24.99',
                          'brand': 'Mad Hatter\'s Hat Emporium',
                          'category': 'Hats/Mens',
                          'variant': 'Purple',
                          'quantity': 1
                        },
                        {
                          'name': 'Felt Fedora',
                          'id': 'MH342',
                          'price': '17.99',
                          'brand': 'Mad Hatter\'s Hat Emporium',
                          'category': 'Hats/Mens',
                          'variant': 'Grey',
                          'quantity': 1
                        }
                    ]
                }
            }
}];
</script>
```

The action is named checkout, and in the actionField object you can specify two additional attributes:

- step indicates which step of the checkout process this is. (It's not required if you have a one-step checkout, but otherwise it's needed.)

- option is an optional attribute to indicate some additional characteristic about the checkout step. For example, it might be used to indicate a shipping method (as in this example) or payment method.

The product data includes all the core attributes, plus a quantity attribute (just like the add and remove actions as before).

You'll repeat this data, changing the step number and options as necessary, on each page that is part of the checkout.

Often, you don't know the value of an option until the subsequent step. For example, on the shipping page, the user has the option to select different shipping methods. You can't fill in that choice in the data layer for the shipping page, because you don't yet know what the user will choose. To accommodate this, there's an additional action called checkout_option that you can use to update the chosen option for a step:

```
'ecommerce': {
    'checkout_option': {
        'actionField': {'step': 1, 'option': 'White Rabbit Delivery Service'}
    }
}
```

The actionField indicates the step and the option value. Typically, you could include this in the data layer for the *subsequent* page (step 2 in this case). The full example might look like this:

```
<script>
dataLayer = [{
    'ecommerce': {
        'checkout_option: {
            'actionField': { 'step': 1, 'option': 'White Rabbit Delivery Service' }
        }
        'checkout': {
            'actionField': { 'step': 2 },
            'products': [ // as above ]
        }
    }
}];
</script>
```

Purchase

Finally, when a purchase is successfully completed, you can use the purchase action.

```
<script>
dataLayer = [{
    'ecommerce': {
        'purchase': {
            'actionField': {
                'id': 'AW699168',
                'affiliation': 'Online Store',
                'revenue': '55.97',
                'tax':'3.92',
                'shipping': '',
                'coupon': 'FREE_SHIPPING'
            },
            'products': [
                {
                  'name': 'Top Hat',
                  'id': 'MH007',
                  'price': '19.99',
                  'brand': 'Mad Hatter\'s Hat Emporium',
                  'category': 'Hats/Mens',
                  'variant': 'Purple',
                  'quantity': 1,
                  'coupon': 'TOPHAT_SALE'
                },
                {
                  'name': 'Felt Fedora',
                  'id': 'MH342',
                  'price': '17.99',
                  'brand': 'Mad Hatter\'s Hat Emporium',
                  'category': 'Hats/Mens',
```

```
                        'variant': 'Grey',
                        'quantity': 2
                    }
                ]
            }
        }
}];
</script>
```

For the purchase action, the actionField object contains a number of attributes that summarize the transaction:

- id is required, and serves as a unique identifier for this particular purchase.

- affiliation is optional, and could denote a particular store (if you have multiple stores) or an affiliate code.

- revenue represents the total revenue for the transaction. (This total can be inclusive or exclusive of shipping and tax, depending on how you want to see revenue in your reports.) If you don't specify revenue, GA uses the total of price for the products in the transaction.

- tax and shipping are optional and represent tax and shipping charges for the transaction.

- coupon is optional and represents a coupon applied to the overall transaction.

Then the products are included in an array for each of the products that are part of the transaction, including the core product attributes as well as the following:

- quantity, as previously seen in add, remove, and checkout actions for the number of items of that particular product purchased.

- coupon is optional and represents a coupon applied to a particular product.

■ **Note**   The same fields used for GA can also be used for purchase tracking for Doubleclick transaction tags (with some additional optional fields that can be used for Doubleclick).

Refunds

You can also record refunds using the refund action. An entire transaction can be refunded, as in the following example:

```
<script>
dataLayer = [{
    'ecommerce': {
        'refund': {
            'actionField': { 'id': 'AW699168' }
        }
    }
}];
</script>
```

The id attribute should match the id of the original transaction.

You can also record a partial refund of only certain products in the transaction:

```
<script>
dataLayer = [{
    'ecommerce': {
        'refund': {
            'actionField': { 'id': 'AW699168' },
            'products': [
                { 'id': 'MH342', 'quantity': 1 }
            ]
        }
    }
}];
</script>
```

Here, the id in the actionField object should match the id of the original transaction, and the id and quantity of each item in the products array should represent which items are being refunded.

Providing refund data in the data layer, as in this example, is a workable approach if users can obtain a refund by completing a process on your website. However, in many cases, refunds might be issued through a customer service process that takes place outside the user interactions on the website (through online or phone support, for example). In a case like this, you can process such interactions using GA's Measurement Protocol to record data from a non-web application (Chapter 13) or by importing the data to GA in a spreadsheet (Chapter 12).

Promotion Data

In addition to product data, you can also provide information about internal promotions: a banner promoting certain products on sale, for example. Just as with products, you can measure both impressions and clicks of such promotions. Data about these promotions, and purchases that result after clicking them, are available in the enhanced ecommerce reports in GA.

Promotions can include the following attributes:

```
{
    'name': 'April Foolery Clearance',
    'id': 'PROMO_0401',
    'creative': 'Tweedle Dee v.1',
    'position': 'Store Home Banner'
}
```

The attributes describe the promotion as follows:

- At least one of name or id is required. They give a label and identifier for the promotion, respectively.

- creative is optional and describes the creative content or format of the promotion.

- position is optional and describes the location or slot in which the promotion was displayed.

Since promotion impression data is available when the page loads, you can include them in the data layer declaration, like all of the product data you've looked at so far. (For promotion clicks, see the "Product and Promotion Clicks" section later in this chapter.)

Promotion Impressions

Promotion impressions can be included in the data layer declaration as follows:

```
<script>
dataLayer = [{
    'ecommerce': {
        'promoView': {
            'promotions': [
              {
                'name': 'April Foolery Clearance',
                'id': 'PROMO_0401',
                'creative': 'Tweedle Dee v.1',
                'position': 'Store Home Banner'
              },
              {
                'name': 'Free Shipping',
                'id': 'FREE_SHIPPING',
                'creative': 'White Rabbit Delivery Service',
                'position': 'Right Sidebar'
              }
            ]
        }
    }
}];
</script>
```

The action is promoView, and the promotions array contains one or more promotions that were included on the page with the attributes described earlier.

Ecommerce Data on User Interactions

In all of the previous examples in this chapter, you included enhanced ecommerce data in the data layer declaration when the page loads. However, for some types of interactions, you may need to send it at a later time. You can do this using dataLayer.push() to add information to the data layer upon a user interaction, and send that to GA using an event.

First, you'll look at the two ecommerce actions that are always user interactions: product clicks and promotion clicks. Then you'll take a look at cart and checkout interactions, which for AJAX sites might need to be handled using these techniques as well.

Product and Promotion Clicks

Earlier in the chapter, you captured data about the impressions of products and promotions (using the impressions and promoView actions). Now you can look at which of those impressions resulted in clicks using the click and promoClick actions. You'll need to trigger these when the appropriate user interaction occurs.

You'll employ the same approached you used in Chapter 5 to capture user interactions; all you'll need to add is the ecommerce data to them. You'll recall that several approaches to tracking user interactions have been discussed:

- Embedding dataLayer.push() code directly in the site to listen for events on an element

- Using GTM's auto-event tracking capabilities to attach events to an element

Either of these approaches is also viable for the product and promotion clicks, so you'll look at each of them in the following sections.

Explicit Data Layer Events in Site Code

The ecommerce object for a product click looks like this:

```
'ecommerce': {
    'click': {
        'products': [{
            'name': 'Top Hat',
            'id': 'MH007',
            'price': '24.99',
            'brand': 'Mad Hatter\'s Hat Emporium',
            'category': 'Hats/Mens',
            'variant': 'Purple'
        }]
    }
}
```

The action is click, and it contains a products array with the core product attributes. (Unless there's something very strange about your site, a user can only click one product at a time, so typically there's just a single product in the array.)

For a promotion click, the ecommerce object looks like this:

```
'ecommerce': {
    'promoClick': {
        'promotions': [{
            'name': 'April Foolery Clearance',
            'id': 'PROMO_0401',
            'creative': 'Tweedle Dee v.1',
            'position': 'Store Home Banner'
        }]
    }
}
```

The action is promoClick, and it contains a promotions array with the promotions attributes.

For each of the product or promotion links on the site, you'd like to capture the click interaction. To do that, you could call the dataLayer.push() function when the link is clicked:

```
<a onclick="dataLayer.push({'ecommerce': { // as above }, 'event':
'ecommerceProductClick' })">...</a>
```

■ **Note**   Although this example uses an inline `onclick` attribute to call the `dataLayer.push()` function, the code could be used in an event listener or any other existing JavaScript code on the site.

The data in the ecommerce object would be filled in by server-side code from your site, just as you fill in data in the data layer at the time the page loads, but it isn't added to the data layer until the link is clicked.

Notice that you've also added an event attribute. This allows you to set up a trigger in GTM to fire a GA event tracking tag, which will send the data (just as the GA pageview tag does for the data in the data layer at the time the page loads).

TRACK EXPLICITLY CODED ECOMMERCE CLICKS

Assuming you've added the `dataLayer.push()` code described earlier, you can create the tag and trigger to use these variables to send an event to GA.

1. Create a new tag. Select Google Analytics ➤ Universal Analytics as the tag type.

2. Use the previously created {{GA Property ID}} variable for the Tracking ID.

3. In each of the Category and Action fields, enter some values to describe the event (see the following screenshot). The example uses a category of "Ecommerce" and an action of "Product Click".

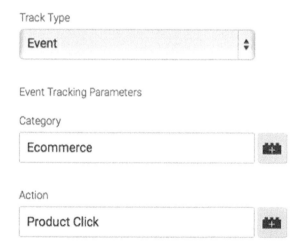

4. Under More Settings ➤ Ecommerce Features, select the check box to Enable Enhanced Ecommerce Features (just as you did previously for the GA pageview tag). Check the box to use the data layer.

5. Choose Continue to specify a trigger for the tag.

    a. Choose More, then select the New button to create a new trigger.

    b. Select Custom Event as the event to cause the trigger. Custom Event allows you to trigger on a `dataLayer.push` with any `event` name.

    c. For Event name to match, enter `ecommerceProductClick` (which corresponds to the name in the code).

    d. Select the Create Trigger button, giving the trigger a name: "Custom Event – Product Clicks". GTM saves the trigger and returns to creating the tag.

6. Save the tag, giving it a name: "GA – Event – Ecommerce Product Clicks".

This example is specifically for product clicks. You could create another tag for promotion clicks (with a different name in the `event` attribute that you'll use as the trigger for that tag).

Using GTM's Auto-Event Tracking

The disadvantage of the approach in the previous section, as also mentioned in Chapter 5, is that it forces you to include tracking JavaScript in the site's code, while one of the reasons you adopted GTM in the first place was to take tracking JavaScript out of the site's code and centralize its control in GTM.

As an alternative, you can use GTM's built-in auto-event tracking to find certain types of links or other elements on which to trigger tags. You'll still need to provide the ecommerce data to be sent for each element, however, which you can do using a `data-` attribute. In HTML, `data-` attributes are basically a reserved namespace of attributes for providing additional, site-specific data about elements. You can use a `data-` attribute on the product link:

```
<a data-ecommerce='{"ecommerce": { // as above }}' class="product" href="/products/fedora">
Fedora</a>
```

Here you've chosen the name `data-ecommerce` for the attribute. You can choose any name that starts with `data-`, making sure to avoid conflicts with any existing attributes in use on your site. The contents of the attribute are the object with all the ecommerce data about the product or promotion click.

■ **Caution**   Although in most cases single quotes (') and double quotes (") are interchangeable in HTML and JavaScript, the JSON (JavaScript Object Notation) specification specifically requires double quotes. JavaScript's `JSON.parse()` function (which you'll use to access this value) respects this and treats the `data-ecommerce` attribute as an object only when the inner quotes are double (otherwise, it will be interpreted as a string). *Long story short: don't swap the quote styles in this example.*

With the data in place on the product and promotion links you'd like to track, you can create a variable in GTM to read this data, and then send it along with an event set up with auto-event tracking.

TRACK ECOMMERCE CLICKS WITH AUTO-EVENT TRACKING

First, you'll create a variable to read the ecommerce data from the `data-ecommerce` attribute. Recall from Chapter 5 that using auto-event tracking automatically adds a message to the data layer that includes a variable called {{Click Element}}, which allows you to access all the properties of the clicked element. You'll use this in a Custom JavaScript variable to return the value of the `data-ecommerce` attribute.

1. Create a new variable.

2. For the variable type, choose Custom JavaScript. Here's the code you'll be using:

    ```
    function() {
        var el = {{Click Element}};
        if(el && el.getAttribute) {
            var data = el.getAttribute('data-ecommerce');
            try { return JSON.parse(data); } catch(e) { return data; }
        }
    }
    ```

    This uses the existing `{{Click Element}}` variable and uses a JavaScript function called `JSON.parse()` to retrieve the `data-ecommerce` attribute, and returns the contents of that attribute as the value of the variable. So long as you've formatted the object correctly in the attribute as discussed earlier, it will be returned as a JavaScript object.

3. Save the variable, giving it a name: "Ecommerce Data Attribute".

Next, you can set up a GA event tag using auto-event tracking to track clicks on the product or promotion.

1. Create a new tag. Choose Google Analytics ➤ Universal Analytics as the type.

2. Use the previously created `{{GA Property ID}}` variable for the Tracking ID.

3. Select Track Type ➤ Event.

4. Fill in the Category, Action, and Label to be sent to GA. You'll want to choose your own conventions for how you'd like to see these in your reports, but one sensible choice might be:

    -   Category: Ecommerce

    -   Action: Product Click

    -   Label: `{{Click Text}}` (the anchor text of the link)

5. Under More Settings ➤ Ecommerce Features, select the check box to Enable Enhanced Ecommerce Features. Instead of selecting the box to use the data layer (as you've done in the rest of the examples in this chapter), choose the `{{Ecommerce Data Attribute}}` variable that you created earlier.

6. Choose Continue to specify a trigger for the tag.

    a. Choose Click, and then select the New button to create a new click trigger.

    b. Choose Some Clicks.

    c. Specify some criteria to trigger this tag on appropriate clicks. In this example, the product links have a class attribute with the value product, so you could use that. (See Chapter 5 for more in-depth discussion of triggers for auto-event tracking).

        `{{Click Classes}} – contains – product`

    d. Name the trigger. Then choose Link Click as the trigger type.

    e. Filter pages on which the trigger should listen for product clicks (if needed). If you want to restrict this trigger to only listening for product clicks on certain pages, you can use a condition or regular expression to match certain pages. To listen on all pages, use a regular expression to match any URL:

        `{{Page URL}} – matches RegEx – .*`

    f. Select the Create Trigger button, giving the trigger a name: "Product Clicks". GTM saves the trigger and returns to creating the tag.

7. Save the tag, giving it a name: "GA – Event – Ecommerce Product Clicks".

This example is specifically for product clicks. You could create another tag for promotion clicks (with a different trigger for that tag to target the appropriate links). The same `{{Ecommerce Data Attribute}}` variable can be used for this tag as well.

AJAX Cart and Checkout Interactions

Earlier in the chapter, you used the add, remove, checkout, and purchase actions to track interactions with the shopping cart and checkout process, and you assumed that each of the steps in that process was a distinct page, and you added information to the data layer declaration on each of those pages.

A site using an AJAX approach can use dataLayer.push() to add an ecommerce object to the data layer for the action to be measured (add, remove, checkout, purchase):

```
<script>
dataLayer.push({
    'event': 'ecommerceCheckout',
    'ecommerce': {
        'checkout': {
            'actionField': {
                'step': 1,
                'option': 'White Rabbit Delivery Service'
            },
            'products': [
                {
                    'name': 'Top Hat',
                    'id': 'MH007',
                    'price': '24.99',
```

```
                    'brand': 'Mad Hatter\'s Hat Emporium',
                    'category': 'Hats/Mens',
                    'variant': 'Purple',
                    'quantity': 1
                },
                {
                    'name': 'Felt Fedora',
                    'id': 'MH342',
                    'price': '17.99',
                    'brand': 'Mad Hatter\'s Hat Emporium',
                    'category': 'Hats/Mens',
                    'variant': 'Grey',
                    'quantity': 1
                }
            ]
        }
    }
});
```

```
</script>
```

This code would typically be incorporated in the AJAX response when new content for the page is loaded. This code is identical to the checkout example earlier in the chapter, except for two changes:

- It uses `dataLayer.push()`

- It includes an event attribute

Since the page doesn't reload, you *don't want to declare a new data layer* (using `dataLayer = []`); instead you want to *append to the existing data layer* (using `dataLayer.push()`). Declaring the data layer again after it already exists will overwrite its previous values and can cause GTM to behave unexpectedly.

Also added is an event attribute. You can use this to trigger an event or virtual pageview tag to send data to GA.

■ **Note**   This solution, using `dataLayer.push()` and a custom event trigger, is one approach to tracking an AJAX cart or checkout process, and probably the most straightforward. See Chapter 6 for an in-depth discussion of tracking AJAX processes and other options in GTM, such as form submission and history change triggers.

TRACK AJAX ECOMMERCE ACTIONS

Assuming that you've added the `dataLayer.push()` code described earlier, you can create the tag and trigger to use these variables to send an event to GA.

1. Create a new tag. Select Google Analytics ➤ Universal Analytics as the tag type.

2. Use the previously created {{GA Property ID}} variable for the Tracking ID.

3. Select Track Type ➤ Pageview or Track Type ➤ Event, depending on whether you'd rather use a virtual pageview or event to measure this interaction (see Chapters 5 and 6 for further discussion). Fill in the Page or Category and Action fields (as appropriate).

4. Under More Settings ➤ Ecommerce Features, select the check box to Enable Enhanced Ecommerce Features. Check the box to use the data layer.

5. Choose Continue to specify a trigger for the tag.

   a. Choose More, then select the New button to create a new trigger.

   b. Select Custom Event as the event to cause the trigger. Custom Event allows you to trigger on a `dataLayer.push` with any `event` name.

   c. For the Event name to match, enter `ecommerceCheckout` (which corresponds to the name in the code).

   d. Select the Create Trigger button, giving the trigger a name: "Custom Event – Ecommerce Checkout".

6. Save the tag, giving it a name: "GA – Ecommerce – Checkout".

This example is specifically for checkout actions. You could create other tags for `add`, `remove`, or `purchase` (with different names in the `event` attributes that you'll use as the trigger for those tags).

Summary

- Google Analytics offers two options for ecommerce tracking. Basic ecommerce tracks completed purchases only. Enhanced ecommerce tracks many ecommerce interactions throughout the site. Either must be enabled in Google Analytics. You can also set a preferred currency in your view's settings in Google Analytics, which can automatically convert if you send data in a different currency.

- Basic ecommerce tracking requires implementing server-side code to add ecommerce data to the data layer on the final transaction page of the site. Then a Google Analytics transaction tag is added in Google Tag Manager to be triggered only on this final transaction page, reading the information in the data layer and sending it to Google Analytics. This approach is advantageous because it is straightforward, but limited in the types of insights that can be derived from the data.

- Enhanced ecommerce tracking requires implementing server-side code to add ecommerce data to the data layer on many pages of the site, to record details such as impressions, clicks, and detail views of products, additions to and removals from the shopping cart, purchases and refunds, and impressions and clicks of internal promotions. Enhanced ecommerce data is sent along with an existing pageview or event tag for Google Analytics by reading the ecommerce data from the data layer. For user interactions that trigger ecommerce actions, such as a click or an AJAX checkout process, you can apply approaches like auto-event tracking and virtual pageviews from Chapters 5 and 6 to send ecommerce data. Enhanced ecommerce is advantageous because it provides a much wider pool of data for analysis, but involves more effort to collect these additional types of data.

CHAPTER 8

Cleaning Up and Enriching Data

"When I use a word," Humpty Dumpty said in rather a scornful tone, "it means just what I choose it to mean—neither more nor less."

—Lewis Carroll, *Through the Looking Glass*

You're collecting lots of data; the last several chapters have talked about how to customize and expand the types of data sent to Google Analytics through Google Tag Manager. However, amid all of this data, there are certain pieces that you just don't want to appear in your reports—internal data from testing, for example. And sometimes you'd like to make changes to your data to make it more useful—cleaning up URLs, extracting important information from query parameters, and grouping like pages together.

This chapter begins by looking at the tools for doing these sorts of data cleanup, both in GTM and in GA. The latter half of the chapter will move on to a number of specific scenarios of the most common uses for these tools to see them in action.

Tools for Cleaning Up Data

You have two opportunities to remove or change data that ultimately end up in GA reports:

- In Google Tag Manager, blocking or changing data at the point of collection using triggers and variables.

- In Google Analytics, excluding or changing data in a view after it's received, using filters and other settings.

Let's take a look at the options available.

GTM: Blocking Triggers and Overriding Default Values

First, let's talk about the ways that GTM can remove or change data.

In GTM, you can prevent data from being sent at all to GA by an appropriate use of triggers. You also have the opportunity to change or override the default values collected by GA tags or other tags in GTM by using variables.

Blocking Triggers

GTM uses triggers to say "fire this tag when" some set of criteria occurs. It could be a pageview, an auto-event like a click or form submission, or a custom event pushed to the data layer. (Refer back to Chapter 5 for more examples of triggers.)

You can also specify blocking triggers. The combination of firing triggers and blocking triggers say "fire this tag when X occurs, except when Y occurs"—that is, you can set some exceptions that prevent the tag from firing.

You can add blocking triggers to a tag in the same way that you set firing triggers, choosing Create Exceptions in the tag setup flow (see Figure 8-1).

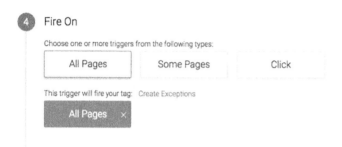

Figure 8-1. *Adding a blocking trigger*

A trigger must always include an event pushed to the data layer. If you select the trigger type for pageviews, the built-in `gtm.js` event is used. If you select click, form, or one of the other auto-event options, the auto-event labels (`gtm.click`, etc.) are used (see Chapter 5). If you're specifying custom criteria, you need to specify which event or events the trigger should block on.

■ **Tip** In many cases, the firing trigger and blocking trigger will operate on the same event: "Fire on all pageviews, except pageviews where the URL contains `/blog`", for example. However, sometimes you may want to block based on some variable for all events (pageviews, clicks, etc.). "Fire on X (any trigger), except when GTM is in preview mode" might be one example. In this case, you can use a custom event trigger and specify a regular expression of "`.*`" (match anything) to block when any event occurs. Then you can reuse this trigger as a blocking trigger across many different types of firing triggers for tags. You'll see several examples throughout this chapter.

Overriding Default Values in a Tag

In the GA tag, several fields are filled in automatically, including the page and referrer URLs, campaign information (see Chapter 9), and more. You can, however, override these values if you need to use the settings under More Settings ➤ Fields to Set (see Figure 8-2).

Figure 8-2. *Using Fields to Set to override values in a GA tag in GTM*

You've used these settings before to tell GA to do something other than the default, such as in setting up cross-domain tracking (see Chapter 2), or in creating a URL label for virtual pageviews (see Chapter 5). Fields to Set can be used any time you'd like to manually override the values that GA uses by default for some field.

Each field is specified by a name, and you provide a value (usually a variable) that you'd like to use. There's a long list of possible fields accessible in the drop-down menu. Several will be discussed in this chapter and in subsequent chapters of this book, and you can find a complete list in the GA documentation.[1]

GA: Filters and Views

Next, let's take a look at how you can change data with GA.

As you'll recall from Chapter 1, your site's tracking code corresponds to a property in GA. Each property can have one or more views, which are different buckets of data about that site.

Creating a view is as easy as simply selecting Create New View from the bottom of the view drop-down menu in the rightmost column of the Admin tab in Google Analytics (see Figure 8-3). Keep in mind that the view begins accumulating data from the property from the time it's created, but is not filled with data retroactively.

Figure 8-3. *Creating a new view*

Filters allow you to include or exclude specific data from a view (include just a subsection of a site, for example, or exclude your own employees' interactions on the site). They can also enable you to make changes to data (to clean up URL formats or other information).

---

[1]https://developers.google.com/analytics/devguides/collection/analyticsjs/field-reference

In a view's settings (the rightmost column) you can see Filters listed as one of the options (see Figure 8-4). Each view can have different filters applied, resulting in a different set of data. You can see any existing filters applied to the view in this list. Selecting a filter from this list allows you to edit it or remove it from the view.

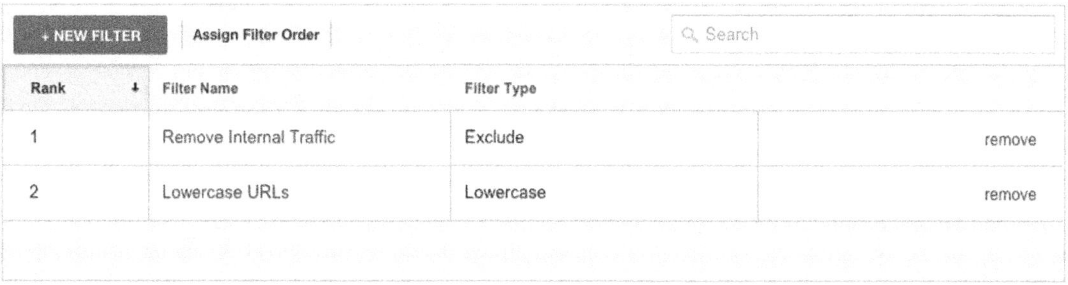

+ NEW FILTER	Assign Filter Order			Q Search
Rank ↓	Filter Name	Filter Type		
1	Remove Internal Traffic	Exclude		remove
2	Lowercase URLs	Lowercase		remove

Figure 8-4. *The list of filters on a view in GA's Admin settings*

Filters can be added to a view in one of two ways:

- Apply an existing filter from the account to the view.
- Create a new filter to apply to the view.

Once created, **filters are stored at the account level**. This means that you can create a filter once and apply it to as many views within the account as you like. (It also means that a user needs Edit access at the account level to create new filters.) You can see a list of all filters in the account listed in the Admin area under All Filters in the account column (the leftmost column), where you can also quickly apply a filter to multiple views.

To apply an existing filter or create a new one, select the button at the top of the list of filters. You have the option to apply one or more existing filters, or to create a new filter (see Figure 8-5).

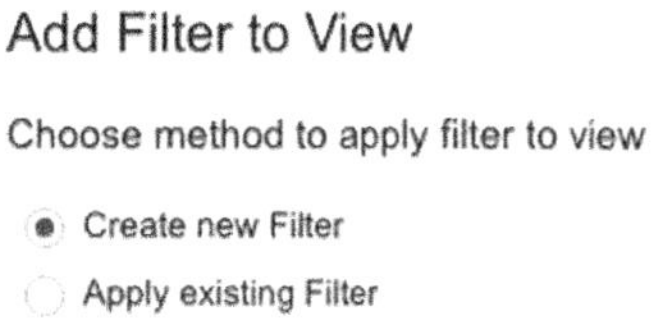

Add Filter to View

Choose method to apply filter to view

- ● Create new Filter
- ○ Apply existing Filter

Figure 8-5. *Creating a filter for a view*

Types of Filters

When creating a new filter, you have two main choices:

- Predefined filters cover a handful of common use cases, with easy-to-use drop-down menus to define the filter options.
- Custom filters allow more flexibility and the use of regular expressions to match patterns.

Predefined Filters

The predefined filters use a series of drop-down menus to specify data to include or exclude in the view that cover a few common use cases, such as excluding an IP address or including only a specific subdirectory of the site. (You'll see both of those examples later in the chapter.)

Custom Filters

For more complex needs, custom filters offer a variety of options (see Figure 8-6).

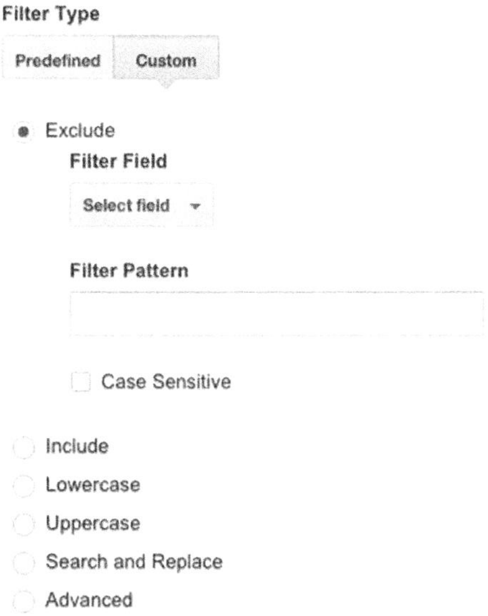

Filter Type

Predefined	Custom

● Exclude

Filter Field

Select field ▾

Filter Pattern

☐ Case Sensitive

○ Include
○ Lowercase
○ Uppercase
○ Search and Replace
○ Advanced

Figure 8-6. *Custom filter types and options*

First, there are a number of different types of custom filters:

- *Exclude*: exclude data that matches a regular expression
- *Include*: include only data that matches a regular expression
- *Lowercase*: convert a field's alphabetic characters into lower case
- *Uppercase*: convert a field's alphabetic characters into upper case
- *Search and Replace*: find a regular expression match in a field and replace it with text
- *Advanced*: find regular expression matches in one or two fields and rearrange the text from those fields

You'll see each of these filter types in action in applications later in the chapter. When you choose one of these filter types, you'll see that GA provides a very long drop-down list of fields to filter on (see Figure 8-7).

Filter Field

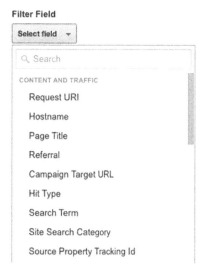

Figure 8-7. *Fields available in filters (partial list)*

This list includes all the fields you might expect, but there's a little challenge: the names used for fields in this list don't always match up very well with how corresponding dimensions are named in the reports in GA. For example, this menu includes Request URI, which is the same as the dimension simply referred to as Page in GA's reports. As you look at examples in this chapter, you'll see several of the most commonly used fields from this list that may be useful, and there's a full accounting in the GA documentation if you can't quite decide which field is the right one.[2]

All of the filter types which allow you to match values in a field (Include, Exclude, Search and Replace, Advanced) use regular expressions as input. This allows you to be as specific (one exact value) or as broad (multiple values, or some common pattern across values) as you need to be.

■ **Caution**   In regular expressions, characters like the dot (.) and question mark (?) have special meaning. Sometimes these appear in the strings you are matching, however (consider a URL like /alice.html?potion=drink-me). You need to be careful, and for any special regular expression characters you'd like to use as the literal character, preface it with a backslash (\). Characters that require a backslash to be treated as ordinary characters are: \ . ? + * [(^ $

Testing and Troubleshooting Views and Filters in GA

For changes you make in GTM, you can use GTM's preview mode and other browser tools to inspect the data being sent to GA (see Chapter 4). But what about changes you make with views and filters in GA? These are applied after the data is received, so browser-based testing tools don't help you.

---

[2]https://support.google.com/analytics/answer/1034380

The critical characteristic of any changes you make in GA's Admin interface is that they take effect only **from the time you make the change going forward**. Changes don't retroactively affect the data in the reports in a view. This has important repercussions for testing changes. Suppose you add a filter to a view, and later (an hour, a day, a week) you find there's a typo, and you accidentally filtered out something you didn't mean to. There's no way to undo this retroactively in the view's data. You can correct the typo in the filter, which fixes data going forward, but for the intervening hour or day or week where the data was wrong, it stays wrong.

With this constraint in mind, to help with testing and troubleshooting filters and other view configuration settings, you'll also want to create the following views:

- An ***unfiltered view*** for troubleshooting and backup. If you're filtering traffic out, how do you know what you've removed without an unfiltered set of data to compare it to? An unfiltered view gives you a point of comparison. Create this view and don't apply any filters to it. The other advantage of an unfiltered view is as a backup: if something goes wrong and you accidentally lose some data, you can always refer to the unfiltered view.

- One or more ***test views*** to test changes to filters and other view configuration settings and ensure that they work properly. In this way, you have a place to try changes with no adverse consequences if you make a mistake (since you're not actually using the data in these test views).

These views would, of course, be in addition to any views you actually use for reporting and analysis of your site.

▪ **Tip**   If you're setting up a site from scratch, create these views at the same time you set up the site in GA, so that the data goes back to the very beginning. If you're inheriting a site that has been previously set up, create these views right away so that they start gathering data to aid you as you make changes and updates going forward.

Once you've created a test view, you can use it to try out configuration changes in the Admin settings, and then look at the data in the reports of the test view to make sure they match your expectations.

Because the data in GA is typically reported on by day, and the changes only take effect going forward, changes made in the middle of a day can result in a mixed set of data (both before and after the change) for the day when the change was made. To get a clear view of whether a filter is working correctly and the data is "clean," you generally need to wait until the next day. The process typically goes something like this:

1. Make a change to a filter or other view configuration setting in the test view.

2. Wait until sometime in the next calendar day.

3. Check the relevant report(s) in GA, **changing the date range to the current day**.

4. Did you get it right?

   - If everything looks good, go ahead and apply the same filter or change the same setting in the reporting view(s).

   - If not, repeat this process from step 1.

■ **Note** For certain types of data, you may be able to use the Real-Time reports to see the effect of a newly applied filter, but those reports don't have full coverage of the types of data in GA, and may be difficult to use in comparing two sets of data.

Partitioning Internal Traffic

One of the most common desires is to separate website traffic by internal users from that of the general public, the customers and prospects whose website behavior is of interest to you. Internal users have very different behavior from customers, are excluded from the targets of your marketing activities, and are often engaged in testing website functionality. Although data about these activities may be useful to you, it's useful in ways different from the activities of external users, so you'd like to be able to separate them.

The following sections explore two main topics connected to this challenge:

- Removing (or separating out) traffic from internal users to avoid "polluting" your customer data.

- Dealing with multiple versions of a site for development, testing, and staging to keep testing activity separate from your live website.

Removing Internal Traffic

"Internal traffic" includes your organization's employees, as well as third parties who work on your website on your behalf, like advertising agencies or web developers. Usually you're not interested in their usage of your website in the same context as external users—your actual audience—so you'd like to eliminate or separate them out.

There are several different ways to identify and block this internal traffic (by IP address in GTM or in GA, or by Service Provider in GA), which you'll explore in the following sections. Different organizations define and treat internal traffic differently, so assess all of the options available to understand what will work best for your situation.

■ **Note** None of these methods can be absolutely perfect: your employees sometimes travel, or work from home, or other situations in which it would be hard to identify them as "internal." Do your best, but you should expect some data will leak through in any case.

Using IP Addresses

If you're targeting particular IP addresses to exclude internal traffic, you have two potential options:

- Apply a blocking trigger to your GA tags in GTM. This prevents your site from sending any data about the internal IP addresses.

- Apply a filter to a view in GA. This allows you to exclude internal traffic, while still collecting internal traffic data in an unfiltered view in GA.

If your only goal is to exclude internal traffic, either method works just fine. However, in many cases you might be interested in including *only* internal traffic in some views in GA. For example, imagine you have a university website, and you wish to create views for both on-campus and off-campus traffic based on IP addresses. In this case, you need to collect data for all IP addresses using GTM, and filter the data in views in GA (the latter method).

SIDEBAR: BLOCKING INTERNAL TRAFFIC IN NON-GA TAGS

Although this book has primarily focused on using GA tags in GTM, using a blocking trigger in GTM for internal traffic applies equally well to other tags deployed via GTM. You will want to exclude your internal traffic from other kinds of measurement tools, and especially from ad tracking and targeting tools. (There's no need to market to your own employees, for example!)

Like GA, other tools will often have the ability to filter or remove internal traffic, using IP address or other characteristics. But if you have to do this separately in each tool, that's a pain. Using a set of blocking triggers in GTM allows you to have a centralized way to do this for all tags you want to prevent from firing for internal traffic. And if your IP addresses should ever change or need to be updated, you can do it in one spot.

Whether you separate internal traffic in GA or in GTM, first you need to know what IP addresses to filter out. Although you can check your own IP address (Googling "what is my IP address" does the trick), what you won't know from that is whether everyone in your office network shares a single IP or a range, whether there are additional IP addresses for other office locations, and other details about your internal network. You'll need to get a comprehensive list or range of IP addresses from a networking guru in the IT department to reliably filter out your internal traffic

---

■ **Note**　Often a device has both an internal IP address (assigned by your network's router) as well as an external IP address (the address(es) of the router itself on the internet at large). You need the external IP addresses to filter in GA or GTM. Internal IP addresses usually start with a first number of 10, 172, or 192, so if you receive a list with these IP addresses, ask again and make sure to specify the external address.

Now let's take a look at the two different methods of removing traffic by IP address, starting with blocking triggers in GTM. GTM doesn't have a built-in variable for IP address, and it's not a value accessible via JavaScript alone, so you need to provide GTM a way to access the value. The natural way to do this is simply to add it to the data layer declaration:

```
dataLayer = [{ 'ipAddress': '93.184.216.34' }];
```

This is quite straightforward to do with any server-side programming language.

■ **Note**　Although it may be tempting to pass the IP address as a custom dimension to GA, don't do it. IP addresses are considered potentially personally identifiable information and prohibited from being included in reports in GA. (See Chapter 11 for more information on custom dimensions.)

PREVENT SENDING TRAFFIC BY IP ADDRESS IN GTM

First, you need a variable for IP address. Let's assume it's already in the data layer, as shown earlier.

1. In GTM, create a new variable.

2. For the variable type, choose Data Layer Variable.

3. For the data layer variable name, enter `ipAdress` (or whatever label you used for the IP address in the data layer).

4. Save the variable, giving it a name: "IP Address".

Now you can create a trigger based on the {{IP Address}} variable. For the trigger type, you'll need to use a regular expression to match any event, since you want to match pageviews, auto-event triggers, and any other events that occur.

1. In GTM, create a new trigger.

2. For the event, choose Custom Event.

3. For the event name, select the Use Regex check box and enter `.*` (as seen in the following screenshot).

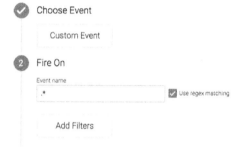

4. Select Add Filters to apply a condition.

5. For the condition, choose the {{IP Adress}} variable and an appropriate condition and value for the specific IP address(es) you'd like to exclude (as seen in the following screenshot). If there's just one, "equals" might be appropriate, or if you'd like to match a range you might use "matches RegEx" to use a regular expression.

6. Save the trigger, giving it a name: "Blocking – Internal IPs".

You can repeat the preceding steps to create multiple triggers if there's a list of IP addresses you'd like to block. Now you're finally ready to apply this trigger to block a tag.

1. Select your GA pageview tag (or any other tag) in GTM to edit.

2. Select Fire On to edit the triggers for the tag.

3. Select Create Exceptions.

4. Choose the Blocking – Internal IPs trigger you created earlier. If you created multiple blocking triggers (for multiple IP addresses), you can choose multiple triggers.

5. Save the changes to the tag.

Don't forget to preview and publish the changes to the container so the new blocking trigger takes effect.

Next, let's take a look at the second method of using IP address, with a filter in GA. GA automatically captures the IP address, so there's no need for a variable for that value in the data layer. Additionally, GA will not only allow you to exclude one or more IP addresses, but also to include only internal traffic in a view.

FILTER TRAFFIC BY IP ADDRESS IN GA

You'll create a filter on a single view, but once it's been created, you can apply it to as many views as you like.

1. In the Admin area of GA, with the appropriate account, property, and view selected, choose Filters in the third column to see the filters for the view. Select the New button to add a new filter.

2. Choose to create a new filter (rather than apply an existing one).

3. Give the filter a name: "Exclude Internal IPs".

4. You can use a predefined filter for simple cases (an exact IP, IPs that begin with a particular value), or a custom filter to use regular expressions for multiple values or ranges:

    •   Select the Predefined tab, and use the drop-down menus to exclude traffic from an IP address (see the following screenshot). "Equals" or "starts with" can both be useful options (for a single IP address and an entire block of IP addresses, respectively).

Filter Type

Predefined	Custom

Exclude ▾	traffic from the IP addresses ▾	that are equal to ▾

IP address

123.123.123.123

- Alternatively, select the Custom tab. Choose Exclude as the filter type and IP Address as the field. Then, enter a regular expression for the IP address(es) you wish to exclude (see the following screenshot).

Filter Type

Predefined	Custom

● Exclude

Filter Field

IP Address ▾

Filter Pattern

123\.123\.123\.12[3-5]

☐ Case Sensitive

5. Save the filter.

Remember that this filter will only affect data going forward. Past data collected from this IP address will not be affected.

If you instead wanted to create a view with only internal traffic, you can simply change the selection of "exclude" to "include" in this filter.

Tip GA starts with the entire set of data for the property, then applies the filters to find what is left over. This means that it can make sense to apply multiple exclude filters (get rid of two different IP addresses, for example). Conversely, however, it does not make sense to apply multiple include filters on the same field—include means *include only*. So if you say, include only IP address A and then include only IP address B, there's nothing left in the resulting data. Instead, you must use regular expressions to match multiple values in a single filter.

Now that you've created this filter, you can apply it to as many views as you need.

Using Service Providers

Google Analytics contains another label that is sometimes useful for filtering internal traffic: a dimension called Service Provider. The Service Provider dimension contains a label for the user's internet service provider, based on their IP.

For many consumers and some businesses, the internet service provider listed will be the telecommunications company through which they have internet access (a phone or cable company). Larger businesses, institutions, and government agencies, however, may be listed as their own service provider for the range of IP addresses they are assigned. In these cases, you can use a filter in GA for the service provider label. This approach has the advantage that you don't need to know the IP address ranges or express them in regular expressions.

You can check if your organization is listed as its own service provider in the Audience ➤ Technology ➤ Network report in GA (see Figure 8-8).

	Service Provider	?
☐	1.	(not set)
☐	2.	time warner cable internet llc
☐	3.	verizon online llc
☐	4.	comcast cable communications holdings inc
☐	5.	comcast cable communications inc.

Figure 8-8. *Service Providers*

Notice that many of the entries are telecommunications providers, but you may also see your own company listed here. Use the search function at the top of the report to search for your organization's name to see if you can find yourself. (Also try various abbreviations for your organization's name, and keep in mind that if you have multiple office locations or subsidiaries, they may be listed in multiple entries.) If the name of your organization appears here, you can create a filter in GA to exclude your internal traffic. (No such luck for you? See the previous section on excluding based on IP addresses.)

EXCLUDE TRAFFIC BY SERVICE PROVIDER WITH A FILTER IN GA

1. In the Admin area of GA, with the appropriate account, property, and view selected, choose Filters in the third column to see the filters for the view. Select the New button to add a new filter.

2. Choose to create a new filter (rather than apply an existing one).

3. Give the filter a name: "Exclude Internal Service Provider".

4. Choose the Custom tab.

    a. Choose Exclude as the filter type.

    b. Choose ISP Organization as the field. (This is an example of poor naming in the filter field drop-down compared to the dimension names in GA: here, ISP Organization, in GA reports, Service Provider.)

    c. Enter a regular expression for the service provider value to match (see the following screenshot).

Filter Type

Predefined	Custom

● Exclude

Filter Field

ISP Organization ▾

Filter Pattern

alice worldwide industries

5. Save the filter.

Remember that this filter will only affect data going forward. Past data collected from this IP address will not be affected.

If you instead wanted to create a view with only internal traffic, you could simply change the selection of "exclude" to "include" in this filter.

Now that you've created this filter, you can apply it to as many views as you need.

Separating Test and Production Environments

In many cases, you may already have taken care of excluding internal traffic in GA (see the previous section in this chapter), which would typically include your employees' or agency's testing of your website. However, you might want to be able to separately view such testing traffic to ensure that everything is working correctly—collecting test data about new site content or features before they go live on the website to ensure they're working and recording data as expected.

Your exact setup will depend on your environments and how you'd like to be able to view the data. Let's assume for example purposes that you have the following environments:

- dev.aliceswonderlandresorts.com
- staging.aliceswonderlandresorts.com
- www.aliceswonderlandresorts.com

You'd like to keep the messy, internal testing data from the development and staging sites separate from the good, clean, customer-oriented data you use to analyze your site's content and marketing on the production site. You can accomplish this by creating additional properties in GA for the development and staging sites and using GTM to route data to the correct property. The next section will walk through this process.

There's another kind of testing traffic you should consider: when you use GTM's preview mode (see Chapter 4) for testing changes to tags and triggers on the live production website (www.aliceswonderlandresorts.com, in this example). You might also want to separate this data into another property. A later section will look at that case later as well.

Using Lookup Tables to Partition Traffic in GTM

Way back in Chapter 3, you created a {{GA Property ID}} variable to hold the property ID for the GA tag in GTM. It might have seemed like an overly elaborate solution back then (can't you just paste in the ID value?). Now, however, you'll be able to replace that variable with one that takes into account your need to change the property ID depending on whether the tag is on the development, staging, or production site.

There's a variable type in GTM called the lookup table. What it allows you to do is provide multiple conditions for an input variable that result in different output variables. In this case, you're interested in using the value of {{URL Hostname}} to change the value of the variable among your GA property IDs (see Table 8-1).

Table 8-1. *Properties for test and development versions of an example website*

dev.aliceswonderlandresorts.com	UA-12345-2
staging.aliceswonderlandresorts.com	UA-12345-3
www.aliceswonderlandresorts.com	UA-12345-1

Let's walk through this step by step.

USE A LOOKUP TABLE VARIABLE TO PARTITION TEST SITES

Let's change the existing {{GA Property ID}} variable to a lookup table.

1. Edit the {{GA Property ID}} variable in GTM.

2. Select the type and change it from Constant to Lookup Table.

3. As the Input Variable, choose the built-in {{Page Hostname}} variable.

4. Add a row to the table.

    a. For the input, enter a hostname, such as dev.aliceswonderlandresorts.com.

■ **Note**   Lookup tables support exact matches only. Avoid regular expressions in the input values.

---

    b. For the output, enter a GA property ID where you'd like data for that site to be routed.

5. Repeat adding rows until hostnames for all of your development, test, staging, and so forth, sites have been added (see the following screenshot).

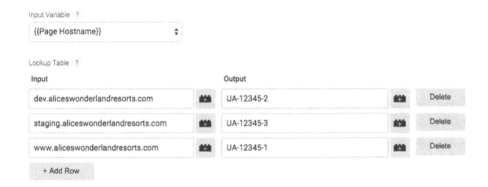

6. (Optional) Set a default value by checking the box and entering a GA property ID. The default value will be used for any hostnames that do not match any row in the table.

7. Save the variable.

No changes to the tags are necessary, since they already use this existing variable. Test and publish the container to start routing your test traffic to different properties.

Lookup tables can be useful in many situations where you want to translate one value into another. In this case, you translated a hostname into a GA property ID. For your production website, however, you also have another type of testing activity: your use of GTM's preview mode to test tags before they are published.

You also want to capture this activity, but separately from the rest of the production site data (as illustrated in Table 8-2). You can layer in an additional lookup table to further separate. Let's see how.

Table 8-2. *Routing testing traffic for an example site, including GTM debug mode*

dev.aliceswonderlandresorts.com	UA-12345-2	
staging.aliceswonderlandresorts.com	UA-12345-3	
www.aliceswonderlandresorts.com	In debug mode?	UA-12345-4
	Not in debug mode?	UA-12345-1

USE A LOOKUP TABLE VARIABLE TO PARTITION PREVIEW MODE

First, you'll create an additional lookup table that separates preview mode.

1. If it's not already enabled, enable the built in variable {{Debug Mode}}. This variable is true if GTM is in preview mode.

2. Create a new variable. Choose Lookup Table as the type.

3. As the Input Variable, choose the {{Debug Mode}} variable.

4. Add a row to the table.

   a. For the input, enter true.

   b. For the output, enter a GA Property ID where you'd like data for that site to be routed when GTM is in preview mode.

5. Set a default value by checking the box and entering a GA Property ID where you'd like data to be routed when GTM is *not* in preview mode.

6. Save the variable, giving it a name: "GA Property ID – Preview Mode".

Now you can use this value in the overall {{GA Property ID}} variable, which you changed to a lookup table in the previous section.

1. Edit the {{GA Property ID}} variable.

2. Select Configure Variable to edit the table.

3. In the row containing the live/production website (in this example, www.aliceswonderlandresorts.com), replace the output with the {{GA Property ID – Preview Mode}} variable.

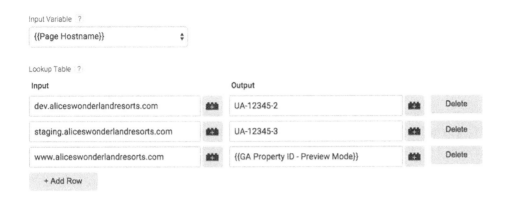

4. Save the changes to the variable.

After publishing this container, GTM will continue to route traffic for the development and staging websites as before. Now, for the live website, if it's in preview mode, it will route to a test property, while the live production data continues to route to the main property.

Cleaning Up and Grouping Content

URLs are just one of many pieces of information captured in GA, but they're often one of the messiest. In an ideal world, you have a site with URLs that:

- are easy to interpret and grouped together in a logical hierarchy,

- contain no extraneous or unnecessary information, and

- uniquely represent a single page.

Often you don't have complete control over the structure and format of URLs on your site (because of particular software being used or historical reasons, for example). In many cases, you need to work with URLs on your website that are made for machines, not for people. By default, Google Analytics captures the URL that you see in the browser's location bar, exactly as it appears. In GA's reports, these URLs are broken up into two dimensions:

- *Hostname*, which contains the domain name (which does not include the protocol and punctuation, such as http:// or https://)

- *Page*, which contains the rest of the URL, including the path and query parameters, but not the fragment

So for example, in the following URL, GA shows these values for the Hostname and Page dimensions:

http://www.aliceswonderlandresorts.com/going/down/?hole=rabbit#lateness

- *Hostname*: www.aliceswonderlandresorts.com

- *Page*: /going/down/?hole=rabbit

Since GA captures these pieces from the URL exactly as they appear, you can encounter inconsistencies in your data that aren't ideal, where there are several variations of a URL that all correspond to what is essentially the same page on your site. These can include inconsistencies in capitalization, query parameters, and more. This section will take a look at each of these issues and some best practices for dealing with them, as well as methods for gathering URLs into groups, such as by topic categories or by internal search results pages.

■ **Important**   Changes to URLs can also affect goal conversions based on those URLs. Make sure to update your goal configurations if necessary (see Chapter 6) after you have made changes to URLs through filters.

Enforcing Case in URLs

Technically speaking, URLs are case sensitive. That is, `http://example.com/jabberwock` and `http://example.com/JabberWock` don't have to go to the same page. However, in practice this is almost never how websites use URLs; usually your web server or content management system will deliver the same page regardless of capitalization.

However, since GA simply captures the URL as it appears, it will potentially show the same URL capitalized in different ways in your reports (see Figure 8-9).

Page ?		Pageviews ? ↓
1. /mad-hatters-tea-party/	⬚	**4,383** (3.26%)
2. /Mad-Hatters-Tea-Party/	⬚	**3,940** (2.93%)

Figure 8-9. *Inconsistent URLs in GA reports*

This isn't very helpful—if you just want to know how many people viewed the page, you have to do the arithmetic yourself. Instead, you'd rather have one, consistent entry for each page in your reports, regardless of capitalization. To do that, you can apply a filter to this data in Google Analytics.

USE A FILTER TO LOWERCASE URLS

1. In the Admin area of GA, with the appropriate account, property, and view selected, choose Filters in the third column to see the filters for the view. Select the New button to add a new filter.

2. Choose to create a new filter (rather than apply an existing one).

3. Give the filter a name: "Lowercase URLs".

4. Choose the Custom tab.

    a. Choose Lowercase as the filter type.

    b. Choose Request URI as the field. (Another example of the mismatch between the filter field drop-down and the dimension names in GA: here, Request URI, in GA reports, Page.)

5. Save the filter.

Remember that this filter will only affect data going forward. Past data collected with mixed case in URLs will not be affected.

■ **Tip** The lowercase filter can be useful for any field that potentially involves human error in entry at some point. This includes both parts of the URL (Request URI and Hostname) as well as the Campaign fields (see Chapter 9). You should look at these values in your GA reports and consider applying lowercase filters for increased consistency.

Default URLs

Another issue with consistency in URLs involves default pages. For your home page, or the default page of subdirectories on a site, a browser can often access the same page via multiple URLs. For example, your home page might be accessible through either of these URLs:

- `http://www.aliceswonderlandresorts.com/`
- `http://www.aliceswonderlandresorts.com/`**`index.html`**

■ **Note** The ending might differ depending on your content management system and web server: index.html, index.php, default.aspx, and so forth. Check your site to see what it uses.

Now you again have a problem in your reporting (see Figure 8-10).

Figure 8-10. *Inconsistent default URLs in GA reports*

Similarly to the capitalization problems described in the previous section, you'd have to add up those rows to understand how many times this particular page was actually viewed. Fortunately, you can fix this in GA as well. There are two options, depending on which version of the URL you'd like to consolidate on:

- There's a view setting that will append `index.html` (or whatever is appropriate) to the end of URLs that end in a trailing slash.

- You can use a filter to remove `index.html` (or whatever is appropriate), leaving only the trailing slash.

Which you prefer is mostly a stylistic choice in the way you'd prefer to see the pages listed in your reports.

USE THE VIEW SETTING TO APPEND DEFAULT TO URLS

GA provides a setting that will automatically append text to the end of any URL that ends in a trailing slash.

1. In the Admin area of GA, with the appropriate account, property, and view selected, choose View Settings in the third column to edit the settings for the view.

2. Scroll down to the setting Default Page.

3. Enter the text you'd like to append to the end of any URL that ends in a trailing slash. (Do not include the slash.)

4. Save the changes to the settings.

Remember that this setting will only affect data going forward. Past data collected for URLs will not be affected.

USE A FILTER TO REMOVE DEFAULT FROM URLS

1. In the Admin area of GA, with the appropriate account, property, and view selected, choose Filters in the third column to see the filters for the view. Select the New button to add a new filter.

2. Choose to create a new filter (rather than apply an existing one).

3. Give the filter a name: "Remove index.php" (for example).

4. Choose the Custom tab.

   a. Choose Search and Replace as the filter type.

   b. Choose Request URI as the field.

   c. For the search string, enter a regular expression for the pattern you want to remove. This might be as simple as `index\.html`, or a more complex pattern if there are multiple possibilities—for example, `(index|default)\.(php|html?)`

   d. For the replace string, leave it blank (to replace with nothing).

5. Save the filter.

Remember that this filter will only affect data going forward. Past data collected with `index.php` in URLs will not be affected.

Query Parameters

The "query string" or "query parameter" portion of the URL is the part after the question mark:

http://www.aliceswonderlandresorts.com/reservation.php**?status=completed&sort=az&session id=123456**

The query parameters consist of name-value pairs joined by equal signs, with multiple parameters separated by ampersands. Sometimes, they tell you something really valuable about the content of the page or the choices of the user (`status=completed`) but other times they're unimportant (`sort=az`) or even detrimental to your data (`sessionid=123456`).

To see how query parameters can muck up your page data, consider that last example, `sessionid`. Web servers sometimes use a session ID or visitor ID to keep track of the user's state in a process. This number is used internally by the web server, but you don't care about it, and furthermore it's different for every single browser session. This is like your capitalization problem from before, but instead of two ways to capitalize the URL, now there are hundreds or thousands! (See Figure 8-11.)

1.	/reservation.php?status=complete d&sort=az&sessionid=123456	⟲	1
2.	/reservation.php?status=complete d&sort=az&sessionid=173940	⟲	1
3.	/reservation.php?status=complete d&sort=za&sessionid=3643783	⟲	1

Figure 8-11. *Query parameter values can cause many variations of the same URL*

Fortunately, you can remove query parameters you'd like to get rid of. There's a view setting in GA that allows you to remove query parameters from the URL, so that you can see one consistent URL with just the query parameters that you want to keep around. Or, if you want to do away with all query parameters, you could use a simple filter.

■ **Tip** Sometimes it might make sense to have multiple views for the site with different settings or filters on the query parameters. For example, one view could keep more detailed query parameter information for more specific reporting (when you really want to know if a user sorted from A to Z or Z to A), while another could remove those parameters for better high-level information about pages.

Before getting started, you're going to need a list of the query parameters you'd like to eliminate. The part of the query parameter you are interested in is the *name* (that is, the part before the equals sign)—for example, status, sort, or sessionid in the example URL. How do you go about compiling this list? If you have existing data in GA, that's one place to begin. (It can be helpful to export the pages into a spreadsheet and use formulas to break apart the query parameters based on delimiters like ?, &, and =.) Looking into the documentation of your content management system or other software used to manage your website may also give insights into query parameters and how they are used.

Once you've established a list of query parameters you'd like to eliminate, you can remove them.

■ **Tip** One type of query parameter you might encounter are parameters relating to an internal site search. For example, in http://aliceswonderlandresorts.com/searchresults.php?q=hats, the query parameter q=hats could indicate that the user searched for the term "hats" using your site's search. Don't remove these with filters or the view setting—they're valuable information, and GA has a special set of reports for dealing with them (and then you can strip them out of the URLs, too). You'll see how in a later section in this chapter.

USE THE VIEW SETTING TO REMOVE SPECIFIC QUERY PARAMETERS

GA provides a view setting that lets you selectively remove query parameters from URLs.

1. In the Admin area of GA, with the appropriate account, property, and view selected, choose View Settings in the third column to edit the settings for the view.

2. Scroll down to the setting Exclude URL Query Parameters.

3. Enter the names of query parameters you'd like to exclude, separated by commas. Note that you should not enter ampersands, equals signs, or other delimiters, merely the name of the query parameter.

4. Save the changes to the settings.

Remember that this setting will only affect data going forward. Past data collected with query parameters in URLs will not be affected.

```
┌──────────────────────────────────────────────────────────────────────┐
│           USE A FILTER TO REMOVE ALL QUERY PARAMETERS                   │
└──────────────────────────────────────────────────────────────────────┘
```

This filter removes everything after the question mark character (?) in your URLs.

1. In the Admin area of GA, with the appropriate account, property, and view selected, choose Filters in the third column to see the filters for the view. Select the New button to add a new filter.

2. Choose to create a new filter (rather than apply an existing one).

3. Give the filter a name: "Remove All Query Parameters".

4. Choose the Custom tab.

   a. Choose Search and Replace as the filter type.

   b. Choose Request URI as the field.

   c. For the search string, enter the following regular expression: \?.*

   d. For the replace string, leave it blank (to replace with nothing).

5. Save the filter.

■ **Caution**   This filter removes everything in a URL after the question mark character. Ensure that you have at least one other view with full, unfiltered URLs should you ever need them.

Remember that this filter will only affect data going forward. Past data collected with query parameters in URLs will not be affected.

Capturing the URL Fragment

You may have noticed in previous examples, or in your GA data, that the Page dimension in GA includes the path and query string of the URL (in bold in this example), but not the fragment (the part after the hash mark):

http://www.aliceswonderlandresorts.com/**tea-party/index.html?location=wonderland**#agenda

The fragment (#agenda, in this example) is often used to link to a particular section of a page. GA discards the fragment by default. If you'd like to capture it, you can grab it with a variable in GTM and override the default page URL with the fragment appended. Here's how.

■ **Note**   If URL fragment changes result from an AJAX application, see Chapter 5 and its information on history listeners to trigger tags to capture that information. The example described here merely captures the fragment in the page's URL to be recorded when an existing tag is triggered.

USE A GTM VARIABLE TO CAPTURE THE URL FRAGMENT

First you'll need to set up a variable to get the URL fragment.

1. Create a new variable in GTM.

2. Choose URL as the variable type.

3. Choose Fragment as the component.

4. Save the variable, giving it a name: "Page URL Fragment".

Now you can alter the GA pageview tag to include the fragment in the URL.

1. In GTM, edit the GA – Pageview tag.

2. Select Configure Tag to make changes to the GA tag settings.

    a. In the Fields to Set section, add a new field.

    b. Select page from the drop-down as the field name.

    c. For the field value, you're going to construct a new URL that includes the site search term from the built-in `{{Page Path}}` variable and the `{{Page URL Fragment}}` variable you just created: `{{Page Path}}#{{Page URL Fragment}}`

> ■ **Note**   If there's no fragment, note that this tag would still append # to the end of the URL. You can easily use a Search and Replace filter in GA to remove the trailing # if there's no fragment. You could also make a clever use of variables in GTM to handle this.

3. Save the changes to the tag.

After publishing these changes, GTM will include the fragment with each page URL sent to GA.

Viewing Hostnames for Subdomains and Cross Domains

Chapters 2 and 3 discussed setting up GA tags to share cookies across subdomains or cross domains, to treat them as a single website. But as you've seen, GA's Page dimension includes only the URL path, not the hostname. Although there is a separate Hostname dimension, in a basic, out-of-the-box report like the Behavior ➤ Site Content ➤ All Pages report, there's no good way to tell which pages are on which site when you have multiple domains (see Figure 8-12).

Page ?		Pageviews ↓ ?
1. /	🗗	**8,142** (4.85%)
2. /locations/	🗗	**4,672** (2.78%)

Figure 8-12. *The All Pages report doesn't indicate which domain or subdomain the pages are on*

You can use filters in GA to prepend the hostname value to the Page dimension, so that these reports become much more easily digestible (see Figure 8-13).

Page ?		Pageviews ↓ ?
1. hotels.aliceswonderlandresorts.com/	🗗	**5,187** (4.85%)
2. parks.aliceswonderlandresorts.com/	🗗	**2,955** (2.78%)
3. hotels.aliceswonderlandresorts.com/locations/	🗗	**1,433** (2.20%)

Figure 8-13. *The All Pages report after adding a filter to include the hostname in URLs*

You'll do this using the Advanced filter type (Figure 8-14), which you haven't seen so far in the examples in this chapter. The Advanced Filter lets you take two different fields in GA (Field A and Field B), extract information from them, and output that information to a field (Output).

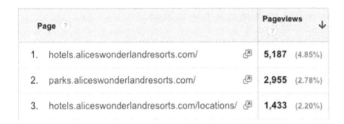

Figure 8-14. *Advanced filter setup in GA*

Field A and Field B each take a regular expression. Any part of the regular expression enclosed in parentheses captures that part of the field to use in the output. The Output takes text as well as variables that refer back to the information captured in Fields A and B. The variables look something like $A1, where $ is the signal for a variable, A refers to field A, and 1 refers to the first set of parentheses in the regular expression.

In this way, you can combine data from two fields into one, which is exactly what you'd like to do with the URL's hostname and path. Let's walk through it.

USE A GA FILTER TO PREPEND HOSTNAME TO URL

1. In the Admin area of GA, with the appropriate account, property, and view selected, choose Filters in the third column to see the filters for the view. Select the New button to add a new filter.

2. Choose to create a new filter (rather than apply an existing one).

3. Give the filter a name: "Prepend hostnames to URL".

4. Choose the Custom tab.

    a. Choose Advanced as the filter type. (See the example earlier in the chapter for cross-domain tracking for more on how the Advanced filter works.)

    b. For Field A, select Request URI in the drop-down menu. Enter the regular expression (.*). This will select the entire contents of the Request URI field, and enclosing it in parentheses lets you use it later in the output.

    c. For Field B, select Hostname in the drop-down. Enter the regular expression (.*). This will select the entire contents of the Hostname field, and enclosing it in parentheses lets you use it later in the output.

    d. For the Output, select Request URI (since you want to overwrite the existing URL with your version). Enter $B1$A1.

    $B1$A1 calls back to the previous fields. $B1 selects the first set of parentheses in Field B (the hostname), and $A1 selects the first set of parentheses in Field A (the URL path). Since you've run them right together with no spaces or punctuation, that's how they'll look in GA's reports, for example, www.aliceswonderlandresorts.com/page.html.

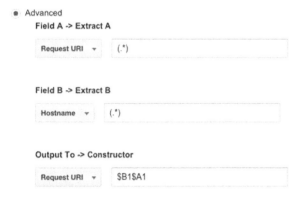

● Advanced

Field A -> Extract A

| Request URI ▾ | (.*) |

Field B -> Extract B

| Hostname ▾ | (.*) |

Output To -> Constructor

| Request URI ▾ | $B1$A1 |

    e. Check the boxes for Field A and B Required and Override Output Field.

5. Save the filter.

Remember that this filter will only affect data going forward. Past URLs will not be changed in reports.

Site Search

Almost every site has a way for users to search for content within the site. Depending on the type of site, this search might be used to find articles, products, or whatever types of information are available. GA has a subset of reports in Behavior ➤ Site Search devoted to measuring searches that users perform and how successful they are in finding answers (see Figure 8-15).

Figure 8-15. *Site search reporting in GA*

To enable these reports, you need to tell GA where to find the information about what a user searched for. There are three possible scenarios a site's search may fall into:

- The search term is contained within a query parameter. For example, a search for "hats" might result in a URL like the following:

  http://www.aliceswonderlandresorts.com/searchresults.php?q=hats

  This is GA's default assumption, and is true for many site search engines. This is easily set up with a view setting in GA.

- The search term is contained in the URL, but not in a query parameter:

  http://www.aliceswonderlandresorts.com/search/hats

  Using a filter in GA, you can pull the term "hats" out of the URL and place it in the appropriate field (the Search Term dimension).

- The search term is not contained in the URL at all:

  http://www.aliceswonderlandresorts.com/searchresults.php

  In this situation, you need to capture the term in the tag in GTM, since it's not already part of the URL.

In addition to the search term, GA can also optionally capture a category, which typically represents a way of limiting or restricting the search to a subset of content on the site. Like the search term, this may be represented in a query parameter, other information in the URL, or not in the URL. In the URL, a category might be something like the color parameter in this URL:

http://www.aliceswonderlandresorts.com/searchresults.php?q=hats&color=violet

Let's look at the process for each of these scenarios.

SET UP SITE SEARCH WITH A QUERY PARAMETER

Suppose your search results URLs look like /searchresults.php?q=hats&color=violet, where "hats" is the search term.

1. In the Admin area of GA, with the appropriate account, property, and view selected, choose View Settings in the third column to see the settings for the view.

2. At the bottom, in the section labeled Site Search Settings, turn site search tracking on.

3. Specify where to find the site search term in the URL:

    a. Enter the name of the query parameter. In this example, it is q. Note that you do not need to enter ampersands, equals signs, or other delimiters, merely the name of the query parameter.

    b. (Recommended) Check the box to strip this query parameter out of URLs. Once this data is in the Site Search reports, you don't need to see it in the URLs.

4. (Optional) Specify where to find the site search category in the URL by turning site search categories on and entering the query parameter. In the example URL, the category was color.

5. Save the changes to the settings.

Remember that this setting will only affect data going forward. Past data collected with site search parameters will not backfill the Site Search reports.

SET UP SITE SEARCH WITH INFORMATION IN THE URL

Suppose your search results URLs look like /search/hats, where "hats" is the search term. Here's how you can use a filter to pull the value out of the URL and into the appropriate field.

1. In the Admin area of GA, with the appropriate account, property, and view selected, choose Filters in the third column to see the filters for the view. Select the New button to add a new filter.

2. Choose to create a new filter (rather than apply an existing one).

3. Give the filter a name: "Site Search Term".

4. Choose the Custom tab.

    a. Choose Advanced as the filter type. (See the example earlier in the chapter for cross-domain tracking for more on how the Advanced filter works.)

    b. For Field A, select Request URI in the drop-down. Enter a regular expression to extract the term portion of the URL (enclosing the desired part of the URL in parentheses). In this example, you might use the following: `^/search/(.*)`

    c. Leave Field B blank. You don't need a second field for this filter.

    d. For the Output, select Search Term. Enter the variable from Field A that corresponds to the search term; in this example: $A1

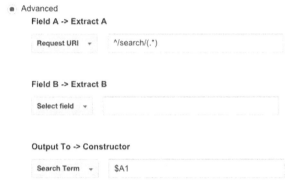

    e. Check the boxes for Field A Required and Override Output Field.

5. Save the filter.

Remember that this filter will only affect data going forward. Past data will not be backfilled into the site search reports.

Like the setup using query parameters in the previous section, you can also capture a category with this method (if applicable to your site search). Create another filter and select Site Search Category as the field, and alter the regular expression to match the relevant portion of the URL.

CAPTURE SITE SEARCH INFORMATION USING GTM

In the final scenario, you have a search results page URL like `/searchresults.php`, where the site search information isn't in the URL at all, so you'll have to supply it in some alternative way. You can include this information in the data layer declaration:

`dataLayer = [{ 'searchTerm': hats' }];`

First, you'll create a data layer variable for this information. Then, you can override the default URL captured in the GA pageview tag to include this information.

■ **Note**   Alternatively, the search term could be extracted from the page's content using a DOM Element variable. However, as discussed in Chapter 5, variables based on page content can be subject to changes in layout and appearance, so a data layer variable is preferred when possible.

---

1.   In GTM, create a new variable.

2.   For the variable type, choose Data Layer Variable.

3.   For the data layer variable name, enter `searchTerm` (or whatever label you used for the search term in the data layer).

4.   Save the variable, giving it a name: "Search Term".

Now you can create a tag that uses this variable to augment the URLs that you send to GA for search results pages.

1.   In GTM, make a copy of the GA – Pageview tag. You can copy a tag by selecting it to edit, then selecting the Copy button at the bottom right.

2.   Select Configure Tag to make changes to the GA tag settings.

   a.   In the Fields to Set section, add a new field.

   b.   Select page from the drop-down as the field name.

   c.   For the field value, you're going to construct a new URL that includes the site search term from the built-in {{Page Path}} variable and the {{Search Term}} variable you just created: `{{Page Path}}?q={{Search Term}}`

3.   Select Fire On to make changes to the tag's triggers.

   a.   Remove the All Pages trigger. You only want this tag to fire on search results pages.

   b.   Select Some Pages.

   c.   Create a new trigger called "Search Results Pages Only", where the Page URL matches your search results page URL(s). For this example: `{{Page URL}}` – equals – `/searchresults.php`

4. Save the tag, giving it a name: "GA – Pageview – Search Results".

■ **Note** Since you've created a specific pageview tag with a trigger only for search results pages, you'll also want to **add this trigger as a blocking trigger for the general GA pageview tag** so that you don't double-count.

After you publish this change to the GTM container, your search results pages will send URLs to GA that look like `/searchresults.php?q=hats`. From here, you can simply proceed with the same setup as though you have query parameters discussed earlier in this section, using q as the query parameter setting.

Grouping Content

In the previous section, you looked at a variety of ways to clean up URLs so that they correspond precisely well to a page, without needing to aggregate across variations of a URL. Sometimes you also have a need to group pages at higher levels: by category, page type, or other classifications.

GA has a number of tools to address this. Sometimes groupings may be obvious in the structure of URLs:

```
http://aliceswonderlandresorts.com/hearts/queen/
http://aliceswonderlandresorts.com/hearts/king/
http://aliceswonderlandresorts.com/spades/ace/
http://aliceswonderlandresorts.com/clubs/deuce/
```

In this case, the Content Drilldown report (located in Behavior ➤ Site Content) groups URLs together based on these subdirectories (see Figure 8-16). You can drill down through up to four levels of subdirectory in this report.

Page path level 1 ?	Pageviews ? ↓
1. ☐ /hearts/	**150,659** (89.80%)
2. ☐ /spades/	**9,486** (5.65%)
3. ☐ /	**3,193** (1.90%)
4. ☐ /clubs/	**2,016** (1.20%)
5. ☐ /diamonds/	**1,482** (0.88%)

Figure 8-16. *Using the Content Drilldown report to group URLs by subdirectory*

In other cases, you may wish to make groupings based on other information in the URL (such as a query parameter) or information not present in the URL at all. You can use a feature in GA called Content Grouping to accomplish this.

Content Groupings are created in a view. Each view can have up to five Content Groupings—that is to say, five different sets of categories for grouping pages (with an unlimited number of categories within each grouping). Useful ways of grouping content will depend on your site and what kinds of content it contains, but common types of content groupings include the following:

- By topic or product category

- By content type or page template (landing pages, article pages, product pages, etc.)

- By author, publication date, or other content metadata

- By qualities of the page content (word count, contains a video, etc.)

Once the Content Groupings have been created, they are available to group pages in the Behavior ➤ Site Content ➤ All Pages report (see Figure 8-17; also other reports with Page as the primary dimension) as well as in the navigational reports such as the Behavior Flow report.

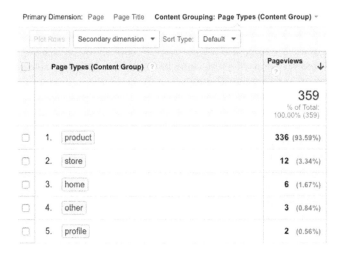

Figure 8-17. *Content Groupings in GA reports (here, the All Pages report)*

Content Groupings can be defined in three ways: by ***extraction***, by ***rule definitions***, and by ***tracking code***. Extraction and rule definitions allow you to use patterns based on the page's URL or title (or custom dimensions; see Chapter 11), while the tracking code option allows grouping based on categories you supply (often provided in the data layer). The following sections explain each type of content grouping with examples of the situations in which it can be used.

Grouping by Extraction

Extraction uses regular expressions to extract group names from the page's URL or title (or from custom dimensions). So, for example, in the following URLs, you might wish to extract the product type (hats, teacups, etc.):

```
http://aliceswonderlandresorts.com/products?type=hats&id=123
http://aliceswonderlandresorts.com/products?type=teacups&id=456
http://aliceswonderlandresorts.com/products?type=croquet&id=789
```

The trick is to write a regular expression to match this pattern, and to capture only the part of the URL you want. The portion to be captured is expressed in parentheses. In this case, the following regular expression might do what you need:

```
/products?type=([^&]*)
```

Recall that GA's Page dimension does not contain the hostname, so you begin with the URL path starting with /products. The [^&] matches all characters that aren't ampersands, and the * says 0 or more of them.

However, you should be careful: what happens if the category parameter isn't always the first one? Consider a URL like this:

```
/products?id=123&type=hats
```

You want to be **as specific as you need to be, and no more**. A better choice for the regular expression, to match the earlier possibility, would be the following:

```
type=([^&]*)
```

Now you're able to accommodate capturing the type parameter's value no matter where it appears in the URL.

Notice that, with the extraction method, you are specifying the **location in the URL** where the content group label appears, but you never have to specify the labels themselves. They're already there in the URL, and this pattern will match as many different category names as appear in the URLs.

■ **Tip** The regular expression pattern shown earlier is especially useful in creating content groups by extraction. It's known as "character class negation": [^*something*], most often used with ampersands, slashes, and other common delimiters in URLs to match all characters *except* those listed.

SET UP CONTENT GROUPING BY EXTRACTION

Let's set up a content grouping by extraction, based on the preceding example URLs.

1. In the Admin area of GA, with the appropriate account, property, and view selected, choose Content Grouping in the third column to see the content groupings for the view. Select the button to add a new content grouping.

2. Enter a name for the content grouping (the label that will appear for this set of categories in the report menus): "Product Category".

3. Choose to group by extraction.

   a. For this example, select Page as the dimension.

   b. Enter the regular expression: category=([^&]*)

   Notice that **the part you'd like to extract should be in parentheses**.

   4.   Choose Save to save the content grouping.

The new content grouping will be available immediately as a choice in the drop-down in reports, but the categories will only be filled in for pages on data from the point the content grouping was created going forward.

Grouping by Rule Definitions

Like the extraction method, rule definitions use the page's URL or title (or custom dimensions). Unlike the extraction method, rule definitions don't just pluck out a piece from this URL or title. Instead, rule definitions let's create a finite list of rules based on the contents of the field.

Suppose you have the following URLs:

```
http://aliceswonderlandresorts.com/hearts/queen/
http://aliceswonderlandresorts.com/hearts/king/
http://aliceswonderlandresorts.com/spades/ace/
http://aliceswonderlandresorts.com/clubs/deuce/
```

If you wanted to group these by suit (hearts, spades, etc.) you could easily do that by extraction. But what if you'd like to group them by color? Hearts and diamonds should be red and spades and clubs black, but "red" and "black" appear nowhere in the URLs. Rule definitions help with this. You can set up rule definitions that look like the following:

   1.   Red:

      • Page – contains – hearts – OR

      • Page – contains – diamonds

   2.   Black:

      • Page – contains – spades – OR

      • Page – contains – clubs

There are a number of options for how to match—*contains*, *starts with*, and so forth—and criteria can be combined with logical OR and AND. Rules are applied in the order they are specified, and the first rule that applies is the label used for that page in the content grouping.

Notice that, unlike extraction, you need to explicitly specify all of the possible labels in the rule definitions. In this example, Red and Black would be the only possible categories assigned, and any URLs that didn't contain "hearts", "diamonds", "spades", or "clubs" would not be assigned to a category (which would appear with the value "(not set)" in GA reports).

SET UP CONTENT GROUPING BY RULE DEFINITIONS

Let's set up a content grouping by rule definitions, based on the preceding example URLs.

1. In the Admin area of GA, with the appropriate account, property, and view selected, choose Content Grouping in the third column to see the content groupings for the view. Select the button to add a new content grouping.

2. Enter a name for the content grouping (the label that will appear for this set of categories in the report menus): "Suit Color".

3. Choose to group by rule definition, selecting the option to add a new rule set.

4. Name the rule set "Red" for this example.

   a. For the first criterion, select Page as the dimension.

   b. Select contains as the matching option.

   c. Enter `hearts` as the text to match.

   d. Choose to add a second criterion by selecting OR, then repeat the previous steps, choosing "Page contains `diamonds`".

   e. Select Done to finish the first rule set.

5. Add another rule set named "Black" and repeat the previous step for "Page contains `spades`" OR "`clubs`".

6. Choose Save to save the content grouping.

The new content grouping will be available immediately as a choice in the drop-down in reports, but the categories will only be filled in for pages from the point the content grouping was created going forward.

Grouping by Tracking Code

In both of the previous methods, content groupings were based on information contained in the URL or other data already in GA. However, in some cases you'd like to group by other information. Consider the following URLs:

```
http://aliceswonderlandresorts.com/blog/2015/09/22/guide-rules-flamingo-croquet/
http://aliceswonderlandresorts.com/blog/2015/10/25/wheres-that-cat/
http://aliceswonderlandresorts.com/blog/2015/11/13/red-queen-proclamation/
```

This structure is pretty common on blog or news articles. If you were looking for the publication date, that would be easy enough to extract with a regular expression (see the earlier section). What if you wanted to group based on, say, the article's author? Or what about article length?

Grouping based on tracking code allows you to supply the label in the page's tags, by having a GTM variable with the correct label. The source of this variable would typically be one of two options:

- *Data layer variable*: For information that comes from the website's content management system or other source. In the preceding example, the content management system knows the author of the article, and so you could include that in the data layer declaration for the page:

```
dataLayer = [{ 'author': 'Alice' }];
```

  This approach can be used for any kind of content metadata that is available from the content management system or other source when the page is rendered.

- *Custom JavaScript variable*: To check for a condition or makes a calculation. In the preceding example, if you wanted to create a content grouping based on article length, you could have some JavaScript code to find the article section of the page, split it by spaces and other punctuation, measure the length, and bucket into categories (like 0–100, 101–200, etc.). Similarly, custom JavaScript variables could check for the presence or number of images, videos, or other kinds of media in the article, or any other information that is present in or can be calculated from the page's content.

■ **Caution**   Although Content Groupings are set up in each view in GA, Content Grouping by tracking code would apply across all views in the property (since the data all comes from the same set of tracking code for the property, you can only supply one value in that slot). Map out how you will be using each of the five Content Groupings across the views within a property to ensure you're not stepping on your own toes anywhere.

SET UP CONTENT GROUPING BY TRACKING CODE

First, you'll set up the Content Grouping in GA.

1. In the Admin area of GA, with the appropriate account, property, and view selected, choose Content Grouping in the third column to see the content groupings for the view. Select the button to add a new content grouping.

2. Enter a name for the content grouping (the label that will appear for this set of categories in the report menus): "Author".

3. Choose to group by tracking code.

   a. Set the Enable setting to On.

   b. Choose the slot you'd like to use (1–5) from the index drop-down.

4. Save the content grouping.

Next, you'll need a variable in GTM that contains the category name for the content grouping. This example assumes you are using a data layer variable, but you could also use a custom JavaScript variable.

1. Create a new variable in GTM.

2. Select Data Layer Variable as the type.

3. Enter `author` as the name (in this example; use whatever name you are using in your data layer).

4. (Optionally) Set a default value by checking the box and entering a value. Otherwise, if the data layer doesn't specify a category, the value will be blank and GA reports will show "(not set)".

5. Save the variable, giving it a name: "Author".

Finally, you're ready to alter the GA pageview tag to include the content grouping.

1. In GTM, edit the GA – Pageview tag.

2. Select Configure Tag to make changes to the GA tag settings.

   a. In the Content Groups section, add a new content group.

   b. For the index, enter the index number you selected when you created the grouping in GA (1–5).

   c. For the Content Group, enter the `{{Author}}` variable you just created.

3. Save the tag.

When you publish the changes to the GTM container, content group data will be passed for each page to GA. The new content grouping will be available immediately as a choice in the drop-down in reports in GA, but the categories will only be filled in for pages on data from the point the content grouping was created going forward.

Other Applications for Filters

The previous section looked at a number of the most common applications of filters and other settings for cleaning up data in GA, as well as a bevy of workarounds using GTM to capture additional information. Filters have many potential uses, but the previous examples capture most of the common use cases.

The other most common purpose for filters is to create views with only a subset of the site's data. This is useful especially when the parts of a site are operated or marketed semi-independently from one another. For example, if there are separate marketing teams for different product lines or brands, each team may desire to have a view with reports that only contain the parts of the site under their influence. Then they are also able to filter and group the data for the view in the ways that are most useful to them and set up conversion goals (see Chapter 6) that are relevant.

Note Keep in mind that the base limit for the number of views per property is 25. This limit can be raised for Google Analytics Premium subscribers and in some cases for other users of GA.

The most common ways to divide a site into these kinds of functional areas are by subdirectories or (sub) domains:

- **Subdirectories:** You want to divide `www.aliceswonderlandresorts.com/hotels/` and `www.aliceswonderlandresorts.com/amusement-parks/` into separate views.

- **(Sub)domains:** You want to divide `hotels.aliceswonderlandresorts.com` and `parks.aliceswonderlandresorts.com` into separate views.

GA has predefined filter types for each of these (see Figures 8-18 and 8-19).

Filter Type

| Predefined | Custom |

| Include only ▾ | traffic to the subdirectories ▾ | that begin with ▾ |

Subdirectory

/blog/

Figure 8-18. *Predefined filter to include a subdirectory*

Filter Type

| Predefined | Custom |

| Include only ▾ | traffic to the hostname ▾ | that are equal to ▾ |

Hostname

hotels.aliceswonderlandresorts.com

Figure 8-19. *Predefined filter to include a domain or subdomain*

If more complex criteria are needed to specify the pages or hostnames in the view, the custom Include filter can be used with regular expressions.

Filtered Views vs. Segments

GA's reporting interface includes a feature called Segments. On its face, applying a segment to a report seems like it does much the same thing as filtering a view: you can include or exclude sessions in the segment based on a long laundry list of dimension and metric criteria. When should you use a segment on a report, and when should you use a filter on a view?

When possible, prefer segments over filters. They have an easy-to-understand interface built into the reports in GA. No knowledge of regular expressions is necessary, the dimension and metric names match up to those in reports, and no administrative access to the view is needed to create and apply segments. And most usefully, as an in-report feature, **segments can be applied to historic data** that already resides in your view.

However, filters have advantages in some situations and capabilities that are not possible via segments (such as rewriting field values), as you've seen in this chapter. If there's **data you always want to exclude** (like internal traffic), if there's **data you need to change** for purposes of cleanup, or if there are **functional reasons to create separate sets of data** in separate views (as discussed earlier), filters are the appropriate tool.

Summary

- Google Analytics and Google Tag Manager include a number of tools that help you clean up data to make it as useful as possible, including filters and view settings in GA and blocking triggers and overriding default values in GTM.

- Like all changes in GA and GTM, it's important to test before applying these tools to the data you use for reporting and analysis. In GA, because changes only affect the data going forward, a careful use of test and unfiltered views to try out and compare results is important.

- The most common needs for cleaning up data include removing internal traffic and standardizing and organizing URLs. There are a number of approaches using the tools in GTM and GA appropriate for different situations, as well as some specialized tools for dealing with specific kinds of content (such as URL query parameters & fragments and site search results URLs).

CHAPTER 9

Measuring Campaigns and Troubleshooting Traffic Sources

In another moment down went Alice after it, never once considering how in the world she was to get out again.

—Lewis Carroll, *Alice's Adventures in Wonderland*

Google Analytics has an entire set of Acquisition reports, dedicated to categorizing users' sources of traffic to the site. Did they come from a search engine, a link on a social media site, or a paid advertisement? This chapter will look at the data GA gathers about traffic sources and how you can influence those data with settings in GA and tools in GTM.

Traffic Sources in GA

In the first hit in a user's session, GA looks at the browser's Referrer value (the URL of the previous page) to determine where the user came from to arrive at the site. Based on this value, it assigns values for two of the dimensions used in the Acquisition reports, **Medium** and **Source**. A medium represents a general category or type of traffic, while the source specifies a specific site within that category.

GA categorizes traffic by default into the following mediums and sources:

- *Organic search traffic*: Medium is organic and Source is the name of the search engine (Google, Bing, Yahoo, etc.). This is traffic that comes from a search engine site.

- *Referral traffic*: Medium is referral and Source is the domain of the site. This is traffic that comes from a link from another site (any site *other* than a search engine).

- *Direct traffic*: Medium is (none) and Source is direct. Direct traffic is traffic that has no other apparent source, typically because the user typed in a URL, used a bookmark, or otherwise directly used the URL. A URL opened in a web browser from an application outside the web browser would also be classified as direct.

These values can be found in the Acquisition ➤ All Traffic ➤ Source/Medium report, and throughout reports in GA.

SIDEBAR: ATTRIBUTION IN GA

Attribution is a term in web analytics that refers to applying a model for **crediting traffic sources for desirable behavior**, such as sessions or conversions. Users often visit the site multiple times via multiple sources, so there are various ways or models you could use to credit those sources: give all the credit to the first one, or all to the last one, or divide the credit equally among all of them, as a few examples.

GA records a traffic source for each session. In all of its standard reports, GA uses what's called "last-click attribution" to report these traffic sources, meaning that however the user got to the site this time (the last click) is the traffic source to which the session will be attributed.

However, there's one important exception to this "last-click" rule: if a session's traffic source is direct, GA remembers the previous traffic source and attributes the session to that. Essentially, *direct never overwrites a previous traffic source*.

What's the rationale here? Recall that direct traffic is basically *no information* about where the user came from. So this rule says that if you know something about how they got here the last time, let's not overwrite that with *nothing*.

The timeout for how long GA "remembers" the previous source for the user is adjustable; it's six months by default. Find the setting in the Admin area in the property settings under Tracking Info ➤ Session Settings.

As noted, this "last-click except direct" rule is used in all of GA's standard reports. However, GA also has a series of reports in Conversions ➤ Multi-Channel Funnels that can look at the source for *every* session over a period of time before a conversion. The Attribution Modeling Tool allows analysis under different attribution rules, such as first-click, last-click including direct, weighted credit among all traffic sources, and so forth.

Beyond the default categorization performed by GA, you can influence these classifications and supply additional detail about how you'd like to label traffic sources to better reflect your site and its audiences. Let's see how.

Adding Organic Search Engines

GA recognizes a wide list of organic search engines by default,[1] but if a particular search engine is not in that list, you can add domains to be counted as search engines (rather than referrals). This is typically used for the following situations:

- Language- or country-specific search engines relevant to your site not included in GA's default list.

- Industry-specific or other niche search engines relevant to your site.

---

[1] https://support.google.com/analytics/answer/2795821#searchEngine

You can add search engines by specifying domains and URL patterns for search results pages in GA's Admin area in the property settings under Tracking Info ➤ Organic Search Sources. When added to this list, referrals from the site will be categorized as organic rather than referrals, just like organic search traffic from other search engines.

Ignoring Certain Referrers

GA also gives you the option to ignore certain referring sites (treating them as direct). This is most common in the following situations:

- Certain types of third-party sites, such as PayPal. It's typical for a user to leave your site, go to PayPal (to complete a transaction), and then return to your site for the final confirmation message. You're not interested in counting the return as a referral from PayPal.

- Cross-domain tracking (discussed further in Chapters 1 and 2 and in the troubleshooting section later in this chapter).

You can specify domains to treat as direct in GA's Admin area in the property settings under Tracking Info ➤ Referral Exclusion List. Any referrals from sites added to this list will be treated as direct traffic.

Campaign Tracking

For links to your site that you control, you can specify exactly the value you'd like GA to use for the medium and source (as well as additional traffic source dimensions). This could include many types of marketing and advertising links:

- Paid search and display advertisements

- Social posts and paid social advertisements

- Links in email marketing, such as a newsletter or promotion

- Links from partner or affiliate sites

- Links in offline advertising, such as print, TV, or radio

▪ **Note** GA can only measure activity *on your website* and how users arrived there. It's not a tool for measuring activity on other sites, such how many people liked or shared a link on a social network. Other tools can be used to gather those types of data.

It's useful to be able to specify your own labels for these types of traffic, since you'll want to break them out from referral, organic, and direct traffic and be able to analyze their effectiveness. You can specify your own values for a variety of traffic source dimensions:

- *Medium* (discussed earlier): The general category of type of traffic. Values such as email, social, display, print, and so forth, are common.

- *Source* (also discussed earlier): Where specifically within a medium the traffic came from. Often this is the domain of another website, such as a social network or a site where a display ad was shown. For an email, it might be the name of the list the email was sent to; for print it might be the name of the publication.

- *Campaign*: A specific promotion or marketing activity. For example, you might promote the Spring Season Ticket Sale across many mediums and sources. You want to be able to bring all of that traffic together under a single campaign.

- *Keyword (optional)*: A keyword used in search advertising.

- *Ad Content (optional)*: A label describing the content or format of the ad. For example, you might use this to distinguish several different display ads with different creative content, or to differentiate different sizes and formats for the ad.

The Acquisition reports allow you to view traffic using any combination of these dimensions.

Campaign Tracking URLs

So how do you provide the values you'd like to use for these traffic source dimensions to GA?

You can specify the values you'd like to use for these dimensions using campaign tracking URLs, or what's commonly called ***campaign tagging*** for GA. (Don't be fooled by the word "tag"; these are unrelated to tags in GTM.) There are specific query parameters you can include in a URL to specify values for these traffic source dimensions. Here's an example of a campaign tracking URL (broken across lines for clarity):

```
http://aliceswonderlandresorts.com/buy-season-tickets/
                    ?utm_medium=email
                    &utm_source=Mad%20Hatter%27s%20Club
                    &utm_campaign=Spring%20Season%20Ticket%20Sale
```

This would be a URL for a landing page you would use in a promotional email (the medium) about the Spring Ticket Sale (campaign) you sent to users on the Mad Hatter's Club mailing list (source). Notice the query parameters begin with utm_ and correspond (in this case) to the Medium, Source, and Campaign dimensions. Like all query parameters, the start of the query string is signaled with a question mark (?), each parameter is a key-value pair separated by an equals sign (=), and each parameter is separated by an ampersand (&). There are five parameters recognized by GA corresponding to the dimensions listed earlier: utm_medium, utm_source, utm_campaign, utm_term, and utm_content. The Source, Medium, and Campaign are required (or at least, very strongly recommended; only Source is technically required), while the Keyword and Content are optional. Note that the values provided are URL-encoded (so that a space character appears as %20, for example).

■ **Tip**   Rather than including all the campaign values in the URL, you can include a single utm_id parameter and use GA's data import features to fill in the rest of the values. See Chapter 12 for more information on data import.

GA provides a tool[2] to help get these URLs in the correct format (see Figure 9-1).

---

[2]https://support.google.com/analytics/answer/1033867?hl=en

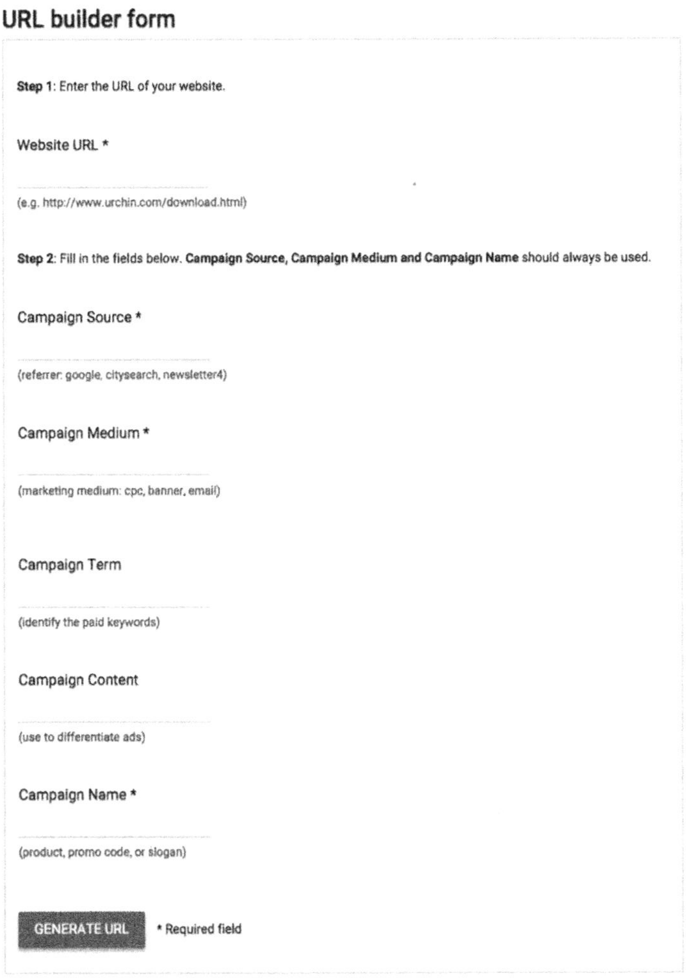

URL builder form

Step 1: Enter the URL of your website.

Website URL *

(e.g. http://www.urchin.com/download.html)

Step 2: Fill in the fields below. **Campaign Source, Campaign Medium and Campaign Name** should always be used.

Campaign Source *

(referrer: google, citysearch, newsletter4)

Campaign Medium *

(marketing medium: cpc, banner, email)

Campaign Term

(identify the paid keywords)

Campaign Content

(use to differentiate ads)

Campaign Name *

(product, promo code, or slogan)

GENERATE URL   * Required field

Figure 9-1. *The URL Builder tool for creating campaign tracking URLs*

This tool is handy, but it's important to note that using it is not required. As long as you provide the parameters in the correct format, when someone clicks this link and arrives at the website, GA will recognize the values and use them for the traffic source dimensions (rather than whatever would have been recorded by default).

Note that there's **nothing you have to do to set up GA beforehand** (telling it a list of the source, medium, and campaign values, for example), and **anyone can create one of these URLs** (they don't need to be an administrator in GA). This creates a very flexible system that empowers everyone in the marketing department to label the marketing and advertising links they're responsible for, but it also means that there's a potential for inconsistency.

Whatever values are in the URL parameters will be exactly what appears in GA. It's important that capitalization, spelling, and formatting are consistent among the parameters used—for example, email, Email, and e-mail will all show as separate values in GA. Filters on views can be used to clean up accidents with campaign URLs (see Chapter 8), but consistency should be your first objective.

The most important planning that you can do for campaign tracking URLs is to define some standard for your organization and how you label your advertising and marketing, and make sure that everyone adheres to those standards. There are a number of technical measures that can help you achieve consistency:

- Google advertising platforms AdWords and DoubleClick have automatic integrations with GA (described later in the chapter), so you don't need to worry about manually applying campaign parameters.

- Many third-party tools have integrations with GA that can automatically tag URLs. For example, MailChimp, a popular email marketing system, can automatically add campaign parameters to links in email campaigns.

- Instead of the URL builder form in GA, you can use a shared spreadsheet (like a Google Sheet) or a web form with some drop-down choices to enforce consistency in the values marketers choose when they create campaign URLs.

Shortening Campaign URLs

Campaign URLs can be long, which is fine if you're using them as the destination URL for an advertisement or in an email. But in a social media post or print, where brevity or readability is important, using a URL shortener can be useful.

It's fine to use a URL shortener (such as bit.ly, the most popular option) with campaign-tagged links from GA. Simply add the campaign parameters first, then enter the campaign-tagged URL as your link to be shortened.

You can also use so-called "vanity URLs" as shortened versions of campaign URLs, by simply using a redirect from a short URL like this:

```
http://aliceswonderlandresorts.com/tickets
```

To a full, campaign-tagged URL:

```
http://aliceswonderlandresorts.com/?utm_medium=print&utm_source=brochure&utm_campaign=Tickets
```

(The details of how to implement a redirect are specific to your content management system and/or web server; consult the documentation there for details. See later in the chapter for some best practices around using redirects with GA.) Vanity URLs are especially useful for a print or other offline advertisement or marketing material where you'd like to include a branded link. Of course, there's no guarantee that people who saw the ad will necessarily use the URL (rather than just visiting directly or using a search engine), but it gives you some indication of the relative response of different offline ads used to drive traffic to your website.

Avoiding Conflicts with Campaign URLs

As you saw earlier, you can specify traffic source dimensions by including parameters in the query string in links to your site. In most cases, a website will simply ignore query parameters it doesn't recognize (such as the utm_ parameters). With some content management systems or web servers, however, unrecognized parameters may cause issues or be disallowed. Specifically, you should ensure that your website is prepared to handle the following query parameters:

- utm_source, utm_medium, utm_campaign, utm_term, utm_content

- utm_id (mentioned earlier and described in more detail for campaign data import in Chapter 12)

- gclid, dclid (described next in the sections on integrations with other Google tools)

Your website should not cause redirects that strip away these parameters, for example. (See later in the chapter for more information about redirects and how to use them safely with GA.)

If, for some reason, you need to avoid using query parameters, GA does provide an alternative. Instead of the URL's query string, you can use the fragment or anchor string portion of the URL (the portion after the #) to include campaign information. Because this part of the URL is used by the browser and not typically interpreted by the server, it's "safe" for situations where your web server or content management system prevent you from using GA's campaign tracking query parameters in URLs.

The format for the campaign tracking information is the same, but is in the URL fragment (note the #):

```
http://aliceswonderlandresorts.com/buy-season-tickets/
                #utm_medium=email
                &utm_source=Mad%20Hatter%27s%20Club
                &utm_campaign=Spring%20Season%20Ticket%20Sale
```

To enable this in GA, there's a setting called `allowAnchor` in the tracking code. In the GA pageview tags in GTM, you can set this value in the Fields to Set section when editing the tag (see Figure 9-2).

Figure 9-2. *Using allowAnchor in the Fields to Set section in a GA tag in GTM*

Setting this value to true allows you to use the campaign labels in the URL fragment.

Specifying Campaign Values with GTM

Sometimes rather than specifying campaign values in a link, using the URL parameters described earlier, you'd like to specify campaign parameters based on the page or pages of your website. This is most commonly used for the following:

- *Adapting legacy tracking URLs to GA*: In some cases you may have a system of labeling campaign URLs that predates your use of GA. You might use a particular URL pattern or query parameter that you'd like to translate into the appropriate campaign dimensions in GA.

- *Links "in the wild" with missing or incorrect campaign tags*: Even with the best efforts at being assiduous and consistent in applying campaign tracking parameters to URLs, sometimes mistakes happen. You can supply values for campaign dimensions based on a landing page or referrer in such cases.

Whatever the reason, you can use GTM to override the campaign dimension values.

SPECIFY CAMPAIGN VALUES IN A GA TAG IN GTM

Let's look at how to override campaign values in a GA tag in GTM.

1. In GTM, in the Tags section, choose a GA pageview tag and select it to edit.

■ **Caution**   Typically you would *not* make this change to the pageview tag on *all* pages. You'll probably only want do this for a particular circumstance defined by a trigger (such as on a particular landing page URL or for a particular referrer) or based on a variable value (such as a query parameter in a URL).

---

2. Click on Configure Tag to make changes to the tag configuration.

3. In More Settings ➤ Fields to Set, enter the following:

   a. For the Field Name, choose one of the following options, depending on which field you'd like to set: campaignMedium, campaignSource, campaignName, campaignKeyword, campaignContent, or campaignId.

   b. For the Value, enter a fixed value or a GTM variable with the value you'd like to use.

■ **Tip**   Variables based on the page or referrer URLs (or portions thereof) are useful for dynamically creating values.

---

4. Repeat step 3 for each additional campaign value you'd like to set.

5. Select Save Tag to save the changes to the tag.

Once published, GTM will now override the default traffic source dimension values with the values specified in the tag.

Channel Groupings in GA

You've seen that there are a number of traffic source dimensions in GA, including source, medium, campaign, and others. Additionally, GA allows you to group combinations of those dimensions into channel groupings. The channel groupings are a way of categorizing the traffic sources into channels that correspond to the way that you think about your marketing and advertising activities. GA provides a default set of channel groupings (which you can find in the Acquisition ➤ All Traffic ➤ Channels report), but you're able to customize them to best fit your circumstances.

The default channel groupings include the following channels:

- *Direct*: Direct traffic, with Source value of direct and Medium of (none) or (not set).

- *Organic*: Organic traffic from search engines, with Medium of organic.

- *Social*: Referral traffic from social media sites, with Medium of referral and Source matching a list of social media sites recognized by GA, or with Medium containing social, social-network, social-media, sm, social network, or social media.

- *Referral*: Referral traffic from all other (non–social media sites), with Medium of referral.

- *Email*: Traffic from email, with Medium of email.

- *Paid Search*: Paid traffic from search engines, with Medium of cpc, ppc, or paidsearch, but not with Ad Distribution Network of Content. (See the AdWords integration description for additional information on AdWords-specific dimensions like Ad Distribution Network.)

- *Display*: Display advertising, with Medium of display, cpm, or banner, or with Ad Distribution Network of Content.

- *Other Advertising*: Medium of cpv, cpa, cpp, or content-text.

- Anything that doesn't fit into one of these categories is labeled (Other).

As you can see, using these channel groupings can help sort out different categories of traffic, such as pulling out referral traffic from social media sites and putting that together with campaign-tagged links from social media (thus grouping together what's commonly termed your "earned" and "owned" social traffic).

However, the default categories may not be sufficient to reflect the types of marketing and advertising you do. Examples might include the following:

- Dividing the Paid Search channel into branded and generic keywords.

- Dividing Display into topic-based advertising vs. remarketing.

- Creating a channel for Partner or Affiliate links.

GA allows you to alter the default channel groupings or create entirely new groupings in the Admin area. You can find these settings in the View settings (third column) under Channel Settings ➤ Channel Grouping. Each channel grouping is based on a set of rules (see Figure 9-3).

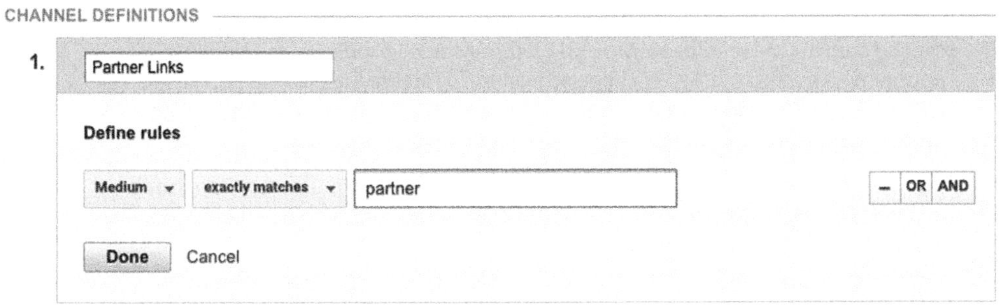

Figure 9-3. *Rules for creating channel groupings*

The rules are applied in the order they appear in the channel grouping settings, and the first rule that matches a session is the label that is applied. Any sessions that don't match any of the rules in the channel grouping displays the value (Other).

Changes to the default channel grouping are applied to all data collected going forward, and do not retroactively change historical data. New channel groupings can be applied at will in reports (much like a segment) to view historical data (but may trigger sampling when applied).

Traffic Data Integrations

Google provides a number of integrations between GA and other Google platforms for data about traffic sources. These integrations can import a number of dimensions and metrics into GA to enrich the interaction data with information such as impressions, click-through rates, and cost.

And don't forget, GTM is useful for tags other than GA tags as well—including tracking and conversion tags for advertising and marketing tools. GTM provides built-in tag types for Google platforms such as AdWords conversion and remarketing tags, DoubleClick Floodlight tags, and Adometry tags, as well as tags for third-party tools. Additionally, GTM offers an integration with DoubleClick Campaign Manager to manage the workflow of creating Floodlight tags.

In the following sections, you'll take a look at the integrations between GA and GTM and Google platforms and tools.

AdWords

GA integrates with AdWords, Google's advertising platform for ads on search results and on its display network. Linking your GA and AdWords accounts enables a number of features:

- *Autotagging of AdWords destination URLs.* Rather than having to manually label campaign URLs as described earlier in the chapter, AdWords can automatically apply a query parameter (`gclid`) that identifies the ad. GA then imports the traffic source dimension data from AdWords, with Medium `cpc`, Source `google`, and the Campaign, Keyword, and Ad Content corresponding to the campaign, bid keyword, and ad headline in AdWords. Additionally, a number of AdWords-specific dimensions are imported, including Ad Group (to group together ads and keyword within a campaign), Matched Search Query (the query that triggered the ad based on the bid keyword), Ad Slot, Placement Domain (for display network placements), and others.

- *Importing AdWords metrics into GA reports.* GA includes a section of AdWords reports under Acquisition that import metrics such as Impressions, Clicks, CTR (click-through rate), Cost, and CPC (cost-per-click). Combined with conversion and revenue data in GA (see Chapters 6 and 7), these can be used to calculate ROAS (return on ad spend) or CPA (cost per acquisition). Having the cost data (from AdWords) and the response data (from GA) in a single set of reports creates a very valuable tool to evaluate the cost-effectiveness of advertising.

- *Importing GA metrics into AdWords reports.* GA metrics such as Bounce Rate can be used in reporting within AdWords, and GA goals and ecommerce transactions can be imported to AdWords as conversion data.

- *Creating remarketing audiences in AdWords from GA segments.* All of the behavioral data in GA can be used to create audiences for remarketing (showing ads to users who have visited the site before or completed a specific action). GA's detailed segmentation tools allow you to tailor specific audience behavior you'd like to target. AdWords audiences can be created in the Admin area in the property settings, or directly from an existing segment in the segmentation drop-down in reports.

To gain all of these advantages, you need to link your AdWords and GA accounts together. **Linking is between an account in AdWords and a property in GA.** Since there are many possible configurations of sites and how they correspond to GA properties and AdWords accounts, multiple AdWords accounts can be linked to a single GA property, and multiple GA properties can be linked to a single AdWords account, as needed.

■ **Tip**   Linking an AdWords account to a property will import AdWords metrics (Clicks, Cost, Impressions, etc.) for *all* of the campaigns in the AdWords account, potentially including campaigns or ad groups that have ads for other sites. It's a good idea to try to organize your AdWords and GA accounts in a similar fashion, with one AdWords account per site (GA property). Even though it's not strictly necessary, it makes it easier to understand how advertising and sites match up.

LINK AN ADWORDS ACCOUNT TO GA

Linking AdWords and GA accounts requires a login that is an Administrator on the AdWords account and has Edit privileges on the GA property to be linked. Ensure that you have the appropriate permissions in both tools before proceeding. (Once linked, anyone with Report & Analyze access to a view in GA can see the imported data, but the linking process requires Edit access.)

1.   In the GA Admin area, with the appropriate account and property selected, choose AdWords Linking in the middle column. Select the New button to add a new AdWords link.

2.   Select one or more of the AdWords accounts you can access to be linked to the property. Then select the Continue button.

3.   Give the link group a title to identify it.

4. Select which views within the property you would like to link. You can select one or more views. The selected views will be enabled for the integration options discussed previously, while unselected views will not contain any of the detailed AdWords data. (You can update these settings later to enable or disable a view after a link has been established.)

 Link configuration

Link group title ⑦

AWR AdWords Accounts|

Linked view(s)

Select view(s) to link ▾

 **Creating this link enables auto-tagging for all linked AdWords accounts.**

Auto-tagging allows Analytics to automatically associate AdWords data with customer clicks.

Advanced settings

■ **Note**   Creating the link enables auto-tagging in the AdWords account by default. You can override this if desired, but using auto-tagging is recommended to gain all the benefits of the AdWords integration with GA.

---

5. Select the Link Accounts button to complete the link.

Like other changes in GA's Admin settings, this data is only imported from the time the link is established going forward.

On the flipside of the advertising coin, GA also provides an integration with AdSense—that is, for publishing ads *from* AdWords *on* your site (for which you get a share of the click revenue from Google). Like AdWords, you can link an AdSense account to GA (in the Admin area in the property settings). Additional reports are available in Behavior ➤ Publisher and additional dimensions and metrics are available from the imported data.

DoubleClick Platforms

Like with AdWords, there is also an integration with Google's DoubleClick advertising tools DoubleClick Campaign Manager and DoubleClick Bid Manager. These integrations are available only for Google Analytics Premium subscribers. Similar to the AdWords integration, DoubleClick supports autotagging (using a `dclid` parameter), importing data into DoubleClick reports in the Acquisition section, and creating remarketing audiences for DoubleClick from GA segments.

DoubleClick Campaign Manager also integrates with GTM, allowing DoubleClick Floodlight tags to be generated in the DCM interface and pushed to GTM for approval. You'll find these in the container settings under Approval Queue (see Figure 9-4). Of course, just like any other change to a container, the container must be published in GTM before taking effect.

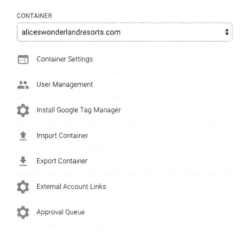

Figure 9-4. *The approval queue for DoubleClick Floodlight tags can be found at the bottom of the container settings in GTM's Admin area*

On the ad publishing side, Google Analytics Premium users also enjoy an integration with DoubleClick for Publishers, which provides similar reports and metrics to the AdSense integration.

Google Search Console

For organic search, Google Search Console (formerly Google Webmaster Tools) provides a multitude of information about how Google's search engine interacts with your site. This includes metrics about search results pages where your site appeared, the keywords and landing pages that were listed, their average rank, and the approximate impressions and clicks. A site in GSC can be linked to a property in GA (in the Admin area in the property settings) to import this information to GA. The imported data is available in the reports under Acquisition ➤ Search Engine Optimization.

Note that, unlike the AdWords and DoubleClick integrations, **the GSC integration does not join external data with session data in GA**. It simply makes reports from GSC available in GA's interface as a convenience, saving you from having to log into GSC and view them separately.

Troubleshooting Traffic Sources

Sometimes, traffic source information can go missing. Let's examine the causes of incorrect traffic source data and see how you can avoid pitfalls.

Redirects

Redirects are a valuable tool to enforce consistency in URLs on a website, to provide alternative (usually shorter) URLs, and to ensure that historical links continue to work. However, you need to be a little careful about how redirects are used on your site to ensure that you don't lose data about how a user arrived at the site. You need redirects to do *both* of the following:

- *The redirect preserves the HTTP Referrer header*. The Referrer header tells the browser what URL was the previous page when a link is followed, and is the signal GA uses to assign the source in referral and organic search traffic. *Server-side redirects* (also called 301 or 302 redirects) typically preserve the Referrer header.

- *The redirect preserves any query parameters in place on the original URL*—specifically any of the campaign tracking parameters described earlier in the chapter. These parameters should be visible in the URL in the final destination page—if you can't see them in the URL, GA doesn't see them either.

You can check for the appropriate behavior using your browser's testing tools on a redirected URL. For example, suppose I know that `www.aliceswonderlandresorts.com` gets redirected to `aliceswonderlandresorts.com` (without the `www`). I can test a link from a referring site to see the type of redirect and that the Referrer header is preserved, and I can test a campaign-tagged link to ensure the campaign parameters are preserved. Here's how.

First, I followed a link from another site to the link (with the `www`). Looking at the Network tab in Chrome's developer tools, you see Figure 9-5.

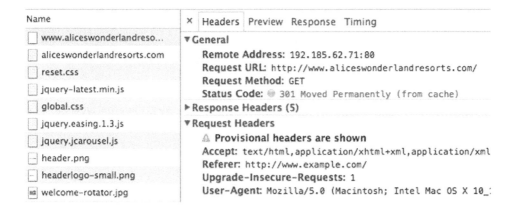

Figure 9-5. *Viewing a server-side redirect in Chrome's developer tools*

Notice that the status code returned by the server is `301 Moved Permanently` (a permanent, server-side redirect), and looking at the request headers you see that the Referrer header appears both in the original request and in the redirected URL.

If this is not the case (i.e., if you don't see either 301 or 302 as the status code), the redirect is a client-side redirect, meaning it happens in the browser itself, rather than on the web server. The effect of this will be that two pages will load in direct succession—first the redirect page, then the actual destination page. Depending on the setup in GTM, you'll have one of two problems:

- You'll have two pageviews in direct succession without any interaction by the user, causing the bounce rate to go to 0% for traffic using the redirect URL.

- You'll have an untracked pageview on the redirect page, meaning the original source information is lost and you'll see a self-referral (see the upcoming section).

Obviously, neither of these is an ideal situation—you're losing one type of data or the other. This is why client-side redirects are not recommended; switch to using a server-side redirect instead. (How you'll go about this will depend on your web server or content management system; consult the appropriate documentation.)

▦ **Note** There are workarounds for using client-side redirects with GA to capture and then provide the original referrer, either through a cookie or a query parameter value. However, client-side redirects are generally harmful to search engine optimization as well, so the best advice is to avoid them entirely in favor of server-side redirects.

Now let's try a campaign link with a redirected URL (see Figure 9-6).

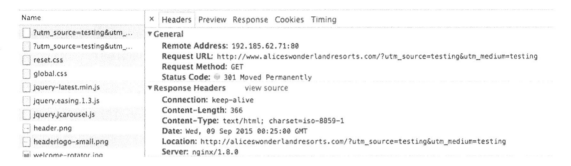

Figure 9-6. *Viewing a redirect with campaign parameters in Chrome's Developer Tools*

Here you can see the campaign parameters are included both in the original request and in the URL after the redirect. Success!

Again, if this is not what you see, you'll need to look at the settings for your web server or content management system to see if there's a way to alter this behavior to preserve these parameters. (Alternatively, you might also be able to use the setAllowAnchor setting described earlier in the chapter to use the URL fragment rather than the query string to transmit campaign tracking information.)

Self-Referrals

One of the most common traffic source problems in GA is seeing self-referrals: your own website appears as a referral source (see Figure 9-7). Obviously this isn't intended—when a user follows a link from one page on your website to another page, that shouldn't count as a referral—it's just navigating through the website!

	Source ?	Sessions ↓ ?
☐	1. t.co	**828** (10.78%)
☐	2. aliceswonderlandresorts.com	**508** (6.62%)
☐	3. facebook.com	**364** (4.74%)

Figure 9-7. *Self-referrals in the Acquisition reports (aliceswonderlandresorts.com is our website)*

Why do self-referrals happen? The two most common reasons are untagged pages and incorrect cross-domain or subdomain tracking.

Untagged Pages

When a user lands on a page and begins a session, GA assigns the source, medium, and other traffic source dimensions discussed earlier in the chapter. However, suppose you have a situation where the user lands on a page where no GA tag fires. What happens?

Since no GA tag fired, no session has yet begun. If the user continues to navigate to a second page—this one with a GA tag—GA begins a session and says, "OK, where did this user come from?" In this case, it's from another page on your site, and GA assigns the medium "referral" and the source as your own domain.

In the Acquisition ➤ Traffic Sources ➤ Referrals report, you can drill down into self-referrals to see the pages they originate from. Check the following things on those pages:

1. *Is the GTM container on the page?* Use the Google Tag Assistant extension or check the page's source code to confirm. Sometimes certain pages might use a different template or layout and you accidentally missed including the container code.

2. *Is there a GA tag set to be triggered on the pageview* (gtm.js *event) for this page?* Use GTM's debug mode to look at the tags and which ones trigger on this page. If no GA pageview tag is triggered, you need to alter the triggers in GTM to make sure you're tracking this page.

Incorrect Cross-Domain or Subdomain Tracking

Recall from Chapter 1 that GA uses cookies to keep track of users. When there are multiple domains or subdomains that you'd like to measure as a single site, you need to ensure that GA has consistent cookie values across these domains. If it doesn't, it will treat each site as separate, with a separate session on each, and you'll see referrals between those domains.

If you have multiple domains or subdomains and you're seeing referrals between them, incorrect settings in the GA tags in GTM are the likely culprit. You need to ensure that all GA tags in GTM include the appropriate cross-domain settings (see Chapters 1 and 2 for details). Check your tag setup carefully and make the necessary adjustments.

Summary

- GA provides a number of dimensions describing a session's traffic source. Beyond the default values assigned, you can use campaign tagging and other features in GA, or override the values in GTM's GA tag, to customize labeling of marketing and advertising sources.

- Google provides a number of integrations between sources of advertising and marketing data on Google platforms with GA and GTM.

- Self-referrals are the most common issue with traffic source data, and commonly result from untagged pages, poorly-behaved redirects, or incorrect subdomain or cross-domain tracking.

CHAPTER 10

■ ■ ■

Tracking Users Across Devices

"Who are YOU?" said the Caterpillar.

This was not an encouraging opening for a conversation. Alice replied, rather shyly, "I—I hardly know, sir, just at present—at least I know who I WAS when I got up this morning, but I think I must have been changed several times since then."

—Lewis Carroll, *Alice's Adventures in Wonderland*

Google Analytics reports a metric called Users, which sounds like it counts the number of people using the site. A "user" should represent a single person's activity over time on the site, right? Unfortunately, it's a little more complicated than that. Google isn't watching us all through our device's cameras and using facial recognition to identify us (yet), and so "user" and "person" are not precisely the same thing.

As you'll recall from Chapter 2, GA uses a cookie that contains a ***client ID***. This is a randomly generated identifier. Since it's stored in a cookie, it's particular to the specific browser and device. By default, this client ID is what GA uses to calculate the Users metric and user behavior across sessions. So "user" truly corresponds to "browser/device," rather than "person." And as you know, people can and do delete their browser's cookies (manually or using "private" browsing modes), as well as use multiple devices (they've visited your website on both their laptop and mobile phone, for example). All of this means that counting users by client ID is inaccurate to some degree.

In some cases, that's the best you can do, and it's a limitation of website measurement that you have to live with. Sometimes, however, you have better ways of knowing who a person is when they interact with your site—a site where users log in, for example. Because they log in, you know exactly who they are regardless of what their cookie says or what device they are using. GA allows us to set an additional identifier, called the ***user ID***, which can be used to arrive at a better approximation of "users" to "people," and shows us the activity by the same person across devices and browsers.

SIDEBAR: SCENARIOS FOR USING USER ID TRACKING

One straightforward scenario for user ID tracking is simply to stitch together website sessions by the same user across devices, using a login, as described above. User ID can also be useful to join up data between:

- Website activity and mobile apps (see Chapter 13). If users log in to both your website and mobile apps, you can unify their activity across those interfaces and devices.

- Website activity and other online or offline marketing activity. If users log in to your website, you may have a profile in your CRM or other systems that include information like an email address, social network usernames, or a loyalty card number (for in-store purchases). Some of this data may be made available in GA through data import (see Chapter 12) or by using the Measurement Protocol (see Chapter 14), or you may join up the data after exporting it, using tools such as using BigQuery for data warehousing and analysis (see the Bonus Chapter) or using the GA APIs to extract data (see the Appendix).

Depending on the internal data you retain about your customers, you may be able to think of additional ways to use this data.

■ **Caution**   When it comes to identifying users, what's *technically possible* extends beyond what's *permitted under GA's policies.*[1] There are a number of techniques for more precise identification of individuals across browsers or when cookies are deleted that would not be permissible (such as re-creating cookies from the Flash shared object or browser fingerprinting, or using a mobile device identifier). Google's policies and the laws of the countries in which you operate are subject to change; check them carefully and seek legal advice if necessary to ensure that you're playing by the rules. Remember that ***reputable websites always clearly inform users how their data will be collected, retained, and used***.

There are three basic steps to setting up user ID tracking in GA:

1. Turn on the user ID feature in the GA property.

2. Create a view in the GA property to report on user ID data.

3. Alter your GA tags in GTM to send the user ID value.

You'll work through these processes in the rest of the chapter.

---

[1]GA's terms of service for your country can be found at www.google.com/analytics/terms/. The additional user ID policy (to which you must agree before turning on the user ID features in GA) can be found at https://developers.google.com/analytics/devguides/collection/protocol/policy.

Set Up User ID in GA

User ID features in Google Analytics are enabled at the property level. Once the user ID is enabled for the property, you can create views within the property that unify users based on the user ID, and show special cross-device reports. All of our existing views will continue to use the old rules (users calculated by client ID). You'll need to create a new view to take advantage of the user ID. User ID can only be enabled at the time the view is created; this setting cannot be changed later.

Views that use the user ID will contain data **only for sessions where a user ID was set**. This means that the user ID views won't contain sessions for anyone who wasn't logged in, for example. As a result, you'll never want to have *only* a user ID view for a property; you'll want at least one with the option turned on (to view cross-device behavior using user ID) and another with it turned off (to show sessions for everyone, including non-identified users).

When setting up the user ID features, you have the option to control the ***session unification***, which relates to whether data collected in a session before the user is identified is associated with the user. For example, consider this sequence of pageviews in a session (see Figure 10-1).

Figure 10-1. A page sequence viewed by a user before and after identification

If you turn session unification on (the default), all the pageviews in this session are associated with the user ID, even though you didn't know the user ID yet on the first two pageviews. (Note that session unification only applies to tracking hits *within a single session*. Non-logged-in sessions are never associated with a user ID or included in the user ID view.) For many websites, turning session unification on is probably the option you want.

However, sometimes you might want to consider only the pages where the user ID is set (the last three pageviews, in this example). This could be the case for policy reasons, or for a computer shared by multiple people who log in, for example. Turning session unification off only includes data in user ID–enabled views where the user ID was set for the tracking hit.

ENABLE USER ID FOR A GA PROPERTY

First, you'll enable user ID tracking in the GA property.

1. In the Admin section of Google Analytics, select the desired property (middle column).

2. In the Tracking Info section, select User-ID.

3. Review the policy and agree to the terms by toggling the switch to On. Select Next Step to continue.

4. GA will display instructions for setting the user ID in the tracking code; you can skip over this for now, as you'll set it up in GTM later in the chapter.

5. Choose to keep session unification on or to turn it off by toggling the switch. (See earlier discussion on session unification settings.) Select Next Step to continue.

6. The last step will prompt you to create a user ID–enabled view. You can select the Create button to start that process, or see the next section if you need to create a new user ID enabled view for this property at any time in the future.

CREATE A GA VIEW TO DISPLAY USER ID REPORTS

1. In the Admin section of GA, select the View drop-down (third column) and choose Create new view at the bottom of the list. (Alternatively, if you are following along from the previous steps, clicking the Create button at the end of that process gets you to the same place.)

2. Select Website for the type of view.

3. Enter a name for the view (such as "Logged In Users", for example) and choose a time zone.

4. Change the User-ID view setting to On.

5. Select the Create View button to complete creating the view.

Once the view is created, don't forget to change any additional settings you need to, such as applying filters (see Chapter 8) or setting up conversions (see Chapter 6) or Channel Groupings (see Chapter 9).

In your new user ID–enabled view, only sessions and hits where the user ID was specified will appear, and the Users metric will be based on the count of unique user IDs. Additionally, you'll find some extra reports in Audience ➤ Cross-Device (see Figure 10-2) that show cross-device behavior by users.

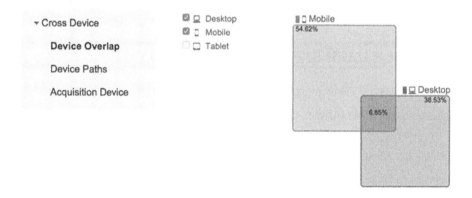

Figure 10-2. *Example of cross-device reports available in a user ID view in GA*

Send User ID Data with GTM

Now that you've enabled GA to receive and use user ID data, you need to set up your site and GTM to send it.

Provide a User ID Value

Your site needs to provide a user ID value for GTM to use. The most direct way to do this is to include an entry in the data layer declaration (the information included in the data layer *before* the GTM code):

```
dataLayer = [{
                'userId': 'alice0214'
        }];
```

Then you can simply use a data layer variable in GTM to access this value. Getting this value in the data layer typically involves some server-side website coding to insert the appropriate value (much like the ecommerce data placed in the data layer in Chapter 7, for example).

Depending on your site, there may be other possible ways to find the user ID value: in a cookie, or even using an element on the page where it says "Welcome, Alice0214!". Using a data layer variable ensures that other changes to the site (e.g., changing the layout where the "Welcome, Alice0214!" element is placed on the page) don't affect your tracking setup. As with many other variables discussed in this book, using the data layer to organize information for GTM is always safer and more reliable than relying on page content or other scripts (which are potentially out of your control).

■ **Tip** There isn't a GA report where the user ID value is directly visible. In many cases, you're interested in reporting on the user ID value to match up with data from other sources, so it's a good idea to *also* send this variable in a custom dimension (see Chapter 11), which you can use in reports and exported data.

Set Up GTM to Send User ID to GA

Now that you have the user ID provided in the site's data layer, you'll need to set up GTM with a variable to capture that value, and then alter the GA tag to send the variable as the user ID. Let's walk through the process.

SET UP USER ID ON A GA TAG IN GTM

First let's create a variable to capture the user ID from the data layer.

1. In GTM, in the Variables section, select the New button to create a new user-defined variable.

2. Choose Data Layer Variable as the variable type, and then select Continue.

3. As the data layer variable name, enter the name you used for the data layer entry (in the example earlier in the chapter, it was userId).

4. Select Create Variable to save the variable. Give it a name: "User ID".

Now you'll need to alter the GA tags in GTM to pass the value of this variable. Let's start with the basic pageview tag.

1. In GTM, in the Tags section, choose the GA – Pageview tag and select it to edit.

2. Click Configure Tag to make changes to the tag configuration.

3. Under More Settings ➤ Fields to Set, choose `userId` as the field name. As the value, use the `{{User ID}}` variable that you created previously (see the following screenshot).

4. Select Save Tag to save the changes to the tag.

You'll want to make this change on all Google Analytics tags within the container, so that you send the user ID value along with any tracking hit where it applies. Of course, you'll need to test and then publish the new version of the container before this data shows up in GA. Once these changes are published on the site, you will begin to see data for logged-in users in the user ID view in GA.

Summary

- Google Analytics typically counts users with the client ID, an identifier stored in a cookie that is particular to a specific browser and device. For sites where users log in or you can otherwise identify them, GA supports using a user ID instead for a more accurate count of users across devices.

- Privacy concerns, policies, regulations, and appropriate disclosures to your site's users are important considerations when collecting user ID data. Review them carefully.

- User ID features are enabled in GA at the property level, choosing to use session unification (counting hits before the user logs in) or not. Within that property, user ID–enabled views can be created, which show only data with an associated user ID along with additional cross-device reports.

- In GTM, the user ID is captured from the website, typically by inserting the user ID value into the data layer. GA tags in GTM are altered to include this user ID variable.

CHAPTER 11

■ ■ ■

Providing Additional Data About Users

"Take some more tea," the March Hare said to Alice, very earnestly.

"I've had nothing yet," Alice replied in an offended tone, "so I can't take more."

"You mean you can't take less," said the Hatter: "it's very easy to take more than nothing."

—Lewis Carroll, *Alice's Adventures in Wonderland*

Previous chapters covered how to get information from your site into Google Analytics using Google Tag Manager. You've looked at ways to measure both the basics—user interactions like loading a page, which you track with pageviews—as well as more specific actions—for example, watching videos or downloading files, which you measured with events.

In this chapter, you'll learn how to include additional, custom data that pertains to these pageviews or events to give more information about your site's content, the users who access it, and their actions. In many cases, your website may know additional information about users and what they do—information that comes from your user registration database, content management system, or other sources you can capture with GTM—that you'd like to connect with the interaction behavior data in GA. You'll use GA's ability to accept custom dimensions and metrics to layer in this additional data. This data, which will be unique to your organization and your website, can be valuable to have in GA to be used in more detailed analysis and segmentation.

■ **Note**　Custom dimensions and metrics are an updated set of features that replace ***custom variables***, a legacy feature in GA that accomplished similar customization. If you've used custom variables in the past, they will continue to work, but custom dimensions and metrics are the preferred method going forward.

Custom Dimensions and Metrics

Recall (from Chapter 1) that GA's reports are organized into ***dimensions*** and ***metrics***. Each hit you send to GA fills in certain built-in dimensions and metrics. However, GA also gives you the ability to add *custom* dimensions and metrics to the hits you send. Let's look at each of these and some of the reasons you might want to use them.

Dimensions

Dimensions are labels to bucket data into categories. Each type of hit, like pageviews and events, has predefined dimensions that you're able to populate with different pieces of data.

For example, with pageviews you have a dimension called Page, which is generally the path of the page that you're on (although in Chapter 6, you were able to customize this to represent any URL that you like).

With events you have more generic dimensions to work with, such as Event Category, Event Action, and Event Label. You're able to put anything you like in these fields; for instance, you can use `Downloads`, `PDF`, and `example.pdf` respectively to tell Google Analytics that someone initiated a download, that the file type was PDF, and that the particular file they started to download was named `example.pdf`.

In addition to dimensions that are associated with each hit, there are others that may apply to the entire session, to the user, or even to a particular product (in ecommerce data). All of these dimensions are predetermined and gathered in the GA tags in GTM. ***Custom dimensions*** allow you to supply your own labels for additional ways of categorizing data that goes beyond these.

With custom dimensions, you have complete control: you get to name the dimension and then decide what to store in that dimension. If you know the author who published a blog article, or a user's registration status, or a product's weight, you can store that in GA. GA allows you to create 20 custom dimensions per property. (GA Premium subscribers get up to 200 custom dimensions per property.)

When you create a custom dimension, you need to specify a ***scope***, which indicates what data in GA it relates to, or how long GA should "remember" the custom dimension. There are four possible scopes:

- *User:* The information provided adds more information about a particular user (as determined by the client ID cookie in the browser—see Chapter 10) and will be remembered every time that user comes back. User-level custom dimensions are used for qualities of the user that should apply to their current session and all future sessions (unless you change or update the value). Possible examples could include the following:

  - Demographic information such as age, gender, income, occupation, and so forth.

  - Customer information such as a user ID, status, subscription level, or renewal date.

  - Cumulative data over the user's relationship with the site, such as lifetime value or total shares.

  - User cohort information, such as date of first purchase, date of registration, and so forth. (Date of first session is a built-in dimension in GA, so you won't need a custom dimension for that, but other "firsts," like product purchases, could be useful.)

▪ **Tip**   If you're collecting user IDs as described in Chapter 10 for unifying sessions across devices, you should also create a custom dimension for the user ID, since GA doesn't make this value available in reports as a built-in dimension.

- *Session*: The information provided describes that particular session. Examples might include the following:

    - Behavior that occurred during the session, such as logged-in status or whether a particular type of content was viewed.

    - Engagement with a particular feature of the site, such as faceted navigation or whether anything was added to the shopping cart.

- *Hit*: The information provided describes only this particular hit, like a pageview or an event. Examples might include the following:

    - Page level information such as author name, publication date, or page category.

- *Product*: The information applies to a particular product, beyond the basic dimensions that you can use with GA's ecommerce tracking. Examples could include the following:

    - Product weight, sourcing information, internal tracking IDs, and so forth.

▓ **Warning**   With custom dimensions, you're given free rein with the fields you create and populate. Keep in mind that GA's terms of service prohibit collecting personally identifiable information—so custom dimensions that contain the user's name, email address, and so forth, are definite no-nos. Make sure that you read and adhere to the policies.[1]

Metrics

Whereas dimensions are labels that sort hit, session, or user data into categories, metrics are measurements assembled from counting those hits. Metrics are numbers in various units, such as total pageviews or events, which simply count up from zero; or a time element, like session duration; or dollar amounts for ecommerce and goal values.

As with dimensions, you can also create your own ***custom metrics***. When creating a custom metric, you can choose the format to be an integer, a decimal currency, or a time measurement. GA formats the metric appropriately based on this type in reports. GA allows you to create 20 custom metrics per property. (GA Premium subscribers get 200 per property.)

You also must choose a scope. There are only two scopes for custom metrics:

- *Hit*: The custom metric represents a measurement associated with the hit to which it is attached, such as a pageview or event.

- *Product*: The custom metric represents a measurement associated with a particular product in an ecommerce transaction.

▓ **Note**   Custom metrics are always totaled across some dimension, which also has a scope. As a result, you'll get the total for a custom metric for a given hit by using a hit-scoped dimension (like Page), for a session by using a session-scoped dimension (like Campaign), and so forth.

---

[1]The terms of service may vary by the country in which you operate; find the terms in your country and language here: http://www.google.com/analytics/terms/

SIDEBAR: DIMENSION OR METRIC?

When you have some piece of data from your website that you'd like to use in GA, you have to decide: Is this a dimension or a metric?

Sometimes, the choice is easy. If the value is text, it is certainly a dimension. Metrics are always numbers. So anything you'd use text for—a category for pages or other hits, a label or identifier for users or sessions—must be a dimension.

So, you might wonder, is the inverse true: If it's a number, it must be a metric? This requires a little more thought. *Metrics are always numbers* (an integer, currency value, or length of time), but *not all numbers have to be metrics*.

To find examples, look at the list of built-in dimensions in GA. You'll find that some of them *are* numbers: Page Depth (the number of pageviews that occurred during the session), Day of Week (0 to 6 for Sunday to Saturday), and many others. What's going on here?

In some cases, a number is just a label for something. This is the case in the Day of Week dimension, for example: the numbers 0 to 6 are simply labels for Sunday to Saturday, not measurements of any kind, and it would be nonsense to total them up.

In other cases, like Page Depth, those numbers *are* based on measurements. There are already metrics that measure "how many pageviews?"—that metric is just Pageviews! Why would you ever need a dimension for this when you already have a metric?

To find the reasoning behind this choice, remember that dimensions are used to categorize or bucket together hits, sessions, users, or products. The Page Depth dimension, then, gives you a way to say "Show me metrics for all the sessions that had exactly 1 pageview" (or 2, or 3, etc.). **Dimensions are used as the rows of reports, whereas metrics fill out the columns.** If you want to be able to see metrics across some list of categories, that category is a dimension.

	Dimension ?		Metric ?	↓ Metric ?	Metric ?
			123,023	4,083	00:03:40
			% of Total: 100.00% (123,023)	% of Total: 100.00% (4,083)	Avg for View: 00:03:40 (0.00%)
☐	1. dimension value	⎘	12,160 (9.88%)	30 (0.73%)	00:06:05
☐	2. dimension value	⎘	3,973 (3.23%)	6 (0.15%)	00:04:16
☐	3. dimension value	⎘	3,111 (2.53%)	39 (0.96%)	00:04:59
☐	4. dimension value	⎘	2,580 (2.10%)	15 (0.37%)	00:03:51
☐	5. dimension value	⎘	2,564 (2.08%)	2 (0.05%)	00:05:57

Additionally, remember that **metrics get totaled up** across hits, sessions, users, and so forth, whereas dimensions are simply labels.

When thinking about the custom dimensions and metrics that you desire for your own site, think about what you'd want the report to look like. The row labels are dimensions; the column values are metrics.

Accessing Custom Dimensions and Metrics in GA

Once you've sent data into custom dimensions or metrics, there are a few different ways to access this information in GA's reports. Custom dimensions are available in most standard reports as a secondary dimension (see Figure 11-1).

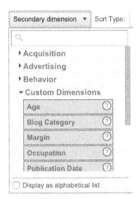

Figure 11-1. *Custom dimensions are available in the secondary dimension drop-down in reports*

You can also use custom dimensions and metrics in custom reports and dashboards (see Figure 11-2).

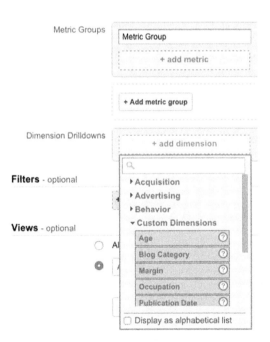

Figure 11-2. *Custom dimensions and metrics in a custom report*

Custom reports are the most flexible and useful way to access this custom data. (Custom dimensions and metrics are also available in GA data in BigQuery and the reporting APIs; see the bonus chapter and appendix for details.)

Setting Up Custom Dimensions and Metrics

Now that you have an understanding of why you might want to use custom dimensions and metrics, let's look at the process to implement them in GA and GTM. There are three steps to begin sending data in custom dimensions or metrics:

1. First, you need to create and label the custom dimension or metric to store the data in GA.

2. Next, you'll need to actually generate the data that you're going to use from the content of your site or other metadata (most often by placing it in GTM's data layer).

3. Finally, you need to send this data to GA by including the custom metric or dimension with a GA tag in GTM.

The following sections walk through this process, beginning with a relatively simple example. Suppose users of your site can register for the Alice's Wonderland Resorts Mad Hatter Club, which signs them up for special offers and discounted park admissions. When they sign up, they specify their preferred park location, which helps you target the offers that you send to them. You want to record this information in GA.

You need to ask yourself several questions before you begin:

- *Is this a dimension or a metric?* This is a dimension, as it's a label for various categories (park locations for the Mad Hatter Club membership). You want to be able to use these labels as the rows in reports, to say something like what's shown in Figure 11-3.

Mad Hatter Club Location ?	Sessions ? ↓
	5,137 % of Total: 100.00% (5,137)
1. Schenectady, NY	**2,841** (55.30%)
2. Peoria, IL	**395** (7.69%)
3. Athens, OH	**314** (6.11%)
4. Muskegon, MI	**139** (2.71%)
5. Fort Wayne, IN	**118** (2.30%)

Figure 11-3. Mad Hatter Club Location as a dimension

- *What's the scope?* Since the Mad Hatter Club Location applies to the same user every time they return, you'll want the scope to be **user**. GA applies the value to every session in which they return with the same cookie.

- *Where will the data come from?* You have to already have this data somewhere! There's some database or application connected to the website where users sign up for the Mad Hatter club, and when they sign up or log in, you'll look up that information. You'll explore this in more detail shortly, but the answer to this question is always specific to your site's platform and tools, since the data ultimately comes from some existing information.

Creating a Custom Dimension or Metric in GA

When creating a custom dimension or metric, you get to choose the name that will appear as the label of the dimension or metric in GA's reports. You'll want the name to be something descriptive that makes sense to those who will be using the data. Since all other field names in GA have the first letter of each word capitalized, it is recommended to do the same. For this example, you'll name the dimension "Mad Hatter Club Location".

CREATE A CUSTOM DIMENSION OR METRIC IN GA

You'll add a custom dimension in GA, using the Mad Hatter Club Location example.

1. In the Admin area of GA, with the appropriate account, property, and view selected, choose Custom Definitions ➤ Custom Dimensions (or Custom Metrics) in the middle column to see the custom dimensions for the property. Select the New button to add a new custom dimension.

2. Enter a name for the custom dimension (or metric): "Mad Hatter Club Location".

Add Custom Dimension

Name

    Mad Hatter Club Location

Scope

    User ▾

Active

    ✓

3. Choose a scope from the drop-down menu appropriate to the dimension or metric. For Mad Hatter Club Location, you'd choose User scope (as discussed earlier).

4. *(Metrics Only)* Choose the formatting type for custom metrics: integer, currency, or time.

5. *(Metrics Only)* Enter optional minimum and maximum values. GA will ignore values outside this range. This is useful to prevent accidental nonsense values (like a miscalculated currency value of $100 billion) from overwhelming the total for a custom metric.

6. Check the box to activate the dimension or metric. (Unchecking this box deactivates the dimension or metric and ceases collecting data.)

7. Select the Create button to create the custom dimension or metric.

Each custom dimension or metric is assigned to a specific index number from 1 to 20. Keep a note of the index number for the dimension or metric that you've created, as you'll need it later in the process to fill in its values. Just like with goals, custom dimensions and metrics cannot be deleted, just turned on or off. You can, however, rename them if you need to reuse a specific slot.

Generating Custom Data

Now that you've set up the name of the custom dimension and the scope where you're going to send the data, you need to tackle the more difficult part: finding the data to send.

You need to already be gathering the information that you want to send to GA, and then make it available in some way. For instance, if you wanted to send in information that describes users' gender and age, logically you need to first know their gender and age—GA and GTM can't automagically create this data for you!

There are several ways that you can gather such data, but they all fall into two general categories:

- Surfacing information from an internal database, such as a content management system with information about pages and content, a user database for information about users who log in to the site, or an ecommerce system with product data.

- Collecting information from a user, either directly through a form or indirectly through their behavior on the website.

■ **Note** In this chapter, you are considering how custom dimensions and metrics are filled directly from a website. It's also possible to fill in values for certain dimensions and metrics (including custom ones) using the data import features of GA, taking a bulk set of values and associating it with GA fields (see Chapter 12 for details).

Using existing information in a system connected to the website is the more common option, so let's consider that situation first. (You can use GTM's form trigger to capture form field values; more on that in a later example.)

Whatever the source of the data, you need to figure out how to get it to the website's code, where it can be read by GTM. Sometimes it may be readily available on the site. For instance, imagine a blog or news site that would like to pass in content metadata such as publication date, author, or tags with every article. Usually this information is already present in a content management system and can be inserted into the site's template.

Sometimes this information is a little trickier to retrieve. Maybe you have a user database available with all sorts of information about users when they log in, like the user's contact information, their Mad Hatter Club status and preferred city, their hat size, and whatever else you know about them. This information is only accessible when a user logs in and you're able to match them to their personal information.

■ **Tip** Consider ways to incentivize users to sign in to your website! This gives more information about the site's audience and allows passing in custom information more frequently. Additionally, signed-in users enable cross-device tracking if you've configured your User ID View correctly (see Chapter 10).

If you know the information, then there's a relatively easy way to pass this information to GTM: the data layer. Accessing the value and inserting it into the data layer will be specific to your site's tools and platforms, of course.

Using the Data Layer

You've used the data layer declaration (before the GTM container in the page) a number of times in this book to provide information to GTM. You can do the same for the Mad Hatter Club Location information:

```
dataLayer = [{
            'hatterClub': 'Schenectady, NY'
        }];
```

The value (Schenectady, NY, in this example) is inserted based on the location chosen by that particular user as their favorite park location.

You can continue to add to the data layer with any piece of information that you'd want to pass to GA as a custom dimension or metric. In GTM, you'll be able to simply use a data layer variable to retrieve these values.

Depending on your site, there may be other possible ways to find the values you're looking for, such as by using a DOM element variable if the data appears in the content of a page. However, using a data layer variable ensures that other changes to the site don't affect your tracking setup and that the value is available as soon as GTM loads. As with many other variables discussed in this book, using the data layer to organize information for GTM is always safer and more reliable than relying on page content.

■ **Note** For product-scoped dimensions or metrics, include the metric in the product object in the ecommerce data you've already included in the data layer, using a name like dimensionXX or metricXX, where XX is the number of the index for the dimension: for example, 'dimension2': 'blue'. Since you've already set up GTM to use the data layer to fill in ecommerce values, it will automatically capture these (see Chapter 7 for details on including ecommerce data in the data layer).

Sending Custom Information to GA

Once you have the desired values in your data layer, it's relatively simple to pass these to GA using the tags you've set up in GTM. Custom dimensions and metrics get sent with an existing hit, so you can add them to an existing tag, such as a pageview or event tag. You just need to find a hit that is already going to GA and then you'll hitch a ride.

Depending on the scope of the dimension or metric, you might want to include it with all hits (tags) or just some. For a hit-scoped dimension or metric, you'd only want to include it with the appropriate kinds of hits, and thus possibly only with certain tags. For example, a custom dimension for an article's publication date might only apply to pageviews (the articles), not to events.

For session- or user-scoped dimensions, you only absolutely need to send the value once during the session, or once for the user. For the Mad Hatter Club Location variable, for example, you would only need to set this value when the user first signs up for the Mad Hatter Club. However, in many instances you want to send the value again (say, every time the user logs in, or even on every page). This helps reinforce the value if the user switches devices or browsers, clears their cookies, or if the value changes.

If you specify values more than once for session- or user-scoped dimensions, *the last value wins* for that session. (Previous sessions' values remain unchanged.)

SEND CUSTOM INFORMATION FROM THE DATA LAYER

Let's take the Mad Hatter Club Status information from the data layer and insert it into a GA tag in GTM.

First, you'll create the variable to capture the value from the data layer.

1. In GTM, in the Variables section, select the New button to create a new user-defined variable.

2. Choose Data Layer Variable as the variable type, then select Continue.

3. As the data layer variable name, enter the name you used for the data layer entry (in the example, it was hatterClub).

4. Select Create Variable to save the variable. Give it a name: "Mad Hatter Club Location".

Now you'll need to alter the GA tags in GTM to pass the value of this variable. In this case, you'll simply include the value in the basic pageview tag. Any time the data layer value is present on a page, you'll send the custom dimension along with that pageview.

1. In GTM, in the Tags section, choose the GA – Pageview tag and select it to edit.

2. Click Configure Tag to make changes to the tag configuration.

3. Under More Settings ➤ Custom Dimensions, click the Add Custom Dimension button to add a new custom dimension.

    a. Fill in the index number of the custom dimension that corresponds to the custom dimension that you created in GA earlier.

    b. For the Dimension Value field, use the {{Mad Hatter Club Location}} variable you created in steps 1–4 (see the following screenshot).

4. Select Save Tag to save the changes to the tag.

You'll need to test and then publish the new version of the container before this data shows up in GA. As always, you can verify that it's working properly using the GTM Debug Panel or the GA Debug mode in the console.

Once these changes are published on the site, you'll begin to be able to see data for the custom dimension or metric in custom reports or by using a secondary dimension in the standard reports. (Remember, there's no built-in standard report that automatically includes custom dimensions or metrics, so you'll have to create one to see the values.)

Additional Examples

The previous section looked at a basic example of a custom dimension. Now let's look at a couple of additional examples to explore the possibilities: a custom dimension based on form input, and a custom metric based on an interaction.

Custom Dimensions from Form Input

Besides using data from another system in the data layer, another way to collect data for a custom dimension would be to scrape some information from a form that a user fills out. This might be information that is given only once and is not available to you later, after the form is submitted.

Suppose you have a contact form on your website. You might ask for a user's gender or perhaps ask them to identify themselves in a certain bucket, like *Teacher*, *Student*, or *Parent*. If you can intercept that data from the form as its being submitted, you may be able to take those fields that they filled out and store them as a user-scoped custom dimension.

Chapter 6 discussed using GTM's form trigger to listen for a specific form to be submitted. Capturing a custom dimension from a form is another great application for the form trigger but requires you to dig in a bit deeper.

Like the click trigger (discussed in Chapter 5), the form trigger adds information about the form submitted to the data layer. It looks something like the following:

```
{
        event: "gtm.formSubmit",
        gtm.element: form#contact-form,
        gtm.elementClasses: "",
        gtm.elementId: "contact-form",
        gtm.elementTarget: "",
        gtm.elementUrl: "http://aliceswonderlandresorts.com/contact-thankyou"
}
```

You've already learned about how to grab the ID and classes of the form, which work exactly the same way as clicks. The really exciting part here is that GTM adds the entire DOM object to the data layer as `gtm.element`. That means that everything about that form is now accessible inside of GTM, including all the form fields and their current values at the time of submission.

Accessing the various parts simply involve navigating the DOM object for the form to find the field that you want. For form fields, the DOM structure is actually quite simple: each form field is nested under `gtm.element` in the order that it appears in the form, listed by number, starting with 0. Under each form field, there's an attribute called `value` that will be the value of the form field at the time it was submitted. (You can explore the DOM elements in the data layer using your web browser's tools; see Figure 11-4 for an example from Chrome.)

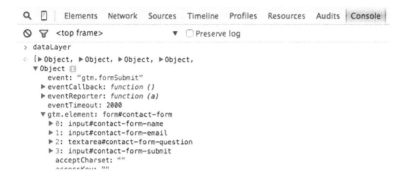

Figure 11-4. *Viewing a form's fields (numbered 0–3, in this example) in the data layer using Chrome's JavaScript console*

To get this information into GTM, you'll find the specific form field that you care about, then grab its value from the data layer using a data layer variable. The data layer uses periods to indicate nested values, so the preceding path would look like the following in the data layer variable:

`gtm.element.0.value`

This data layer variable, when coupled with a form trigger, will return the value of the first field in the form that was just submitted. (Use a different number for a field other than the first one.)

Now you can use that variable to fill in a custom dimension, just like the earlier scenario using an explicitly provided value in the data layer.

■ **Note** This example assumes there's already a tag using the form trigger on this form. Remember that a custom dimension or metric always needs to be sent with a hit such as a pageview or an event. If there's no tag currently triggered by this form, you could simply add a GA event tag to trigger on the form submission to include the custom dimension. (See Chapter 6 for more on form triggers.)

Custom Metrics from Interactions

You can also create custom metrics based on the count of some other interaction you're measuring with a pageview or an event.

Why would you duplicate an event or pageview count with a custom metric? Again, simply to make reporting easy. Although there are metrics in GA such as the total number of pageviews or events, you'd need to employ creative filtering or segmentation to get just the number of pageviews or events of a certain kind. What if you'd just like a column with the count of a certain kind of pageview or event? A custom metric is the perfect solution.

For example, suppose you're using events to track downloads on your site. You could create a custom metric for Downloads and easily see that as a column in reports.

CREATE A CUSTOM METRIC FROM AN INTERACTION

You'll first need to create a custom metric in GA according to the instructions earlier in the chapter. Name it "Downloads" and choose Integer as the formatting type. Make a note of the index of the custom metric; you'll need it in the steps that follow.

You'll also already need a tag in GTM with an event to track downloads (see Chapter 5).

1. In GTM, in the Tags section, choose the GA event tracking tag for downloads and select it to edit.

2. Click Configure Tag to make changes to the tag configuration.

3. Under More Settings ➤ Custom Metrics, click the Add Custom Metric button to add a new custom metric.

   a. Fill in the index number of the custom metric that corresponds to Downloads.

   b. For the Metric Value field, simply use the value 1.

4. Select Save Tag to save the changes to the tag.

Of course, you'll need to test and publish in GTM before the changes take effect.

Once published, every time a file is downloaded and the event is sent to GA, the count of the Downloads metric will be incremented by 1.

Summary

- Custom dimensions and metrics allow you to send custom information to GA for reporting and analysis. Dimensions are category labels, typically represented as rows in reports. Metrics are measurements (a count, currency amount, or length of time) and typically represented as the columns in reports.

- You can specify a name and scope for a custom dimension or metric in GA. The scope affects what data the dimension or metric is associated with in GA. Custom dimensions and metrics are configured at the property level, and there are 20 slots for each in each property.

- The values for custom dimensions and metrics inserted into a tag in GTM may come from the site's server via the data layer, or from the page and the user's interactions with it. GTM's variable make it easy to grab such values.

PART III

Collecting Data from Other Sources

CHAPTER 12

■ ■ ■

Importing Data into Google Analytics

Alice didn't think that proved it at all; however, she went on: "And how do you know that you're mad?"

"To begin with," said the Cat, "a dog's not mad. You grant that?"

"I suppose so," said Alice.

"Well then," the Cat went on, "you see, a dog growls when it's angry, and wags its tail when it's pleased. Now I growl when I'm pleased, and wag my tail when I'm angry. Therefore I'm mad."

"I call it purring, not growling," said Alice.

—Lewis Carroll, *Alice's Adventures in Wonderland*

In Chapter 11, you learned about using custom dimensions and metrics in GA to fill in additional data about your users and their behavior. You supplied those custom dimensions and metrics as additional data sent along with a hit in GTM. GA provides another option to fill in these values, through its data import features. Data import allows you to fill in the data using files uploaded directly to GA. This can be useful in situations such as the following:

- The data isn't available to the site at the time the hit occurs—for example, because it's stored in a separate system. You can upload data from such systems to GA.

- The data is extensive, and including it directly on the site would be a development burden, or would exceed the character limits for data included in a hit. You can reduce the data sent from the site to certain key dimensions and fill in other values later.

- The data is sensitive and you wouldn't want to include it on the site, such as certain kinds of user or product data.

You'll look at the process for importing data in detail in the next section, and then examine the several types of data import available and their applications.

Data Import Process

The basic process for data import works like this:

1. You create a data set associated with a property in GA, to configure the dimensions and metrics that will be imported.

2. You upload a text file with the data to be imported. GA takes this and processes it into the data in reports.

3. You update the data set as necessary to update the data going forward.

Later in the chapter you'll take a look at the specific types of data import possible in GA, but the basic process for each is the same. Let's walk through it.

Creating a Data Set

Creating a *data set* in a GA property configures the dimensions and metrics that will be imported and creates a schema for the text files you will use to upload data. The data set acts as a container for the uploaded files and controls how the imported data is applied to GA.

The different types of data sets available in GA each support one or more *keys* (a dimension that already has a value in GA that the imported data will be associated with) and one or more imported dimensions or metrics (the data that will be added by the import).

SET UP A DATA SET FOR IMPORT

Data sets are created in a property in GA.

1. In the Admin area of GA, with the appropriate account, property, and view selected, choose Data Import in the middle column to see the data sets for the property. Select the New button to add a new data set.

2. Choose a type for the data set (see the following screenshot; more on the types later in the chapter). Select the Next Step button.

① Data set type

Select one of the data types below. **Learn more about data types**.

Hit Data Import ——————————————————————————

○ **Refund Data**

Import refund data for Ecommerce transactions.

Extended Data Import ——————————————————————

◉ **User Data**

Import user data such as customer segment, lifetime value, or contract renewal month.

○ **Campaign Data**

Import campaign metadata such as source, medium, content, referral path, or custom campaign data.

○ **Geography Data**

Group cities, regions, or countries by importing geographic data.

○ **Content Data**

Import content metadata such as article, author, or category.

○ **Product Data**

Import product metadata such as brand, category, variant, or custom product data.

○ **Custom Data**

Create a custom Data Set to import data for your specific use case.

Summary Data Import ——————————————————————

○ **Cost Data**

Import cost data for non-Google marketing campaigns.

3. Enter a name for the data set to describe the data being imported.

4. (*For some data import types only*) Choose the views within the property where the imported data will be shown.

5. Select the dimensions and metrics for the import (see the following screenshot). Depending on the data import type selected, different options will be available for the key dimension(s) and the imported data.

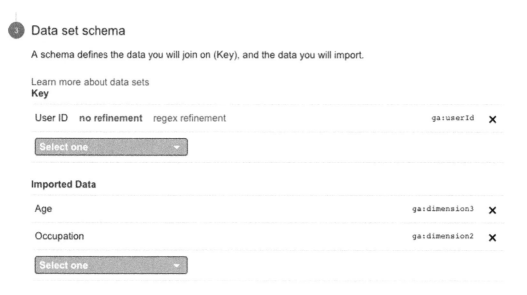

6. *(For some data import types only)* Choose options for overwriting data (this is discussed shortly, with the individual data types).

7. Select the Save button.

After you save the data set, GA displays two buttons with links to get the schema for uploading data, or to get the ID for use with the API. You'll take a look at how to use these shortly.

GA allows you to create up to 50 data sets per property. There are additional limitations on the number and size of uploads. GA Premium subscribers are allowed higher limits.

Once the data set is created, you'll be able to upload data for import.

Data Import Schema

The text files you'll use to import data into GA are in CSV (comma-separated value) format, which is a text file format used to represent the rows and columns of a spreadsheet. CSV files are easily generated using a spreadsheet application like Google Sheets or Microsoft Excel, and they are also widely supported as an export format from many applications.

As you saw earlier, when you create a data set, GA offers a sample schema file that you can download. The schema file contains the headers that describe the dimensions and metrics included in the data set and shows the appropriate file format. (Note that the headers used in data set schemas match the way that dimensions and metrics are labeled in GA's APIs; see the Appendix for more details.) Here's a sample upload file with a few lines of data to be imported:

```
ga:userId,ga:dimension3,ga:dimension2
alice0214,Student,7.5
madhatter13,Milliner,35
queenofhearts<3,Royalty,65
```

As long as you provide the data in this format, GA doesn't care where it comes from or what tools were used to create it. It could be assembled by hand, reformatted from an export from another system or tool, or generated by a script that automates the data import.

Uploading Data

Files for data import can be uploaded to GA manually, through the Admin area, or they can be automated through the API. This section describes the manual process. See the Appendix for more details on GA's APIs.

UPLOAD DATA TO A DATA SET

Let's take a look at how to manually upload data for import to GA. Let's assume you already have your data file, properly formatted to the schema as described earlier.

1. In the Admin area of GA, with the appropriate account, property, and view selected, choose Data Import in the middle column to see the data sets for the property.

2. In the listing of data sets, select the "Manage uploads" link on the right for the data set you'd like to upload. GA displays a list of previous uploads (see the following screenshot).

3. Select the "Upload file" button at the top of the list.

4. Choose the file(s) from your computer to upload and select the Upload button.

The file will be uploaded and the status marked Pending until GA has completely processed the file. If there are no formatting errors, the status will be updated to Complete. Once this occurs, GA will begin applying the data import.

Updating Data Sets

Once uploaded, the data will be applied to data going forward. Some types of data import may rarely need updating after the initial upload, and for those the manual upload process described earlier is an easy solution.

Other data import types may need regular updates, however—potentially even daily, for certain kinds of data that may change frequently. The manual upload process could be cumbersome for these kinds of applications, so using the API (see the Appendix) is recommended.

■ **Tip** There are a number of off-the-shelf tools that already exist to use the GA API to import data from other systems, such as cost data from advertising platforms. You should seek out tools that help you automate these repetitive tasks.

Updating or deleting data sets generally only affects data going forward, like all changes in GA's Admin area. Historic data is unaffected. The different types of data import behave slightly differently in how they are affected by updates; see the next section for details by type.

Data Import Types

There are three basic categories of data import available in Google Analytics: hit data (directly import hits to GA), extended data (import several kinds of dimension or metric values to be applied to existing hits in GA), and summary data (import metrics for data already aggregated in certain dimensions). You'll take a look at the potential uses of each in the following sections.

Hit Data Import

Hit data import lets you directly import hits to GA. Once imported, they are treated like any other hit and are processed according to the filters applied to the property's views. There is only one type of supported hit data for import: refund data for ecommerce transactions.

Refund Data

Refund data is used to import full or partial refunds of ecommerce transactions. You can use this to add data to GA about refunds that occur outside the context of the website, using the ecommerce or order-processing platform to supply the data. Once a refund is added to GA, the transaction it corresponds with is updated to show the appropriate revenue and products after the refund is applied.

Refund data must include the Transaction ID dimension. For a full refund, only the Transaction ID is needed. The entire transaction, including all products, is refunded in GA. For a partial refund, there are two options:

- Specify a Product SKU and Quantity from the transaction to be refunded. All listed products will be refunded and subtracted from the transaction revenue.

- Specify an amount of refunded Transaction Revenue to be refunded. That portion of transaction revenue will be refunded, but all products will remain in the transaction.

■ **Warning**   Once refunds are imported into GA, there is no way to remove or modify them. Be careful and test refund data in a test property first to ensure that you know how the process works before applying to your production data.

Extended Data Import

Extended data import lets you extend existing hits in GA with additional information. They include one or more "key" dimension values from existing data to match up with imported values for dimensions or metrics. Most often, this is used to fill in values for custom dimensions or metrics, but it can also be used to overwrite values for existing dimensions.

Extended data import occurs during GA's processing, which means that the data import is applied as new hits are collected. You can choose which of the property's views the data will appear in. Because the data is incorporated during processing, if you make changes to a data set, those changes will only take effect going forward, not on historical data.

▓ **Note** GA Premium subscribers have the ability to designate data import to occur at *processing time* or at *query time*, meaning the imported data can be applied to historical data in reports and updated at will.

There are six different kinds of extended data import. Let's take a look at applications for each.

User Data Import

User data can be imported to GA to enhance the information about individual users. You could use it to import user data from a CRM or other system with information to aid in user segmentation, like demographics, lifetime value or purchase information, and so on.[1]

Chapter 11 discussed a number of such ideas for user-scoped custom dimensions. The only difference with user data import is that you are simply passing in a single dimension on the site to identify users, and importing the rest of the dimensions later, in GA.

User data can be imported based on the User ID (see Chapter 10) or a user-scoped custom dimension. The imported data can be a user-scoped custom dimension.

Campaign Data Import

Campaign data import can be used to fill in campaign-related dimensions such as source, medium, and campaign. It uses a key dimension called Campaign ID, which can be provided through campaign URL tagging (see Chapter 9).

Campaign data import can be used to accomplish one of the following:

- Simplify campaign URL tagging by enabling you to provide a single parameter (utm_id) in campaign URLs, rather than each individual parameter for source, medium, and so on (utm_source, utm_medium, etc.). The full set of descriptive dimensions can then be imported based on the Campaign ID value.

- Fill in campaign-related fields that don't have corresponding campaign URL parameters, such as the Ad Group or Referral Path dimensions, or a custom dimension.

The imported dimensions can include Medium, Source, Campaign, Ad Group, Ad Content, Keyword, Referral Path, or a session-scoped custom dimension.

Geographical Data Import

Geographical data import can be used to create custom geographical regions or groupings with GA's geographic data. For example, in the United States, maybe you'd like to group cities by county, or states into regions such as "New England" and "Midwest".

The key dimension for geographic data can be any one of the following, from broadest to most specific:

- A subcontinent code according to the UN M.49 standard.[2] These are numeric codes corresponding to subcontinent regions such as "Western Europe" or "Caribbean".

---

[1]Remember, personally identifiable information isn't allowed within GA. See Chapters 10 and 11 for more information.

- A country code according to the ISO 3166-1 alpha-2 standard.[3] These are two-letter codes corresponding to countries, such as "US" for the United States or "UK" for the United Kingdom.

- A region ID from Google's list of geographical criterion IDs.[4] These are the geographic divisions used in Google advertising targeting, but they must correspond to an area in the Region dimension in GA. Regions in GA are subcountry divisions, such as the states of the United States, the provinces of Canada, and so forth.

- A city ID from Google's list of geographical criterion IDs. These IDs must correspond to locations in the City dimension in GA.

The imported values can be any session-scoped custom dimension.

■ **Tip**   You can find the Subcontinent Code, Country Code, Region ID, and City ID in the list of dimensions available in custom reports in GA. If you're not sure if you're using the right values, create a custom report to check.

Content Data Import

Content data import can be used to import hit-scoped custom dimensions based on the Page (URL). Chapter 11 discussed a number of potential hit-scoped custom dimensions, such as a page's author, publication date, and so forth. Content data import provides an alternative method to bring these data into GA.

Product Data Import

Product data import can be used to import product-related data based on the Product SKU. Imported data can include product dimensions such as the Product Category or Product Brand, or product-scoped custom dimensions or metrics. Product data import can be useful for the following situations:

- Simplifying the site's ecommerce tracking. Rather than including all the data about products in the ecommerce data in the data layer (described in Chapter 7), you could simply include the SKU (along with quantity and price) and then fill in the additional descriptive fields later, using import.

- Importing dimensions or metrics that are too sensitive to include in data directly on the site, such as the product's profit margin.

Custom Data Import

Custom data import can be used for other associations between dimensions and metrics to be imported (typically custom dimensions and metrics, but also supporting certain built-in dimensions). As the key dimensions, you can select up to two dimensions from a variety of built-in dimensions, as well as custom dimensions of any scope. The imported values can also be a variety of built-in dimensions and custom dimensions or metrics of any scope.

---

[2]https://en.wikipedia.org/wiki/UN_M.49
[3]https://en.wikipedia.org/wiki/ISO_3166-1_alpha-2
[4]https://developers.google.com/analytics/devguides/collection/protocol/v1/geoid

Summary Data Import

Summary data import differs from extended data import because rather than importing data corresponding to individual hits, data is imported for aggregate measures. Summary data import is applied to GA's reports after processing, so it can be updated at a later point in time to apply data retroactively.

There is only one type of supported summary data for import: cost data for advertising and marketing campaigns.

Cost Data Import

Chapter 9 discussed GA's integration with AdWords and DoubleClick platforms to import impression, click, and cost data for advertising on those platforms.

Similarly, you might wish to import data for advertising on other networks. Although there's no automatic integration with GA for other advertising networks and platforms, you can use cost data import to bring in this data.

At a minimum, cost data import must contain the following:

- The Medium and Source dimensions.

- At least one of the metrics Impressions, Clicks, or Cost.

- The dates to which the data apply.

Additionally, you can be more specific by including more dimensions such as Campaign, Ad Group, Keyword, and so forth. Additional metrics are also calculated from this data, such as Cost per Click and Return on Ad Spend.

When you create a cost data import set, you can choose whether new data uploads should be added to any existing data for that date (summing the impressions, clicks, and cost), or whether it should overwrite existing data.

Summary

- GA supports importing dimension and metric values in bulk, based on one or more key dimensions that already have values in GA. This can be used to join GA data with other systems, reduce the amount of data that needs to be sent from the website, or protect sensitive information from being exposed on the site.

- Data import works by creating a data set associated with a property in GA, and then uploading files to the data set. The upload can be automated if it is updated frequently.

- There are a number of different types of data import supported by GA, for ecommerce transaction refunds and product data, user data, campaign tagging and cost data, geographic data, content data, and custom data.

CHAPTER 13

Collecting Data from Mobile Apps

When the Rabbit actually took a watch out of its waistcoat-pocket, and looked at it, and then hurried on, Alice started to her feet, for it flashed across her mind that she had never before seen a rabbit with either a waistcoat-pocket, or a watch to take out of it.

—Lewis Carroll, *Alice's Adventures in Wonderland*

So far this book has focused on using GTM to implement GA (and potentially other tags) to measure *websites*. But websites aren't the only way our customers interact with us. Another important channel is the use of *native apps* for mobile devices—the kind you can download and install on a phone or tablet, rather than visiting a website in a browser.

GTM and GA can be used to collect data from mobile apps as well—specifically, from Android and iOS apps (on any devices using those operating systems). Using these tools for measurement provides a number of advantages:

- A single reporting tool (GA) for websites and apps, using all the same data cleanup and reporting functions that you already know.

- A single deployment tool (GTM) for websites and apps, using the same structure and publication mechanisms that you already know.

- A way of updating between published versions of the app. (Typically, apps must be updated through an app store in a publication process, which can be cumbersome.)

There are, of course, some differences in the data collected in GA and the ways you can collect it in GTM, since we're talking about different environments from websites. This chapter looks at these differences, the platforms on which GA and GTM can be used, and the process for deploying these tools through their software development kits (SDKs) in mobile apps.

Note Keep in mind that this chapter isn't intended to teach you how to *develop* an Android or iOS app. While the implementation within GTM for apps is similar to websites, implementation in the app's code is best left in the hands of a capable Android or iOS developer. This chapter is designed to give you the necessary knowledge to interact with that developer to achieve a successful implementation.

GA for Mobile Apps

Before you take a look at how to collect data in mobile apps, let's examine the data itself that will be collected in GA. The data is similar to website data, with some differences:

- Rather than the *pageview* hit type, mobile app data contains *screenviews*, which represent a screen loading within the app. The screenviews are identified by a dimension called Screen Name (rather than the Page dimension containing URL for pageviews).

- Mobile apps also support an additional hit type for *exceptions*; that is, errors and crashes that occur within the application that you'd like to capture.

- Additional dimensions such as Application Name, Application ID, and Application Version are available in mobile apps, whereas other website-specific dimensions like Hostname may not apply to app data.

- The hit types for *event* and *social* interactions are available in mobile apps, just as in website data (see Chapter 5), to track interactions such as video plays, button clicks, or social media interactions.

- Ecommerce and enhanced ecommerce features are available in mobile apps, just as in website data (see Chapter 7), to track in-app purchases.

- Campaigns work somewhat differently in apps. Campaigns can be used in two distinct ways:

  - Tracking the original installation source of an app—how a user arrived at the Google Play Store (for Android) or the iTunes Store (for iOS) to download and install the app.

  - Tracking app launches from URLs—when a link in a web browser launches the app for a user.

Because of these differences, in GA you can create app-specific properties and views, which rearrange the default reports to better reflect the data for apps.

App Properties and Views

When creating a new property or view in GA (see Chapter 8), you can make the choice of whether the property or view should be for an app or a website (see Figure 13-1).

What would you like to track?

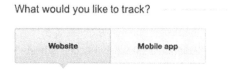

Figure 13-1. *Decide the type of tracking when creating a property or view in GA*

This choice affects the structure of reports available in the view. (Making this choice when creating a property affects the default view created with the property, but subsequently created views can be for either website or app data.) Choosing a view for mobile apps rearranges reports in the view to focus on app data (see Figure 13-2).

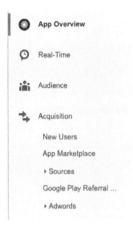

Figure 13-2. *App views in GA contain app-specific reporting such as the App Overview report*

For example, you'll find that rather than the Behavior ➤ Site Content ➤ All Pages report (which focuses on pageviews), instead you have Behavior ➤ Screens report for screenview data. In the Acquisition reports, you'll find reports for the iTunes and Google Play stores. Although this list of reports differs for apps, you'll find that all the familiar GA reporting functions are available, such as segments, dashboards, and many other tools.

Like website data, you can use the view and property settings to customize mobile app data, including creating goals (see Chapter 6), using filters and content groupings (see Chapter 8), and so on.

SIDEBAR: COMBINING OR SEPARATING WEB AND APP DATA

Note that it's possible to include both website and mobile app data in the same property. (They can then be separated when desired using filters.) Should you combine data for mobile apps or keep it separate?

For websites and apps where users log in, you can use the User ID features of GA to connect their activity across these platforms (see Chapter 10). However, a drawback of combining mobile app and website data is that GA doesn't contain reports where data about content (pageviews and screenviews) can be easily combined, mitigating some of the advantages of this approach. Ultimately, the choice is up to you. You should evaluate your needs for analysis and the utility of combining these types of data together in GA.

Google Analytics Premium subscribers can use Roll-Up Properties to combine data from separate properties, giving additional flexibility. Mobile app and website data can remain in separate properties, but be combined in a roll-up property for analysis together.

Other solutions for combining the data include using the GA APIs (see the Appendix) to extract data from properties and combining them in reports outside of GA.

Mobile App SDKs

GTM has official SDKs for the Android and iOS platforms. Additionally, GA has an SDK for the Unity game engine.

■ **Note** For any platform you'd like to track outside those with an official SDK, data can be sent to Google Analytics via the Measurement Protocol (see Chapter 14).

Android and iOS

The GTM SDKs for Android and iOS share many similarities. Although the details of their implementation will differ (in Java for Android apps and Objective-C or Swift for iOS), conceptually they both follow the same basic framework:

- The GTM SDK is included in the app.

    - The GTM SDK for Android comes bundled with the Google Play Services SDK, a collection of SDKs for Google services such as Google Drive, Google Maps, and others. The GTM SDK allows the developer of the Android app to embed a GTM container in the app's Java code to push events and values to the data layer.[1]

    - The GTM SDK for iOS can be loaded into an iOS app. Objective-C or Swift code can be used to push events and values to the data layer.[2]

- Unlike a website, which fetches a new copy of the container every time it loads, a default container is included with the application. Apps can run on devices that aren't guaranteed to be online, so it's important that a default container is included for tracking functionality if the container cannot be updated over a network connection when the app launches.

- Code embedded in the app pushes events and values to the data layer. Note that, unlike a website where the data layer is re-created with each page load, the data layer in an app persists for the entire session.

- Just like with websites, GTM can trigger tags based on data layer events. According to the tags and triggers you've set up in the container, data is dispatched to GA (or other tools with other tags).

- As noted earlier, apps may run on devices that may not currently have a network connection. GTM attempts to send hits to GA or other tools, but if there is no network connectivity, it queues hits to send later. (In the case of long delays, hits older than four hours may not be processed by GA.) Even with network connectivity, GTM batches hits to dispatch at regular intervals to preserve battery life.

A detailed look at the GTM container and data layer for apps appears later in the chapter.

---

[1]https://developers.google.com/tag-manager/android/v4/#push
[2]https://developers.google.com/tag-manager/ios/v3/#push-datalayer

Unity

In addition to iOS and Android, Google Analytics also provides an SDK for the Unity platform. Unity is a game engine in which a single set of code can be compiled into apps on multiple platforms.

Although there is a *GA* SDK for Unity, there is no *GTM* SDK. This means you won't be able to manage tags via GTM. Instead, code within your Unity app directly specifies to send screenview, event, or exception data to GA (akin to implementing GA directly in the JavaScript of a website, for example).[3]

GTM Containers for Mobile Apps

You can create a container for a mobile app by creating a new container from the account overview screen. When creating a container, GTM allows you to choose whether the container is for a website, an Android app, or an iOS app (see Figure 13-3).

Figure 13-3. *Choose the container type when creating a container*

Differences from Website Containers

A GTM container for mobile apps works in basically the same way as with websites, containing tags, triggers, and variables. However, there are some differences in the options available and in the testing processes with mobile apps. Let's take a look.

Tags

Like website tags in GTM, for mobile apps there are a number of built-in tags, as well as custom tags. The tags include the following:

- Built-in tags for GA, AdWords, and DoubleClick. These have the same options as with websites.

- A Custom Image tag for custom tracking pixels. Again, this tag has the same options as with websites.

- A Function Call tag that can be used to call a function within the app, including arguments if necessary.

---

[3]https://developers.google.com/analytics/devguides/collection/unity/v3/

Note that, unlike Custom JavaScript tags on a website, custom code (Java for Android, Objective-C or Swift for iOS) cannot be directly included in a tag. However, the Function Call tag can be used to call to a function that already resides in the app.

Triggers

There is only one kind of trigger in GTM mobile app containers, the Custom Event trigger. As with websites, this is used to trigger tags when an event value is pushed to the data layer (see Chapter 5 for examples).

■ **Tip** As with web traffic, you should employ triggers (and blocking triggers) to separate testing data on mobile apps. Specifically, using the {{App Version Code}} or {{Advertiser ID}} variables may be especially useful for mobile app testing triggers.

Variables

Mobile app containers include built-in variables that provide commonly used values. These include the following:

- App-related variables, including the app ID, name, and version, and the version of the GTM SDK being used.

- Utility variables that are identical to website containers, including the GTM container ID and version, the custom event value from the data layer, and a random number variable. Additionally, mobile apps offer a variable that indicates whether the user has advertising tracking enabled or has opted out. (Android and iOS both offer system-wide options to opt out of interest-targeted advertising.)

- Device-related variables, including platform (Android or iOS), OS version, device type, language, screen resolution, and advertiser ID, which is a persistent but user-resettable device identifier (which differs from the permanent device hardware identifier) that both Android and iOS offer to track devices. This value—often referred to as "IDFA" or ID for Advertising from its name in iOS—takes the place of a cookie (as for the GA cookie for client ID) for device identification for mobile apps.

Additionally, you can create custom variables of the following types:

- Constant and Data Layer Variable types work identically to website containers.

- The Function Call variable type allows you to call a function within the app and use the returned value.

- The Value Collection variable type allows you to specify a list of key-value pairs that can be used in the app.

- The Google Analytics Content Experiment variable allows use of GA's content experiment features[4] to switch among several sets of values for value collection variables.

---

[4]https://support.google.com/tagmanager/answer/6003007

SIDEBAR: APP CONTENT DELIVERY VIA GTM

Like with websites, GTM in mobile apps can provide tracking capabilities (via tags like GA or AdWords conversions), as well as actual content or functionality for the app (via variable values and custom tags). It's generally recommended not to provide content or functionality for *websites* via GTM, for several reasons:

- It muddies the purpose of GTM (providing a system for managing tracking tags) when there are other options (content management systems, web servers) for providing such data dynamically to websites.

- It leads to bloating of the GTM container (which has a maximum size of 200 kilobytes) with content that would be better managed elsewhere.

- If critical functionality depends on content in GTM and the container is for some reason unavailable, the website cannot work properly.

However, the balance of factors is somewhat different in apps. The app update process (via app stores) tends to be lengthy and cumbersome, and as a result, you'd want to update apps as seldom as possible. Thus, the ability to make minor changes via GTM between app store updates can be very valuable, but unfortunately there's no such thing as a "content management system for apps," which is a role that GTM can help fill. Additionally, unlike websites, apps always incorporate a copy of the container as a fallback, even if a refreshed container can't be retrieved from GTM, so the risk of an unavailable container is mitigated.

For these reasons, it's more common to use GTM to provide configuration data or to launch functions in mobile apps. Value collection variables are often used for providing configuration settings or other content to the app. For example, suppose you have a value collection variable with the following values:

```
{
    "suit": "hearts",
    "card": "queen"
}
```

Our app can retrieve these values (via the `container.getString()` function in Android or `[container stringForKey:@{}]` in iOS) and use them in the app:

Value collection variables can be used to contain configuration values or URLs that are inputs to functions in the app, text strings used in the app's interface, or any other pieces of information useful for altering the content or behavior of the app. This functionality is one of the key advantages of using GTM in mobile apps.

The Data Layer in Mobile Apps

The data layer in a mobile app works much the same way as on a website: a running queue of events and values used to trigger tags and supply variable values.

On websites, each new page loading causes the browser to clear away any JavaScript from the previous page. As a result, the data layer is renewed on each page. In mobile apps, however, the data layer persists until the app quits. This has several consequences:

- It's useful to have a persistent data layer, because you don't need to refresh persistent values continually throughout a user's session (like you would with a website). For example, user- or session-scoped custom dimensions, user ID, or other values that stay the same throughout the session remain in the data layer and need not be re-added.

- On the other hand, you need to manually clear transient values that shouldn't apply later. Enhanced ecommerce values, for example, apply to a specific hit, but not to subsequent hits. You need to clear those values (or overwrite them with new ones) to send the appropriate data for each hit.

Also note that there are no default data layer events (gtm.js, gtm.dom, gtm.load) as there are for websites. Everything you'd like in the data layer needs to be explicitly pushed from the app's code. The Android and iOS SDKs provide functions for pushing information to the data layer. For Android, use the DataLayer.pushEvent() function, and for iOS, use the [dataLayer push:@{}] function.

Deployment and Testing

Deployment and testing follows a somewhat different flow on mobile apps, because our update processes are different from websites and different tools are available to us.

First of all, the debug panel you've used with websites isn't available in mobile apps. The GTM SDKs do have built-in logging that can be enabled to view detailed logging information during the development phase. Enable this in Android with TagManager.setVerboseLoggingEnabled(true) or in iOS with [self.tagManager.logger setLogLevel:kTAGLoggerLogLevelVerbose].

When making changes in GTM, you have two ways of previewing the changes to the container in an app:

- If the app is still in development, you can download a binary file representation of a container to be included in the app. The Download option can be found in the list of actions in the version list for a mobile app (see Figure 13-4).

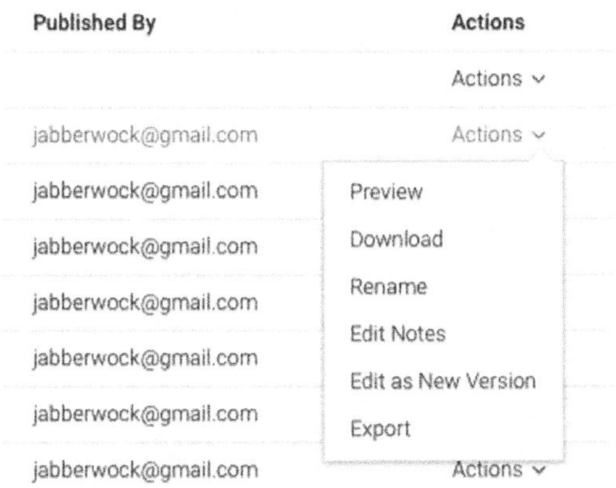

Figure 13-4. Download a binary version of the container to compile into the app

---

■ **Note**   You should include a copy of a testing, fully functional container in the compiled app binary before submitting to the app store or distributing to users.

- As with websites, you can use a preview link (or a QR code) to preview changes to a container in an app—including a published, live app. Before using this link, you must register the URL scheme in your app's code. Then you can select the Preview option in the list of actions in the version list to obtain the link (see Figure 13-5). (Notice that you can also generate a link to *end* preview mode on the device.)

Share Preview

Share a preview of **Version 1** of **Container** .

Enter the name of the app where you would like to preview the container version

Alice's Card Shuffler

Generate begin preview link   Generate end preview link

Visit the following preview link from your device or scan the QR code to preview the container version

https://tagmanager.google.com/mcpr/Alice's%20Card%20Shuf
fler?id=GTM-WQTHQZ&gtm_auth=zH3xv2hO5_iiGI6jnyt-
xA&gtm_preview=1

Figure 13-5. *Enable a preview of a container version in mobile apps with a link or QR code*

For testing mobile app containers on live apps on devices, a packet sniffer (monitoring the outgoing network traffic from the device) may be useful (similar to the use of browser developer tools for websites). And of course, you can monitor incoming data to GA to ensure that it matches up to what you expect.

■ **Note**   When using GA's Real-Time reports to monitor testing activity, remember that the mobile app SDKs batch hits and dispatch them on an interval. As a result, you won't quite see things in real time—instead, several hits will arrive in a burst after a short delay. This is normal behavior for app data.

Summary

- GA can collect data from mobile apps using the screenview hit type, in addition to the event, social, and other hit types discussed previously, plus some additional dimensions that apply specifically to mobile apps. GTM provides SDKs for Android and iOS to enable the use of containers in mobile apps, including GA tags.

- Mobile app containers include tags, triggers, and variables. The selection of tags and variables differs from websites, and the only types of available triggers are for events pushed to the data layer.

- GTM can be especially valuable for mobile apps when the Value Collection variable type is used to provide updates to content or provide configuration values to a mobile app between app store versions.

- Mobile apps use a data layer that persists throughout the session, unlike websites.

- Mobile app testing tools include a preview mode and also the ability to download a container to be compiled into the app.

CHAPTER 14

■ ■ ■

Sending Data from Other Sources Using GA's Measurement Protocol

Curiouser and curiouser!

—Lewis Carroll, *Alice's Adventures in Wonderland*

The bulk of this book has focused on sending data to Google Analytics via Google Tag Manager. These official methods of collecting data in GA extend to websites (JavaScript) and mobile apps (iOS and Android SDKs). However, there are many potential sources of data that you might wish to incorporate into GA beside websites and mobile apps.

To facilitate additional sources of data, GA provides the Measurement Protocol. The Measurement Protocol is a **specification for how data is sent to GA**, and it doesn't matter what the source of that data is. As long as you send it in the proper format, GA can use the data, alongside all the usual data that is collected from websites or mobile apps.

There are many potential applications of the Measurement Protocol for sending data to GA:

- Send data from systems with offline or non-web interaction data about users, such as a call center, or a point-of-sale system in a retail store.

- Send data in contexts where JavaScript cannot be used, such as in an HTML email.

- Send data from environments or devices where an official SDK does not exist, such as Windows Phone, set-top boxes, and other Internet-connected devices.

Since the format specification of the Measurement Protocol is not dependent on the source of the data, it doesn't matter what methods, programming languages, or techniques you use to capture this data (all of which will be platform- and context-dependent). As long as you send data in the same way, it will be received and processed by GA, just like data from the official collection sources for websites, iOS, and Android.

■ **Note** The only official code libraries for GA are analytics.js (for websites) and the iOS and Android SDKs (for mobile apps). You can use the format of the Measurement Protocol to send data from any source, but it's up to you to create the code to do so in whatever programming or scripting language you are working in.

Sending Data

Sending data with the Measurement Protocol simply involves making an ***HTTP request*** (just like requesting a web page in a web browser) that includes a ***payload***, which is a collection of parameters comprising the data being sent.

HTTP Request

The Measurement Protocol makes an HTTP request to the following URL:

```
http://www.google-analytics.com/collect
```

You'll already recognize that this is the same place analytics.js (for websites) and the mobile app SDKs (for iOS and Android) send data! The Measurement Protocol lets any other source send data exactly the same way. You can also use this URL for secure requests over SSL:

```
https://ssl.google-analytics.com/collect
```

Both work the same way.

The Measurement Protocol request can use either a GET or POST request. (You're already familiar with both of these, even if you didn't know it: in a web browser, items such as pages and images use GET, whereas forms typically use POST.)

The ability to use a GET request means that you can send data even from a static environment, like an HTML email, by including an image with the Measurement Protocol URL:

```
<img src="http://www.google-analytics.com/collect?...payload..." />
```

However, GET requests are limited to 2000 bytes for browser compatibility reasons (that's 2000 characters in the URL, unless there are double-byte characters, such as for Asian languages). Unlike GET, POST supports up to 8192 bytes in the payload. A POST request typically requires some kind of script to generate the request (as an extension of a back-end application, for example).

Payload Parameters

The "payload" refers to the data that is sent to GA with the HTTP request. It consists of a series of standardized parameters. For a GET request, these are appended to the URL as query parameters:

```
http://www.google-analytics.com/collect?v=1&tid=UA-XXXX-Y&cid=12345&t=pageview&dp=%2Fhome
```

In a POST request, the payload parameters are sent as the body of the request, in the same format as query parameters (key-value pairs separated by ampersands).

■ **Note**   Payload data should use URL encoding, meaning that characters such as spaces, slashes, and other reserved characters in the URL format should be replaced by encoded characters. For example, in the preceding URL, in the parameter dp, the page /home uses %2F to encode the slash. Typically, your programming or scripting language will have functions that encode and decode URLs.

The Measurement Protocol documentation covers all of the possible parameters to be used in the payload and their acceptable values. (You'll recognize them as all the same fields available in "Fields to Set" in a GA tag in GTM.) Every Measurement Protocol hit must contain at least these four parameters:

- *Protocol Version*: `v=1`. This value is always 1 (until GA updates the Measurement Protocol someday).

- *Tracking ID*: `tid=UA-12345-1`. The GA web property ID.

- *Client ID*: `cid=12345`. The client ID, corresponding to the client ID analytics.js stores in its cookie (more on this follows).

- *Hit Type*: `t=pageview`. The type of interaction; one of pageview, event, social, transaction, item, screenview, exception, timing. (The same types of interactions that you can choose from in GA tags in GTM.)

For different hit types, additional fields may be required. For example, if the hit type is pageview, the Page Path parameter (`dp`) should be set, and if the hit type is event, Event Category and Event Action (`ec` and `ea`) should be set. The available parameters include all the types of data in GA discussed in this book for the Web and mobile apps, including all the basics from pageviews and events down to highly customized information like custom dimensions and enhanced ecommerce data.

Client ID and User ID

Two fields used for aggregation of data by users bear special mention, the Client ID (`cid`) and User ID (`uid`).

The client ID typically represents a device identifier—in analytics.js on websites, it's the value stored in the cookie. For Measurement Protocol hits, depending on their source, you could set this to a new randomized ID, or to an existing client ID pulled from a cookie. For example, consider the following scenario:

1. A prospective customer comes to your website via a campaign link.

2. They browse around, but don't convert. Instead, they decide to call into your call center to complete their conversion.

3. They're presented with a phone number that is randomized from a pool of phone numbers.

4. Your call center receives the call from the phone number. The call center software integrates with the website to keep a correspondence of client IDs and phone numbers, and a Measurement Protocol hit is sent to GA with an event indicating that a phone call started.

5. The customer completes a purchase during the call. As the customer service representative enters this into the call center software, another Measurement Protocol hit is sent to GA with an event indicating the purchase.

Because this process uses the same client ID throughout, in GA you'll see a session by this user that spans from the Web to the phone. Pretty amazing!

User ID helps you take this one step further by providing an identifier for an individual *across* devices, even when interactions happen over time (that is, in multiple sessions). If you know a user's name, email address, or other information, you can link that to a persistent identifier (in your CRM system, for example) and any time that person is identified (by logging in to the website or mobile app, by calling into the call center, etc.), you'll know that it's the same person. (For more information on User ID, see Chapter 10.)

Request Data Outside the Payload

In addition to the payload parameters, the Measurement Protocol also uses several additional pieces of information from the HTTP request:

- The *IP address* from which the request was received, to assign geographical dimensions such as country and city.

- The *user agent* header, which indicates the type of browser and device making the request.

- The *time* the request is received, to assign the hit a date and time.

However, in some cases you might want to override these values. For example, suppose you're using the Measurement Protocol to collect data from your call center logging application, where customers call in to make a purchase. If all the requests come from an internal system on your own server, they'll all have the same IP address, but that doesn't accurately represent the geographic location of the customers who are calling.

There are payload parameters to override the IP address and/or geographic location and user agent, and to specify a latency gap for time (for offline hits that are sent later when connectivity is available, or for hits that are batched together and sent later):

- *IP Override*: The uip parameter can be used to specify an IP address. The standard GA processing for interpreting its location is then applied.

- *Geographic Override*: The geoid parameter can be used to specify a location. The values can be a two-letter country code,[1] or an AdWords location criterion ID,[2] which is a world-wide set of identifiers for countries, cities, and regions used for ad targeting in AdWords, and as geographic identifiers across a number of Google tools.

- *User Agent Override*: The ua parameter can be used to specify a user agent. The standard GA processing for determining the device type, operating system, and browser is then applied.

- *Queue Time*: The qt parameter can be used to specify a time (in milliseconds) that elapsed between when the data was collected and when it was sent. Hits with queue times greater than four hours may not be processed by GA.

Cache Busting

Browsers often cache requests—that is, if the browser makes a request that's identical to a previous one, the browser first checks whether the resource is in its cache, and if so, it loads from there and there is no reason to contact the server with a new HTTP request.

This obviously isn't what you intend with Measurement Protocol hits, however. If you make a second request for a hit that happens to have the same payload, it's because the user actually viewed that page a second time and you want the request to be sent to the server.

To ensure that requests to the Measurement Protocol aren't cached, you can use a parameter in the payload called a ***cachebuster***. (The analytics.js library automatically handles cache-busting, but using the Measurement Protocol, you need to take care of this yourself.) The parameter (z) just contains a random

---

[1]ISO 3166-1, which are also used in the language codes in the Audience ➤ Geo ➤ Languages report in GA.
[2]http://developers.google.com/analytics/devguides/collection/protocol/v1/geoid

number, so that requests that are otherwise identical are differentiated and requested from the server. For example, here are two pageview requests for the same page by the same client ID, but they are differentiated by a different, randomized value for the cachebuster parameter.

```
v=1&tid=UA-12345-1&cid=12345&t=pageview&dp=%2Fhome&z=384585985785
v=1&tid=UA-12345-1&cid=12345&t=pageview&dp=%2Fhome&z=214492387598
```

Validation

To test Measurement Protocol hits and ensure that they are formatted correctly, GA provides some prototyping and testing tools.

The Hit Builder tool provides a form that allows you to fill in values for payload fields to build a Measurement Protocol request (Figure 14-1).

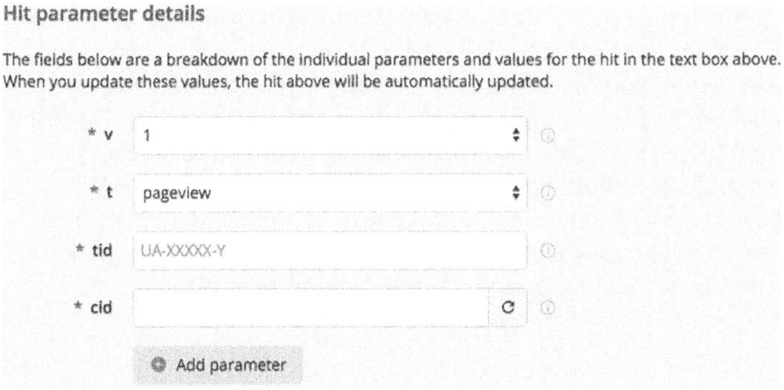

Hit parameter details

The fields below are a breakdown of the individual parameters and values for the hit in the text box above. When you update these values, the hit above will be automatically updated.

* v	1
* t	pageview
* tid	UA-XXXXX-Y
* cid	

⊕ Add parameter

Figure 14-1. *The Hit Builder tool for prototyping Measurement Protocol requests*

GA's Validation Server allows you to send a hit to test whether the payload contains the required parameters in the correct formats. You can send any Measurement Protocol hit to this endpoint to test it:

`http://www.google-analytics.com/`**`debug/collect`**

This endpoint functions just like the normal endpoint, with two differences:

- Data sent to the Validation Server endpoint will not show up in reports. It's only for testing purposes and will be discarded.

- The Validation Server sends a detailed response in JSON format, showing whether the request was valid and any error messages that were generated:

```
{
  "hitParsingResult": [ {
    "valid": false,
    "parserMessage": [ {
      "messageType": "ERROR",
      "description": "A value is required for parameter 'dp'. Please see
                      http://goo.gl/a8d4RP#dp for details.",
```

```
      "messageCode": "VALUE_REQUIRED",
      "parameter": "dp"
    } ],
    "hit": "GET /debug/collect?v=1\u0026t=pageview\u0026tid=UA-12345-1\u0026cid=12345 HTTP/1.1"
  } ]
}
```

You can test any Measurement Protocol hits you generate using the Validation Server first to ensure that they are formed correctly.

Data Processing in GA

Once data is received by GA (assuming it passes validation), it is treated just like any other data for the property. Filters and other settings are applied and the data is placed into reports in the views.

Note that there is currently no specialized reporting for Measurement Protocol data; it appears alongside web and app data (and can be filtered just like that data). For data sent using the Measurement Protocol to be associated with existing users in GA, you should include a client ID or user ID that matches an existing value in your web data (see Chapter 10).

It's up to you to decide how to interpret "pageviews" and other web-centric metrics in the context of Measurement Protocol data, and you should think about how you would like to use the data in GA before you design a solution to send it. Custom dimensions and metrics may be very helpful in recording qualitatively different kinds of data that do not necessarily fit into a web-centric paradigm (see Chapter 11), and custom reporting and segmentation may be useful in presenting this data in useful ways.

Summary

- The Measurement Protocol is a specification for sending data to Google Analytics from any source. It is a specification for an HTTP request containing a payload of data to be accepted by Google Analytics.

- The Measurement Protocol can be used to collect data from sources other than websites and mobile apps, such as back-end applications or environments where official SDKs are not available.

- The payload data can contain all of the same fields as web or mobile app hits. GA provides tools to prototype and validate the data. Once data is received by GA, it appears in reports just like data from websites and mobile apps.

CHAPTER 15

■ ■ ■

Using Google Analytics with BigQuery for Big Data Analysis

Google Analytics provides a wide set of reports and tools in its web interface. The standard reports are designed to provide answers to many of the most common questions about websites, while custom reports, segments, and other tools facilitate further exploration. However, there are some kinds of questions that can't be easily approached through the aggregated session data in GA's reports—especially applications like data mining and applying statistical models, which generally require disaggregated hit-level data. Some of the types of problems and scenarios that such tools can address include the following:

- Finding associations in behavior, such as "users who purchased product X also purchased product Y" or "users who read article X also read article Y".

- Sophisticated attribution modeling, especially models that incorporate additional conversions, marketing data, or customer data from outside GA.

- Algorithmic user segmentation into audiences and predictive models of customer value or likelihood to convert.

These techniques and the technical tools used to accomplish them typically fall under the umbrella of the term "Big Data". GA provides a conduit to access data for just such purposes by supporting an export of data, hit by hit, to another Google tool called BigQuery. BigQuery is a tool designed to make analyzing and querying large datasets easy and fast, without needing to worry about the underlying technologies and computing resources to support. This chapter examines the integration between GA and BigQuery, the data available, and how you can make use of it.

The GA integration with BigQuery is available *only to Google Analytics Premium subscribers.*

■ **Note** This chapter examines BigQuery and the tools it can provide to access and query GA data. The statistical models and data mining tools themselves are outside the scope of this discussion.

This chapter begins with an introduction to BigQuery and tools for accessing it. Further sections look at details of the query language and applying it to GA data within BigQuery. The final section takes a step back to the big picture, to discuss strategies for making use of the data available for BigQuery in applications like those discussed earlier.

About BigQuery

BigQuery is a tool that allows you to store, query, and extract data. It's a separate tool from GA and GTM, part of Google's Cloud Platform, but you can access it with a Google account login in the same way as other Google tools. Although there is a web interface for using BigQuery (which you'll see later in the chapter), the web interface is primarily for exploration and testing of queries. Typically, BigQuery would be used as a service that acts a source of information for other applications, much like any other database. Like any other database, it supports a query language to select subsets of data based on criteria of interest, and it returns the values for further processing in a report, visualization, statistical model, or other application.

■ **Note**   There are charges associated with storing and querying data in BigQuery.[1] The example queries in this chapter would cost you a few pennies to perform. Your Google Analytics Premium subscription includes a monthly credit for BigQuery expenses to offset usage charges, but if you exceed the monthly credit, you will be charged for any additional usage.

What BigQuery Is Not

BigQuery is not a polished set of reports. (After all, you already have those in GA!) It can be used with a variety of reporting and business intelligence tools to create reports, but there are no reporting capabilities built directly into BigQuery.

BigQuery is also not a traditional relational database. If you're already familiar with traditional relational databases and the SQL query language, you'll find it easy to pick up knowledge of BigQuery, but there are some differences. BigQuery is optimized to operate over large, distributed data sets, and its structure can include nesting and repeating values. Because of this, the BigQuery query language is "SQL-like" but does not conform in all ways to the SQL standard. Data in BigQuery tables cannot be changed or updated; a table may only be appended to.

GA and BigQuery Integration

Google Analytics Premium subscribers can contact their account manager to enable the GA-BigQuery integration. You can select one or more views in GA to be exported.

BigQuery is structured into a hierarchy of ***projects***, ***datasets***, and ***tables***. Typically, you have one project that contains all of your GA data. Each GA view you export is a separate dataset in BigQuery.

Once enabled, data from GA is exported on a regular basis to BigQuery. The data includes the details of each hit (pageview, event, etc.) in GA, arranged into sessions. (A later section in the chapter explores the schema used for GA data in more detail.) Each day's data is exported after the end of the day and becomes a separate table in the BigQuery dataset. There are also several intraday exports (at approximately 8-hour intervals) that are available before the table of data for the day becomes final, if you have a need to work with the current day's data before the day is complete.

---

[1]https://cloud.google.com/bigquery/pricing

Accessing BigQuery

BigQuery data can be accessed in multiple ways:

- Through a web interface where queries can be entered and results data viewed or downloaded. This is particularly useful for exploration and testing of the data.

- Through a command-line interface to enter queries and obtain results. This can be useful for one-off exports of data or simple automated scripting to retrieve data from BigQuery.

- Via APIs, which you can use with existing tools (such as Google Sheets or Tableau) to report and visualize data from BigQuery, or to write custom integrations with your own applications or export data to a data warehouse that resides elsewhere.

This chapter shows the web interface, but all the queries discussed work the same way across any of these methods of accessing BigQuery data.

Web Interface

If you're logged in with a Google account that has access to your BigQuery project, you can access the BigQuery web interface (see Figure 15-1).[2]

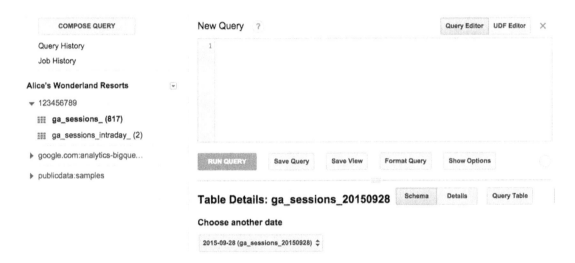

Figure 15-1. *BigQuery web interface, showing a dataset exported from GA*

The left-hand navigation shows the hierarchy of projects, datasets, and tables. The project in this example is named "Alice's Wonderland Resorts". There is a dataset (123456789), the name of which is the view ID number from GA for the view being exported. It contains tables that are named beginning with ga_sessions_ and then the date (as well as the intraday tables for the current day beginning with ga_sessions_intraday_).

---

[2]https://bigquery.cloud.google.com

There are also a few sample datasets included in this project. The dataset [publicdata:samples] is a set of general sample data included in all BigQuery projects. The dataset [google.com:analytics-bigquery:LondonCycleHelmet] is a sample dataset of GA data. It contains one table with one day's worth of data from an example bicycle ecommerce website, and it can be useful for exploring queries with a small set of data before you apply them to larger sets on your own website.

On the right, you can enter a query in the BigQuery SQL-like query syntax and retrieve the results. Here's a simple example query to try out:

```
SELECT
    hits.type,
    count(hits.hitNumber)
FROM
    [google.com:analytics-bigquery:LondonCycleHelmet.ga_sessions_20130910]
GROUP BY
    hits.type
```

This gets the count of hits by type from the sample dataset. (Don't worry too much about the syntax of this query just yet—you'll see more details of how the query language works shortly.) Figure 15-2 shows the results of this query in the BigQuery web interface.

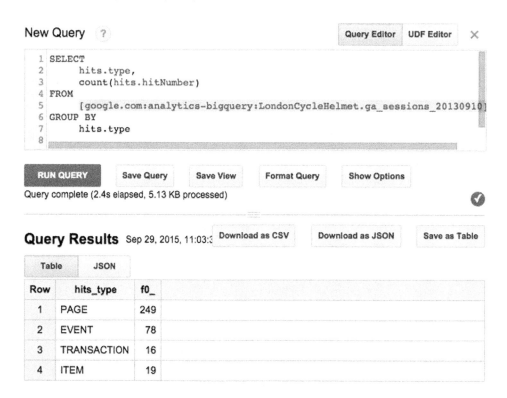

Figure 15-2. *Query results for a query entered in the web interface*

At the top, you can see the query entered. After selecting the Run Query button, BigQuery runs the query and displays the results below (a table with rows by hit type and a column of the count). Note that buttons above the results allow you to download as a CSV or JSON file, or to save the results as a new table in BigQuery.

GA Data Schema in BigQuery

The data that GA exports into BigQuery represent disaggregated, hit-level data for the selected view, after any filters for the view have been applied (see Chapter 8 for more information on filters). Each record in the table of data represents a session, and nested records within the session represent the hits (pageviews, events, etc.). You can select one of the tables in the web interface to see the details of the fields included in GA data (see Figure 15-3).

Table Details: ga_sessions_201: Schema   Details   Query Table

Schema

visitorId	INTEGER	NULLABLE	Describe this field...
visitNumber	INTEGER	NULLABLE	Describe this field...
visitId	INTEGER	NULLABLE	Describe this field...
visitStartTime	INTEGER	NULLABLE	Describe this field...
date	STRING	NULLABLE	Describe this field...
totals	RECORD	NULLABLE	Describe this field...
totals.visits	INTEGER	NULLABLE	Describe this field...
totals.hits	INTEGER	NULLABLE	Describe this field...
totals.pageviews	INTEGER	NULLABLE	Describe this field...
totals.timeOnSite	INTEGER	NULLABLE	Describe this field...
totals.bounces	INTEGER	NULLABLE	Describe this field...
totals.transactions	INTEGER	NULLABLE	Describe this field...
totals.transactionRevenue	INTEGER	NULLABLE	Describe this field...

Figure 15-3. *Schema details for a GA table in BigQuery as shown in the web interface*

The Schema tab shows the field names, structure, and type. You can also select the Details tab to see the data in the first few records in the table to get an idea of how it's filled in.

The schema for GA data is extensive, including over 150 fields that represent many of the pieces of information captured by GA, including information about each pageview, event, or other hit; session-level information such as the traffic source and geographic location; enhanced ecommerce data included with hits (see Chapter 7); and custom dimensions and metrics (see Chapter 11). The fields are named similarly enough to the dimension names in GA that you should have little trouble interpreting them, but the documentation for the schema gives additional clarification.[3]

---

[3]https://support.google.com/analytics/answer/3437719

The schema is a nested structure, where the names of nested fields are separated by a dot (`.`). For example, the `totals` record includes `totals.hits`, `totals.pageviews`, and a few other counts for totals for the entire session. The `trafficSource` record includes `trafficSource.source`, `trafficSource.medium`, and other traffic source dimensions. The most important nested record is `hits`, which is a repeatable record containing the data for each hit, such as `hits.type` (for the different hit types: pageviews, events, etc.), `hits.page.pagePath` (the URL path of the page), and so on. The values of a field can be a string, integer, Boolean (`true` or `false`), or other types. A field can have the value `null` if it is blank.

One major difference you'll notice in this data (versus the data in GA) is that it mostly consists of dimension values, with only a few basic metrics, and lacking many of the metrics you may commonly use in GA such as Bounce Rate, Time on Page, and many others. Since you have the disaggregated hit data in BigQuery, you can calculate whatever metrics you choose by whatever formulas you choose. You can re-create metrics from GA—like Bounce Rate and Time on Page—by calculating them, but you're also not limited by the metrics in GA—you could create new metric calculations like Revenue per User, for example.

Since the data in BigQuery represents the entirety of data in a GA view, queries are never subject to sampling, table row limits, or other limitations of reporting in the GA interface. (See Chapter 1 for more information on sampling.)

Another major advantage of the disaggregated data in BigQuery is detailed, hit-level data *by user*. You can look at a user's entire behavior over time (across many sessions) to classify them in detailed ways. Within GA, this is possible in a limited way by using segments, but user-based segments can only be applied over a limited time frame and are subject to sampling.

BigQuery's Query Language

BigQuery uses a modified SQL syntax to query datasets. If you're new to SQL and database query languages, this section provides some basic examples to get you started. If you are familiar with using SQL in databases such as MySQL, PostgreSQL, MS-SQL, or Oracle, you'll already know the basics of constructing a query, and the following examples provide guidance on where there are differences from more traditional SQL dialects.

For the examples, you are using the London Cycle Helmet sample dataset. The London Cycle Helmet dataset has a single table, [`google.com:analytics-bigquery:LondonCycleHelmet.ga_sessions_20130910`], which you'll use in all of these queries. You should have access to this sample dataset in your GA project in BigQuery.

■ **Note**   The London Cycle Helmet dataset uses a slightly older version of the schema than the current one used by GA. The current schema is backward compatible. You can run any of the following queries against your current Google Analytics exports.

A query is a statement of the desired results from the dataset that can include the following clauses:

```
SELECT
FROM
WHERE
GROUP BY
HAVING
ORDER BY
LIMIT
```

You can think of this as writing a sentence for the data you would like to retrieve:

```
SELECT some fields
FROM some tables
WHERE the record is interesting
GROUP BY some field I want to be unique
HAVING some aggregate I find interesting
ORDER BY some fields
LIMIT to the top so many
```

Let's begin with some basic examples to illustrate the clauses of this sentence and how they work.

■ **Note**   This chapter contains a collection of examples relevant to GA data in BigQuery, but it's not a comprehensive reference to the query language. The GA-BigQuery integration documentation[4] and the BigQuery documentation[5] contain more information and examples.

Selecting Data from Tables

The SELECT keyword allows a query to pick out specific fields FROM a table, rename fields, and perform calculations on data. SELECT and FROM are the two core clauses of any query.

Often, it's not practical or useful to look at every field in a table. Selecting only the fields you need declutters the results you'll examine, and decreases the amount of data and processing power required to complete the query. Using SELECT, you can use the field names (from the schema) or * as a wildcard to select all fields. (SELECT * is not usually recommended, because it is not allowed when there are multiple repeatable fields in a schema. See "Flattening Tables with Repeated Fields" later in this section.)

A very simple example of a query would be the following:

```
SELECT fullVisitorId, totals.hits
FROM    [google.com:analytics-bigquery:LondonCycleHelmet.ga_sessions_20130910]
```

This selects two fields (fullVisitorId, which corresponds to the client ID in GA, and totals.hits, which gives the number of hits in the session) from the London Cycle Helmets sample table. The results look something like this:

	fullVisitorId	totals_hits
1	380066991751227408	8
2	712553853382222331	12
3	881288060286722202	3
4	881288060286722202	1
5	881288060286722202	7

---

[4]https://support.google.com/analytics/topic/3416089
[5]https://cloud.google.com/bigquery/docs

Here just the first few results are shown. If you're using the web interface, it paginates through results showing a few at a time. (The LIMIT clause can also set a maximum number of rows returned; just end your query with LIMIT 5, for example.)

■ **Note** Capitalization and spacing are not important in SQL syntax. Feel free to insert line breaks as necessary to make your queries readable. It's also customary to capitalize the clause keywords like SELECT and FROM.

You can use the AS keyword to rename a field in results, like so:

```
SELECT fullVisitorId AS Client_ID, totals.hits AS Hits
FROM   [google.com:analytics-bigquery:LondonCycleHelmet.ga_sessions_20130910]
```

This would return the same results as previously, but the column headers now correspond to the names you chose:

	Client_ID	Hits
1	380066991751227408	8
2	712553853382222331	12
3	881288060286722202	3
4	881288060286722202	1
5	881288060286722202	7

It is helpful to give the results columns meaningful names, especially as you create new columns to represent new metrics.

Computation Functions

In addition to selecting the values of a field, you can also perform calculations on a field.

Computations can take fields in a single record, combine them, and return a result. For example, you can add, subtract, multiply, or divide numbers (using the operators +, -, *, /) or concatenate strings (using CONCAT()).

For example, suppose you'd like a unique identifier for each session. There's no field for this in the schema, but you can create one by concatenating the client ID (fullVisitorId) and the timestamp when the visit began (visitId):[6]

```
SELECT CONCAT(fullVisitorId, ".", STRING(visitId)) AS Session_ID
FROM   [google.com:analytics-bigquery:LondonCycleHelmet.ga_sessions_20130910]
```

---

[6]As noted in the schema documentation.

This example uses the CONCAT function to combine two field. Notice the insertion of a dot character between them for a visual indication of the parts. Also notice the use of STRING() to coerce the type of the visitId field to a string, since it's actually an integer field (as noted in the schema). The results look like this:

	Session_ID
1	380066991751227408.1378805776
2	712553853382222331.1378804218
3	881288060286722202.1378803865
4	881288060286722202.1378804975
5	881288060286722202.1378805870

There's a second type of computation available, called *aggregate functions*, as they aggregate values from multiple records into a single row in the results, by counting, averaging or summing values (using COUNT(), AVG(), or SUM()), among others. For example, if you wanted the total number of hits for the day, you could use the following query:

```
SELECT SUM(totals.hits) AS Hits
FROM   [google.com:analytics-bigquery:LondonCycleHelmet.ga_sessions_20130910]
```

This produces the following result:

	Hits
1	362

Notice that using the aggregate function combined all the records of the table into a single result. You can use a similar approach for other metrics. For example, suppose you wanted the bounce rate. You might create a query like this:

```
SELECT AVG(totals.bounces) AS Bounce_Rate
FROM   [google.com:analytics-bigquery:LondonCycleHelmet.ga_sessions_20130910]
```

But here is the result you'll get:

	Bounce_Rate
1	1

A bounce rate of 100%—that's not good! But it's also not correct. Unfortunately (or fortunately, depending on your needs), **aggregate functions do not include null values**, and the value of totals.bounces is 1 for a bounced session and null if not a bounced session (as documented in the schema). Instead, you can either convert the nulls to 0s, or count the 1s and divide by the total sessions, like in this example:

```
SELECT COUNT(totals.bounces)/COUNT(totals.visits) AS Bounce_Rate
FROM   [google.com:analytics-bigquery:LondonCycleHelmet.ga_sessions_20130910]
```

Which gives this result:

```
     Bounce_Rate
1    0.1746031746031746
```

Ah, a bounce rate of 17.5%—much better!

Table Date Ranges

So far the examples have only used a FROM clause with a single table. However, as you've seen, the GA data includes a single table per day, so if you'd like to aggregate data across multiple days, you'll need to query the *union* of multiple tables, treating them as one big table. You can union tables in a query by including them in the FROM clause with commas.

■ **Caution**   If you're experienced with SQL, note that commas in BigQuery indicate unions, not joins. This is one of the major deviations of BigQuery from standard SQL syntax.

Here's an example:

```
SELECT
    fullVisitorId, totals.hits
FROM
    [google.com:analytics-bigquery:LondonCycleHelmet.ga_sessions_20130910],
    [google.com:analytics-bigquery:LondonCycleHelmet.ga_sessions_20130911]
```

■ **Note**   The London Cycle Helmet dataset contains only a single table for one date (September 10, 2013), so this example will fail. Try it on some dates in your own dataset.

That syntax is fine if you just want to list out two or three days, but beyond that, it becomes cumbersome. To help, BigQuery also includes the TABLE_DATE_RANGE() function (and its sibling TABLE_DATE_RANGE_STRICT()). This allows you to match a range of dates. TABLE_DATE_RANGE() works by taking a prefix and appending the dates for each day in the range it's given, unioning all the tables together. (TABLE_DATE_RANGE_STRICT() works similarly, but results in an error if any of the tables in the date range are missing.)

You'll notice that all of your table names in a GA export begin with ga_sessions_ and then include a date in YYYYMMDD format. You can use TABLE_DATE_RANGE() to union across these tables like so:

```
SELECT
    fullVisitorId, totals.hits
FROM
    TABLE_DATE_RANGE(
        [google.com:analytics-bigquery:LondonCycleHelmet.ga_sessions_],
        TIMESTAMP('2013-09-01'),
        TIMESTAMP('2013-09-30'))
```

Flattening Tables with Repeated Fields

Also unlike a traditional relational database, in BigQuery you have repeatable fields. For example, the `hits` record repeats a number of times within a session, with different values each time.

The FLATTEN expression takes a repeated fields and creates one row of results for each value of the repeated field (with all other fields duplicated). BigQuery automatically FLATTENs results if you have a single repeated field in your SELECT clause:

```
SELECT
    CONCAT(fullVisitorId, ".", STRING(visitId)) AS Session_ID,
    hits.page.pagePath AS Page
FROM
    [google.com:analytics-bigquery:LondonCycleHelmet.ga_sessions_20130910]
```

	Session_ID	Page
1	380066991751227408.1378805776	/vests/
2	380066991751227408.1378805776	/vests/orange.html
3	380066991751227408.1378805776	/vests/orange.html
4	380066991751227408.1378805776	/login.html
5	380066991751227408.1378805776	/login.html

This is the same as using the following query, with an explicit FLATTEN statement:

```
SELECT
    CONCAT(fullVisitorId, ".", STRING(visitId)) AS Session_ID,
    hits.page.pagePath AS Page
FROM
    FLATTEN([google.com:analytics-bigquery:LondonCycleHelmet.ga_sessions_20130910], hits)
```

The FLATTEN statement is implicit when there is a single repeated field in the SELECT query (as with hits in this example). However, if you wanted to combine multiple repeated fields, such as both hits and customDimensions, you must first FLATTEN the table on one or the other:

```
SELECT
    CONCAT(fullVisitorId, ".", STRING(visitId)) AS Session_ID,
    hits.page.pagePath AS Page,
    customDimensions.index AS CD_Index,
    customDimensions.value AS CD_Value
FROM
    FLATTEN([google.com:analytics-bigquery:LondonCycleHelmet.ga_sessions_20130910], hits)
```

Here are the results (showing some additional rows to see some interesting data in the CD_Index and CD_Value columns):

	Session_ID	Page	CD_Index	CD_Value
1	3800669917512274408.1378805776	/helmets/foldable.html	*null*	*null*
2	3800669917512274408.1378805776	/helmets/foldable.html	*null*	*null*
3	3800669917512274408.1378805776	/helmets/foldable.html	*null*	*null*
4	3800669917512274408.1378805776	/	*null*	*null*
5	3800669917512274408.1378805776	/vests/	*null*	*null*
6	3800669917512274408.1378805776	/vests/yellow.html	*null*	*null*
7	3800669917512274408.1378805776	/vests/yellow.html	*null*	*null*
8	3800669917512274408.1378805776	/	*null*	*null*
9	7125538533822222331.1378804218	/vests/	2	Bronze
10	7125538533822222331.1378804218	/vests/	3	Yes
11	7125538533822222331.1378804218	/vests/orange.html	2	Bronze
12	7125538533822222331.1378804218	/vests/orange.html	3	Yes
13	7125538533822222331.1378804218	/vests/orange.html	2	Bronze
14	7125538533822222331.1378804218	/vests/orange.html	3	Yes
15	7125538533822222331.1378804218	/login.html	2	Bronze

If you make a query with multiple repeated fields and don't properly FLATTEN them, you'll receive an error:

```
Cannot output multiple independently repeated fields at the same time.
```

Ordering by Fields

Often you'd like information in a specific order: users ordered by the number of pages they've viewed, for example. You can sort the results using the ORDER BY clause to sort in ASCending order (smallest to largest) or DESCending (largest to smallest) order. ORDER BY is useful with LIMIT to, say, get the top (or bottom) 5 values.

```
SELECT
    CONCAT(fullVisitorId, ".", STRING(visitId)) AS Session_ID,
    totals.pageviews AS Pageviews
FROM
    [google.com:analytics-bigquery:LondonCycleHelmet.ga_sessions_20130910]
ORDER BY
    Pageviews DESC
LIMIT 5
```

	Session_ID	Pageviews
1	6865576331513008945.1378805428	15
2	7715166900416604175.1378805776	12
3	8266000033835867941.1378803597	10
4	7236424239009423246.1378806189	10
5	5682534891274575276.1378819500	9

Note that, after renaming a field with AS, you can use the name you've created, as shown in the ORDER BY clause with Pageviews.

Grouping Fields

So far, you've seen how to retrieve fields from tables, and aggregate over the entire set of data. Now let's take a look at how to aggregate values with the data GROUPed BY a field.

For example, so far you've seen how to query the aggregated *total* pageviews for the site, and pageviews *by session* (for each record of the table). What if you wanted the number of pageviews *per user* (based on fullVisitorId)? That's what the GROUP BY clause is for: applying an aggregate function for each row with a specific value in a field. You can apply the SUM() aggregate function, GROUPing BY user:

```
SELECT
    fullVisitorId AS Client_ID,
    SUM(totals.pageviews) AS Pageviews,
    COUNT(visitId) AS Sessions
FROM
    [google.com:analytics-bigquery:LondonCycleHelmet.ga_sessions_20130910]
GROUP BY
    Client_ID
ORDER BY
    Pageviews DESC
LIMIT 5
```

	Client_ID	Pageviews	Sessions
1	68655763311513008945	15	1
2	9007483028904009722	12	3
3	8266000033835867941	12	2
4	77151669004166604175	12	1
5	3878411695083249177	11	2

Now that you've totaled pageviews for each user (Client_ID), even where some users had multiple sessions! For example, row 2 in the results shows a user that had a total of 12 pageviews across three different sessions within the days queried.

Note that if you SELECT both a field value (like fullVisitorId) and aggregate functions (like SUM(totals.pageviews)), you must GROUP BY the field value. The query wouldn't make sense otherwise, and you'll receive an error message.

Finding Data Where a Condition Is Met

Often you might be interested not in the entirety of the data, but in a subset of it: a particular user, page, traffic source, and so forth. Similar to building a segment in GA, you can use the WHERE clause in BigQuery to restrict the query to data that meet one or more criteria.

For example, consider this query:

```
SELECT
    CONCAT(fullVisitorId, ".", STRING(visitId)) AS Session_ID,
    totals.pageviews AS Pageviews
FROM
    [google.com:analytics-bigquery:LondonCycleHelmet.ga_sessions_20130910]
WHERE
    trafficSource.medium="organic"
```

This is the same query you used previously to see pageviews by session, with the added WHERE clause to select only sessions where the traffic medium label is "organic". You can combine multiple condition in the WHERE clause using OR and AND.

Further Google Analytics Examples

Now that you've seen the basic syntax of queries in BigQuery, here are a few more complex examples with practical applications for GA data.

Bounce Rate by Landing Page

An earlier query calculated the overall bounce rate. Let's try that, grouping by landing page:

```
SELECT
    hits.page.pagePath AS Landing Page,
    COUNT(totals.bounces)/COUNT(totals.hits) AS Bounce_Rate,
    COUNT(totals.bounces) AS Bounces,
    COUNT(totals.hits) AS Entrances
FROM
    [google.com:analytics-bigquery:LondonCycleHelmet.ga_sessions_20130910]
WHERE
    hits.type="PAGE" AND hits.hitNumber=1
GROUP BY
    Landing Page
ORDER BY
    Entrances DESC
```

	Landing Page	Bounce_Rate	Bounces	Entrances
1	/	0.13043478260869565	3	23
2	/helmets/foldable.html	0.25	3	12
3	/helmets/	0.2222222222222222	2	9
4	/vests/	0.16666666666666666	1	6
5	/vests/orange.html	0.3333333333333333	1	3

The WHERE clause in this query is an example of combining two condition by AND. It uses hits.type="Page" and hits.hitNumber=1 to get only landing pages (the URL of the first pageview of the session). Note that this query is automatically FLATTENed, since you're selecting from the repeating field hits.

Segmenting by a Custom Dimension

Custom dimensions are included in the GA data in BigQuery as a repeating field with an index and value. (See Chapter 11 for more information about custom dimensions.) One common use for custom dimensions is segmentation: using a custom dimension value to define a particular audience in whom you are interested.

Segmentation is easy enough to do with a field in a WHERE clause (such as the trafficSource.medium example previously), but it's a little more complex with a custom dimension, in a repeated field in two parts.

In the London Cycle Helmet data, there are several custom dimensions. The custom dimension with index 2 is a user-scoped custom dimension for customer type, where the values can be Bronze or Platinum, reflecting a preferred customer status. (Null or no value for this dimension would represent a regular customer.)

Here's a query that finds the users who have Platinum status:

```
SELECT
    fullVisitorId AS Client_ID,
    LAST(IF(
        hits.customDimensions.index=2,
        hits.customDimensions.value,
        "Regular")) WITHIN RECORD AS Customer_Type
FROM [google.com:analytics-bigquery:LondonCycleHelmet.ga_sessions_20130910]
HAVING Customer_Type = "Platinum"
```

This query gives an example of several new concepts:

- IF() is a function that takes a condition, a value to return if true, and a value to return if false. In this example, it returns a value only for a custom dimension with an index of 2.

- LAST() is an aggregation function (like SUM(), COUNT(), etc.) taking the last sequential value. In this example, it returns the last value of the custom dimension (in case someone upgraded from Bronze to Platinum status during their session, for example).

- WITHIN RECORD allows us to use an aggregation function within a single record (in this case, using LAST() to get the last value within the session).

- HAVING is similar to WHERE but can be used to filter results from aggregate function. (WHERE defines conditions for the records to be included in SELECT statement, so aggregate function values can't be used in a WHERE clause.)

Metrics for Custom Dimension Values

Beyond the segmentation in the previous example, you may desire to compare metrics among the values for a dimension, aggregating across a field with more complex selection criteria. Here's an example:

```
SELECT
    Customer_Type,
    COUNT(fullVisitorId) AS Users,
    SUM(totals.transactionRevenue)/1000000 AS Revenue,
    SUM(totals.transactionRevenue)/1000000/COUNT(fullVisitorId) AS Revenue_per_User
FROM
    (SELECT
        fullVisitorId,
        totals.transactionRevenue,
        LAST(IF(
            hits.customDimensions.index=2,
            hits.customDimensions.value,
            "Regular")) WITHIN RECORD as Customer_Type
    FROM [google.com:analytics-bigquery:LondonCycleHelmet.ga_sessions_20130910])
GROUP BY Customer_Type
```

	Customer_Type	Users	Revenue	Revenue_per_User
1	Regular	43	104.12	2.4213953488372093
2	Bronze	12	44.98	3.748333333333333
3	Platinum	8	57.13	7.14125

It turns out, the Platinum customers are worth about twice as much as Bronze customers and about 3 times as much as regular customers, on average. Cool!

This query gives an example of a new concept, the sub-select. Rather than select from a table, the FROM clause can include a nested SELECT statement. In this case, it's used to select a few values (including the custom dimension for customer type from the previous example). Then the outer SELECT clause aggregates across those values and groups by customer type.

Pivoting Dimensions

Finally, let's look at constructing a pivot, to see the intersection of some metric between two different dimensions. For example, suppose you'd like to see product purchases by customer type. Here's an example query:

```
SELECT
    Sku,
    SUM(IF(Customer_Type="Bronze", Quantity, 0)) AS Bronze,
    SUM(IF(Customer_Type="Platinum", Quantity, 0)) AS Platinum,
    SUM(IF(Customer_Type IS NULL, Quantity, 0)) AS none
FROM
  (SELECT
      hits.item.productSku AS Sku,
      hits.item.itemQuantity AS Quantity,
      LAST(IF(
          hits.customDimensions.index=2,
          hits.customDimensions.value,
          NULL)) WITHIN RECORD AS Customer_Type
    FROM [google.com:analytics-bigquery:LondonCycleHelmet.ga_sessions_20130910])
WHERE Sku IS NOT NULL
GROUP BY Sku
```

	Sku	Bronze	Platinum	none
1	VEST-ORANGE-4	2	0	2
2	HELM-HEAVY-2	3	0	1
3	HELM-FOLD-1	0	2	4
4	VEST-YELLOW-5	0	1	2
5	HELM-LIGHT-3	0	2	0

The results place the product SKUs in the rows and the customer types in the columns, with the values the quantity purchased.

This example uses the sub-select concept from the previous example and uses IF() in aggregate functions to pivot the data by customer type. Additionally, the expressions IS NULL and IS NOT NULL can be helpful to exclude blank fields or treat them differently, as seen here.

Joining Data

The foregoing examples have used a single table or set of tables, all with the same schema. Sometimes the most interesting applications of GA data in BigQuery involve combining it with data from other sources. (See the next section for more discussion of such applications.) BigQuery, like other database systems, supports the JOIN statement to combine multiple tables or queries.

As an example, suppose you have data about refunds (from your order processing system) that you'd like to combine with the ecommerce transactions in GA to get a better understanding of revenue, net of returns. The London Cycle Helmet dataset actually includes a sample table, refunds_201309, with just such information. Let's take a look at a query using JOIN to combine this with the GA data:

```
SELECT
    hits.transaction.transactionId AS Transaction_ID,
    hits.transaction.transactionRevenue/1000000 AS Revenue,
    Refund_data.RefundAmount AS Refunded,
    hits.transaction.transactionRevenue/1000000- Refund_data.RefundAmount AS Net_Revenue
FROM FLATTEN([google.com:analytics-bigquery:LondonCycleHelmet.ga_sessions_20130910],hits) AS GA_data
JOIN
    (SELECT TransactionId, RefundAmount
    FROM [google.com:analytics-bigquery:LondonCycleHelmet.refunds_201309]) AS Refund_data
    ON GA_data.hits.transaction.transactionId = Refund_data.TransactionId
WHERE hits.type = "TRANSACTION"
```

	Transaction_ID	Revenue	Refunded	Net_Revenue
1	LCH75081220828	11.15	11.15	0.0
2	LCH99499967532	7.56	7.56	0.0
3	LCH69093459403	12.99	12.99	0.0
4	LCH59885020485	12.99	12.99	0.0
5	LCH62189793867	21.15	10.0	11.15

The JOIN statement includes a SELECT clause FROM the second table, with the ON clause indicating the shared value between the two tables to join them.

The results include the transaction ID, which is the value shared between the JOINed tables, with the revenue from GA and the refund amount from the refunds table, and a calculation of the net revenue as the difference between them.

■ **Note** The example data uses basic ecommerce (rather than enhanced ecommerce; see Chapter 7 for details on the differences). If your site uses enhanced ecommerce, you'll need to change the query to use the transaction ID from the enhanced ecommerce data.

This is an example of what's called an INNER JOIN, meaning only records with corresponding values in *both* datasets are included in the results. Like other SQL dialects, BigQuery also supports OUTER JOIN (LEFT, RIGHT, or FULL) and CROSS JOIN capabilities.

■ **Note**   If you're familiar with JOINs in relational databases, you should be aware that they work somewhat differently in BigQuery. BigQuery works most efficiently on nested, de-normalized record sets and is not optimized for a normalized structure. You should *not* normalize datasets before loading them into BigQuery, and you should use JOINs carefully.

Strategies for Using GA and BigQuery in Big Data Analysis

Now that you've seen some of the capabilities of BigQuery and how it can query GA data, let's take a step back and look at the big picture. How does BigQuery fit into an overall strategy for getting the most out of your data about your website, marketing, and customer relationships?

BigQuery can be both a destination and a source for data (see Figure 15-4). On the left, data flows into BigQuery. Just as GA data can be exported to BigQuery, other systems might also be sources of data, turning BigQuery into a repository for many types of data you'd like to combine and query together.

On the right, data is extracted from BigQuery. Sets of data assembled in BigQuery queries can be routed to an alternative data warehouse system, consumed by reporting or business intelligence tools, or serve as inputs to statistical modeling or data mining algorithms.

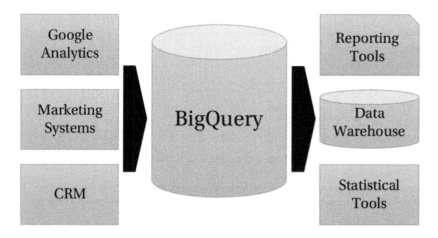

Figure 15-4. *Architecture for data processing with web analytics and other data in BigQuery*

Importing Data into BigQuery

Data from other sources can be imported into BigQuery to be joined with GA data. There are many potential applications:

- Any type of data that can be used with Data Import (see Chapter 12) could alternatively be imported and JOINed with GA data in BigQuery. Advantages to this approach include the ability to enrich historical data (where Data Import only applies to newly gathered data), and the ability to make use of personally identifiable information (which is prohibited within GA).

- Activity stream data like that in GA, from other sources. For example, your email marketing system may contain a record of emails sent to, opened by, and clicked on by a user. Your CRM may contain a timeline of interactions with a user over the phone or in person. You may have records of direct mail or other marketing targeted at a user. BigQuery is a location where all of this information can be combined for identified users.

BigQuery, along with other Google Cloud Platform (GCP) products like App Engine, Cloud Storage, and Dataflow, offers a number of APIs to automate the import of data from such sources.

Using BigQuery as a data warehouse in this manner has several advantages over more traditional data warehouse systems. BigQuery is a fast and reliable engine for querying over large datasets, based on Google's experience and needs for such tools, and represents a next-generation solution from tools such as Hadoop. GCP products run in the cloud, reducing the hardware management challenges of on-premise solutions. Additionally, BigQuery and some of the other key GCP products are fully-managed services, taking much of the guesswork out of provisioning and maintaining a solution.

Extracting Data for Use in Other Applications

Data from BigQuery may also serve as a source for other tools:

- Data from BigQuery may be copied, in whole or in part, into an alternative data warehouse system.

- Reporting, visualization, and business intelligence tools may access data for constructing reports or dashboards. Simple solutions include accessing BigQuery data in Google Sheets. The popular data exploration and visualization tool Tableau offers BigQuery as a data source. Many business intelligence platforms can access BigQuery as a source database.

- Statistical modeling and data mining tools could use query result data from BigQuery as inputs to algorithms for predictive analysis, data reduction, segmentation, association and clustering, and more. This is one of the most fruitful opportunities for using disaggregated GA data in BigQuery, since these kinds of analysis are largely not possible with aggregate data. The statistical programming language R and the Pandas library in Python, the most common toolsets for these applications, both support BigQuery as a data source.

Summary

- BigQuery is a Google Cloud Platform tool that acts as a database that is optimized for queries across large datasets. It uses a SQL-like query language, although it differs from traditional relational databases in some ways. It is accessible through a web interface, a command-line tool, and APIs.

- Google Analytics data can be exported in a disaggregated, hit-level form to BigQuery for Google Analytics Premium subscribers.

- BigQuery can act as a data warehouse for Google Analytics data as well as other data about marketing activities and customer relationships. The outputs of BigQuery can be used to feed data to reporting tools, other data warehouse systems, and statistical models.

Google Tag Manager and Google Analytics APIs

> *But Alice had got so much into the way of expecting nothing but out-of-the-way things to happen, that it seemed quite dull and stupid for life to go on in the common way.*
>
> —Lewis Carroll, *Alice's Adventures in Wonderland*

This book has primarily focused on using the GTM and GA web interfaces for configuration to get data into our reports. However, it bears mentioning that both tools offer APIs for configuration and getting out data.

An *application programming interface* (API) is simply a standardized way for a third-party application or script to read or write data to another tool. Interfacing with an API generally requires facility in a programming or scripting language, such as Java or Python, although there are a number of lightweight possibilities (HTML and JavaScript solutions with the Embed API, for example) for less-proficient developers. This appendix provides an overview of the available APIs and discusses how they can be used, but it does not contain in-depth examples of programming using these APIs. There is extensive documentation and sample code available, and helpful tools if you'd like to explore further.[1]

There is also an existing ecosystem of third-party products, both free and paid, that make use of these APIs. You can find a directory of products that integrate with GA and GTM in the GA partner apps gallery.[2]

Google API Basics

Google provides APIs for many of its products. Most of these APIs share a common infrastructure and design pattern. Some of the common features include the following:

- **Authorization:** Google uses OAuth authorization to provide access to your accounts (equivalent to signing in with your email and password on the website). OAuth provides functionality both for client-side authentication (for scenarios where the user has the appropriate level of access and logs into the product) and for server-side authentication (for scenarios such as automated dashboard updates, scheduled data pipelines, etc.).

---

[1]**GTM:** https://developers.google.com/tag-manager/api/v1/ **GA:** https://developers.google.com/analytics/devguides/reporting/ and https://developers.google.com/analytics/devguides/config/.
[2]https://www.google.com/analytics/partners/search/apps.

- **Client libraries:** The APIs are REST APIs and can be accessed via HTTP by any method. However, official client libraries are available in a number of languages. Coverage varies by API and language. Typically, Java and Python have the most complete libraries and documentation.

- **Quotas:** The APIs have quotas on the number of requests that can be made in a given time period. You can manage your quota usage through the Google API Console.[3] Quota adjustments can be requested if needed for a particular application.

With the Google APIs on a common infrastructure, integrations between GA/GTM and other Google tools—such as Google Sheets and Google Cloud Platform—are simplified. Although the APIs work from any tool or environment, it is common to use multiple Google-provided tools and systems, where appropriate, to achieve your ends with a minimum of bolting components together.

Google Tag Manager API

The GTM API accesses and updates tags, triggers, and variables. As such, it's the basis for convenience tools for setting up containers without using the web interface: making copies of containers, performing automated changes across many containers, and so forth. Remember, GTM doesn't contain any data; it only enables it to be sent to other tools (like GA), so GTM's APIs are focused entirely on configuration.

GTM's API can do all the same things that we can do in the web interface: create accounts and containers; assign permissions; set up tags, triggers, and variables; and publish and manage versions.

GTM Container JSON Format

The GTM API uses a standardized JSON object format to represent a container version's settings, tags, triggers, and variables. This JSON object format is specified in the GTM documentation[4] and it is used in the GTM API to represent the contents of the container or to update a container with new settings, tags, triggers, or variables.

We can also export and import containers from within the GTM interface using this same JSON format. These options are found the container settings of the GTM Admin area (see Figure A-1).

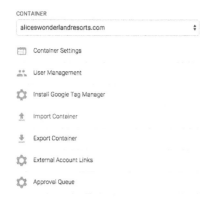

Figure A-1. *Import and export GTM containers in the container settings menu. Google Analytics APIs*

---

[3]https://console.developers.google.com/project

[4]https://developers.google.com/tag-manager/api/v1/reference/accounts/containers/versions

Google Analytics APIs

Google Analytics has two types of APIs: configuration and reporting.

- **Reporting:** The reporting APIs access the same data available in GA's standard and custom reports. You can choose the dimensions and metrics, date ranges, and filtering and sorting options, and apply segments to obtain data from GA, just like in the web reporting interface.

- **Configuration:** Like the GTM API, GA's configuration APIs focus on setup—the things that can be done in GA's Admin area, such as setting user permissions, linking AdWords accounts, setting up views and filters, and creating goal conversions.

Reporting APIs

The main reporting API is the Core Reporting API, which accesses the majority of data in GA. It's supplemented by the Multi-Channel Funnels Reporting API and the Real-Time Reporting API, which access alternative types of data. The Embed API and Metadata API provide additional convenience features around the Core Reporting API.

Core Reporting API

The Core Reporting API allows access to the same data available to standard and custom reports in the GA web reporting interface. The ability to access this data programmatically opens a world of possibilities for custom reporting and dashboarding, integrating GA data into applications or web content, joining with marketing channel or internal application data, and more.

The Core Reporting API is accessed by specifying a query in a request. The API responds with a table of results for that query. Queries in the Core Reporting API have a number of options; an overview follows.

Specifying a View

Each query must specify the ID of a view in GA from which you'd like to pull data. (Of course, the authorized user must have access to that view.) You can find the view ID in the view settings in the Admin area of GA, or by using the Management API.

Dimensions & Metrics

Just as reports in GA's web interface are made up of dimensions and metrics, so are queries in the Core Reporting API. Every query must have at least one metric, and can contain up to ten metrics and seven dimensions.

Not all dimensions and metrics are compatible in the same query. In the GA documentation, there's a tool called the Dimensions & Metrics Explorer.[5] It allows you to see all of the names and descriptions of dimensions and metrics available, along with their names in the GA web reporting interface and their compatibility in API queries. The names of dimensions and metrics in the Core Reporting API are prefixed with ga: (e.g., ga:pagePath or ga:sessions).

---

[5]https://developers.google.com/analytics/devguides/reporting/core/dimsmets

Sort, Filter, and Segment

A Core Reporting API query can be sorted by any of the included dimensions or metrics in ascending or descending order. (Alphabetical order is used for dimensions except dates, which are sorted chronologically; numerical order is used for metrics.) If no sort order is specified, GA sorts by the first dimension, which is almost never what we want! Typically, you're interested in sorting by a basic metric such as `ga:sessions` or `ga:pageviews`, in descending order.

Like a report in the web interface, you can filter the rows of the query result. Filters can include or exclude rows based on a dimension or metric value, including regular expression matches for text. They can be combined with logical AND and OR.

Additionally, like reports in the web interface, you can apply segments. You can select from the built-in segments, a segment you've previously created in the web interface for your user login, or specify the criteria for a segment on the fly.

Date Ranges, Results, and Pagination

Each query includes a time period. The API supports some common shorthand, such as `today`, `yesterday`, and `30daysAgo`. Or you can specify a date range.

By default, the query returns 1,000 rows of results (with whatever sort order is specified). You can specify a number of rows to return from 1 and 10,000. If there are more than 10,000 rows, you can specify a starting row for a request. So, for example, you could request the first 10,000 rows, and then make a second request for rows beginning with 10,001 (up to 20,000), and so on.

Query Explorer Tool

Basically, anything you can imagine doing in a custom report in the GA web interface can also be done via the Core Reporting API. A good tool for exploring the capabilities of the Core Reporting API is the Query Explorer Tool.[6] This tool (Figure A-2) uses a system of drop-down menus to fill in a Core Reporting API request, which you can then submit and see the results (or download in a text file).

---

[6]`https://ga-dev-tools.appspot.com/query-explorer/`

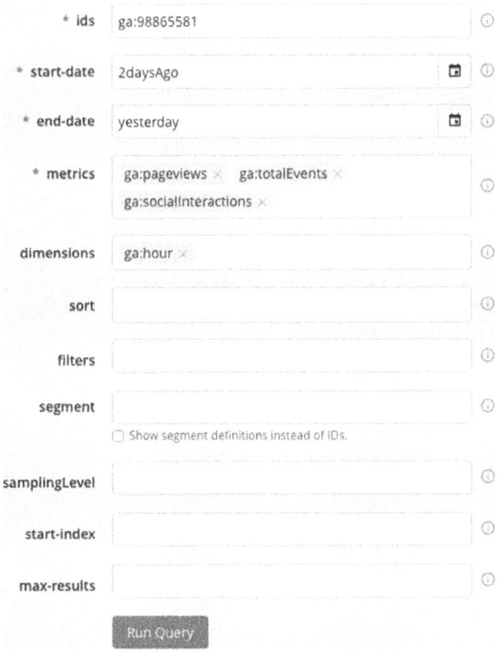

* ids	ga:98865581		ⓘ
* start-date	2daysAgo	🗓	ⓘ
* end-date	yesterday	🗓	ⓘ
* metrics	ga:pageviews × ga:totalEvents × ga:socialInteractions ×		ⓘ
dimensions	ga:hour ×		ⓘ
sort			ⓘ
filters			ⓘ
segment			ⓘ
	☐ Show segment definitions instead of IDs.		
samplingLevel			ⓘ
start-index			ⓘ
max-results			ⓘ

Run Query

Figure A-2. *The Query Explorer Tool is a good way to begin exploring what's possible in the Core Reporting API*

Multi-Channel Funnels Reporting API

The Multi-Channel Funnels Reporting API allows access to the data available in the reports through Conversions ➤ Multi-Channel Funnels in GA. This data deals with traffic sources over multiple sessions leading up to a conversion.

Since this API deals with multi-session data, accessing and handling this data is slightly different from the Core Reporting API (which is based on individual sessions), but its applications are similar: customized reporting and dashboarding, integration with marketing channel data, and so forth. Dimensions and metrics in the Multi-Channel Funnels Reporting API use the mcf: prefix.

Real-Time Reporting API

The Real-Time API allows access to the data available in the real-time reports in GA, including pages, events, goal conversions, geographic locations, and traffic sources. This is a more limited set of data than is available in the Core Reporting API, but unlike that data, it is available in real time. Accessing this data programmatically enables the possibility of real-time dashboarding or alerting. Dimensions and metrics in the Real-Time Reporting API use the rt: prefix.

Embed API

The Embed API is a set of JavaScript functions that provide a wrapper of additional features around the Core Reporting API. It includes a set of components to easily accomplish the following:

- Authorize a user and select from available accounts, properties, and views.

- Run queries against the Core Reporting API.

- Chart the results using Google Charts.

The Embed API is a good starting point if you're just beginning to explore the GA reporting APIs, because it uses JavaScript, it is easily tested and iterated in a web browser, it handles the heavy lifting with OAuth, and it provides built-in visualization capabilities for the data (Figure A-3).

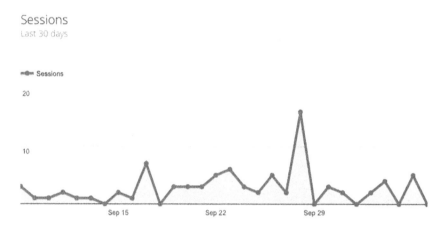

Figure A-3. *A chart created with the Embed API in fewer than 50 lines of HTML and JavaScript*

Metadata API

The Metadata API is a convenience API for GA that lists the dimensions and metrics available in the Core Reporting API. This is similar to the Dimensions & Metrics Explorer tool mentioned previously, but it allows programmatic access to this information.

Configuration APIs

There are two configuration APIs for GA.

Management API

The Management API is used to access and update configuration settings in GA, including the following:

- Create, access, and update the settings of web properties.

- Create, access, and update the settings of views.

- Add and update user permissions.

- Create, access, and update filters and apply them to views.

- Create, access, and update goal conversions.

- Add and update AdWords links.

- Create, access, and update custom dimensions, metrics, and data sources.

- Create, access, and update Content Experiments.

- Create and retrieve unsampled reports (GA Premium only).

Provisioning API

The Provisioning API can be used to create accounts in GA (which can then be managed via the Management API). It is intended for automating large-scale deployments of GA and is available only to invited partners.

Index

W, X, Y, Z

Get the eBook for only $5!

Why limit yourself?

Now you can take the weightless companion with you wherever you go and access your content on your PC, phone, tablet, or reader.

Since you've purchased this print book, we're happy to offer you the eBook in all 3 formats for just $5.

Convenient and fully searchable, the PDF version enables you to easily find and copy code—or perform examples by quickly toggling between instructions and applications. The MOBI format is ideal for your Kindle, while the ePUB can be utilized on a variety of mobile devices.

To learn more, go to www.apress.com/companion or contact support@apress.com.

Apress®
THE EXPERT'S VOICE™

Printed by Printforce, the Netherlands